PRAISE FOR THE ALASKA HERITAGE SEAFOOD COOKBOOK

"This is a book that any lover of seafood—or of Alaska—will enjoy. Not only does it contain recipes for just about any kind of fish you can think of, but it's also filled with tall tales and legends."

> —*Bon Appétit*

"Of several books devoted to seafood this season, *The Alaska Heritage Seafood Cookbook* by Ann Chandonnet stands out. . . . This book is as much fun to read as it is good to cook from."

> —*Washington Times*

"It's not often that you find a cookbook you want to take to bed with you. But *The Alaska Heritage Seafood Cookbook* is just that. It's not only full of tantalizing recipes, and ripe with history, legend and lore, it is also a great read."

> —*Writers NW*

"The author's enthusiasm for her topic is clear and the book is brimming with legends, lore, and recipes that reflect the ethnic diversity of today's Alaskan cuisine."

> —*The International Cookbook Revue*

"Of all the seafood cookbooks that have been published in recent years— and there have been many—this is the most unusual and the most rivetingly fascinating. You'll love it for its connection to the past and present life of the region, its ethnic traditions, and its unique food products and artistic legacy. Add to that great recipes and you have a remarkable cookbook. . . . There are historic photos of Alaskan Eskimos that will sear themselves into your brain. . . . [Chandonnet] has done an admirable job of introducing the folklore and customs of a place like no other in the world."

> —*A World of Cookbooks: The International Cookbook Newsletter*

"Chandonnet's book recalls the wonderful encyclopedic cookbooks of past generations."

> —*Northwest Palate*

"It's a natural—this beautiful, informative and useful seafood cookbook. . . . This book is a delectable bouillabaisse studded with intriguing, fish-related ingredients: legends, journal entries and facts (historical, folklorical, biological, botanical)."

> —*The Third Age* (Seattle)

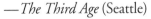

"This cookbook, destined to become a staple in western kitchens, is the author's third. It is more than a mouth-watering browse through tastes, smells, and riches of food. It is a land, a heritage, a people caught in Chandonnet's refreshing style."

—*Hells Canyon Journal* (Oregon)

"It is the most entertaining cookbook I've ever read."

—*Anchorage Daily News*

"*The Alaska Heritage Seafood Cookbook* is the latest in a long line of wonderful cookbooks from Alaska Northwest Books™, and its finest effort to date. More than a compilation of recipes, the cookbook is a love letter to Alaska. . . . Throughout the book, recipes are interspersed with stories of heritage and culture, the history of the halibut club of the Tlingit and Haida, the hooligan amulet of the Inupiat, the workings of prehistoric Eskimo kitchens."

—*Anchorage Press*

"Chandonnet has collected imaginative ways to prepare dozens of varieties of freshwater, saltwater and shellfish. The stories of the people who contributed recipes are fascinating, and Chandonnet includes legends, history and photographs of traditional Alaska, as well as helpful hints and facts."

—*Willamette Week* (Portland, Oregon)

"The book is full of historical references, biological data, personal reflections and Alaska Native legends, all of which move the book far beyond the average cookbook. All in all, it would be a welcome addition to anyone's culinary collection."

—*Alaska* Magazine

"A good read . . . richly illustrated . . . with human interest anecdotes about each recipe's contributor. . . . Like the recipes, this book, too, is a 'many-flavored kettle of fish' —a pleasing medley that engagingly captures the 'flavor' of Alaska sea life including seafood cookery, the people involved in it, and its history and traditions."

—*North Pole Independent* (North Pole, Alaska)

THE ALASKA HERITAGE
SEAFOOD COOKBOOK

GREAT RECIPES FROM ALASKA'S RICH KETTLE OF FISH

ANN CHANDONNET

ALASKA NORTHWEST BOOKS™
ANCHORAGE • PORTLAND

To my husband, Fern, the most important Pisces in my life

Third printing 2002

Library of Congress Cataloging in Publication Data
Chandonnet, Ann.
    The Alaska heritage seafood cookbook : great recipes
from Alaska's rich kettle of fish / by Ann Chandonnet.
        p.   cm.
    Includes index.
    ISBN 0-88240-469-5
        1. Cookery (Seafood)   2. Cookery—Alaska.   I. Title.
TX747.C445 1995
641.5'92—dc20   95-31206
                                                          CIP

Originating Editor: Marlene Blessing
Managing Editor: Ellen Wheat
Editors: Cynthia Nims, Rebecca Pepper
Designer: Elizabeth Watson
Map: Vikki Leib, Steve Podry

Photographs/illustrations. *Front cover:* CENTER: Boy and
king salmon, Juneau, early 1920s. Whatcom Museum of
History and Art, J. W. Sandison Collection, 710.
CENTER BACKGROUND: Plaice. TOP: Aleut kayaker,
Unalaska. Drawing by John Webber, artist with Captain
James Cook, 1778. Center for Pacific Northwest Studies,
Western Washington University. RIGHT TOP: "Some royal
good sport," king salmon, early 1900s. Alaska Historical
Library, Case and Draper Collection, PCA 39-135.
RIGHT CENTER: Petroglyph of fish. *Guide to Indian Rock
Carvings of the Pacific Northwest Coast,* Beth Hill (Hancock
House, 1975). RIGHT BOTTOM: Inuit with speared fish.
Photo by Richard Harrington, *The Inuit: Life As It Was*
(Hurtig Publishers, 1981). LEFT BOTTOM: Octopus.
LEFT CENTER-BOTTOM: Tsimshian sea monster halibut hook.
Indian Fishing: Early Methods on the Northwest Coast, Hilary
Stewart (University of Washington Press, 1977).
LEFT CENTER-TOP: Petroglyph of fish. *Guide to Indian Rock
Carvings of the Pacific Northwest Coast.* LEFT TOP: Salmon
gill netter, Clarence Straits, 1970s. Photo by Joe Upton.
Back cover: TOP: Photo by Joe Upton. BOTTOM: Koodlahlook
(Mrs. Arthur Eide) jigs for tom cod through the ice, Bering
Strait, 1916. Anchorage Museum of History and Art,
B70.28.190. For other credits/permissions, see pages 305
and 307. Every effort has been made to obtain permission
for artwork reproduced here.

Alaska Northwest Books™
An imprint of Graphic Arts Center Publishing Company
P.O. Box 10306, Portland, OR 97296-0306
503-226-2402; www.gacpc.com

Printed in Singapore

SOME ROYAL GOOD SPORT WHERE KING SALMON HIT THE HOOK
JUNEAU ALASKA

FISH AND SHELLFISH RECIPES 22

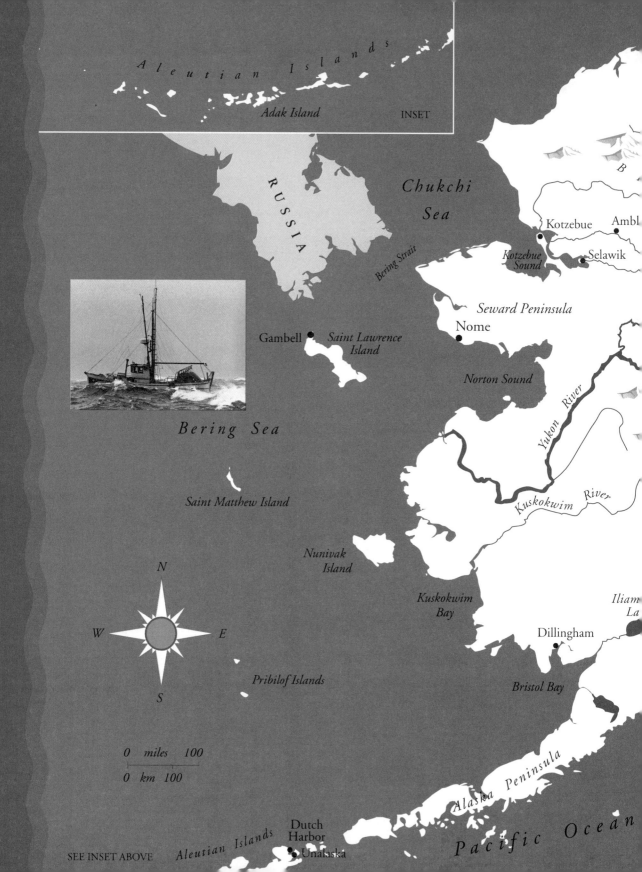

Aleutian Islands

Adak Island

INSET

Chukchi Sea

RUSSIA

Kotzebue •   Ambl

Bering Strait

Kotzebue Sound

Selawik

Seward Peninsula

Nome

Gambell •   *Saint Lawrence Island*

Norton Sound

Yukon River

Bering Sea

Kuskokwim River

Saint Matthew Island

Nunivak Island

Kuskokwim Bay

Iliam La

N

Dillingham

W   E

S

Pribilof Islands

Bristol Bay

0   miles   100

0   km   100

Alaska Peninsula

Dutch Harbor

SEE INSET ABOVE   *Aleutian Islands*   • Unalaska

Pacific Ocean

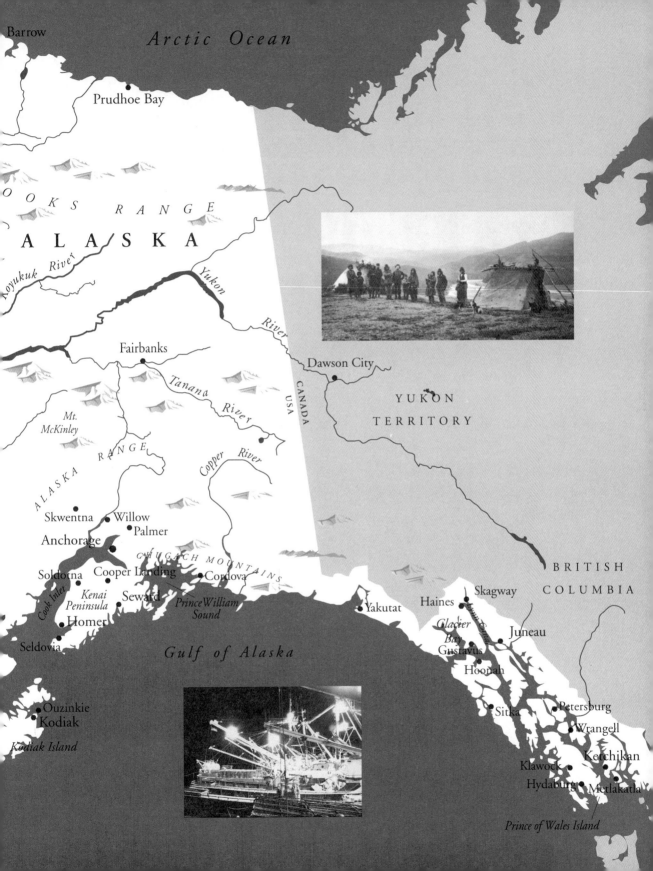

Barrow

Arctic Ocean

Prudhoe Bay

BROOKS RANGE

ALASKA

Noyukuk River

Yukon

River

Fairbanks

Dawson City

CANADA
USA

YUKON

TERRITORY

Tanana

River

*Mt.
McKinley*

ALASKA

RANGE

Copper River

Skwentna Willow
Palmer

Anchorage

CHUGACH MOUNTAINS

BRITISH

COLUMBIA

Soldotna Cooper Landing Cordova
*Kenai
Peninsula* Seward
Cook Inlet *Prince William
Sound* Yakutat Skagway

Homer Haines *Lynn Canal*

Seldovia Juneau

Gulf of Alaska *Glacier
Bay* Gustavus
Hoonah

Ouzinkie Sitka Petersburg
Kodiak Wrangell
Kodiak Island Ketchikan
Klawock
Hydaburg Metlakatla

Prince of Wales Island

Aleuts at Unalaska. Drawing by John Webber, artist with Captain James Cook, 1778

The Freshness, the Freedom, the Farness

Fresh out of graduate school in 1965, I looked around for adventure. I found it in Alaska.

My first morning in the Far North, I was awakened by my bed frame clomping across the floor in an earthquake and my roommate's alarmed yelps from down the hall as her bed danced around too. Teaching high school English on Kodiak Island, just a year after the Good Friday earthquake, I soon learned that Alaskan temblors were not limited to major events; minor ones occurred like clockwork, sometimes as often as twice a week. It became automatic to block the classroom door at even the slightest temblor, so jittery teens wouldn't run into the halls.

My Kodiak landlord, Pat Cannon, was a retired fisherman. Pat was determined I should love Alaska, and his campaign included taking me out for Sunday salmon fishing on his seiner, the *Swallow*. With several other newcomers and Pat's wife, Margaret, we motored to Crystal Bay, where I was mesmerized by the unspoiled shoreline, the limpid ocean awash in tiny translucent jellyfish-parachutes three inches long. The water was so calm and clear we seemed to float on air.

Pat rowed out in a dory to set his purse seine—a procedure I'd only read about before—and we hauled in three big bright silver salmon. Pat gave me one, a gift that gleamed like a diplomat's tea service. My roommate, her fiancé, and I ate fried salmon steaks until it was all gone, finding the treat almost too delicious to be true.

After that year on Kodiak, I married and taught college English back home in Massachusetts. But I wanted to return to Alaska as soon as possible. My husband, Fern, and I did just that in 1973, with our nine-month-old son. Soon Fern was hunting rabbits, and we were moving a moraine to plant a vegetable garden: we were going to stay.

I *did* fall for Alaska, my home now for the last 22 years. I fell for what Klondike balladeer Robert Service called "the freshness, the freedom, the farness." To my taste buds, some of Alaska's most genuine freshness is encapsulated by the riches of land and sea: firm, sweet halibut, wine-dark dewberries, tender venison, and juicy rosewort.

The mountains, the wildlife, canoeing in glacier-carved lakes—all these things keep us here. And then there's the marvelous generosity of established Alaskans to newcomers. For our first Thanksgiving in Chugiak in 1973, we were given bear roast and gravy by a new friend. It was delicious. Over the years, we've received Dolly Varden, caribou

Pacific Bounty

Alaskan waters are host to over 100 species of fish, plus assorted crustaceans and bivalve mollusks. The seafood species selected for the recipes in this book are the most commonly marketed, most commonly sought by sportfishermen, and most commonly cooked in Alaska. But if you live elsewhere, don't let the "Alaska seafood" designation mislead you; many of these species of fish are not limited to Alaska's waters, but are also found along the entire Pacific Coast as far south as Baja. And, of course, many close cousins of Pacific species swim in the Atlantic, as well.

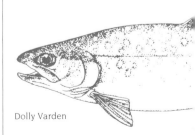

Dolly Varden

Inuit with speared fish

Nori, or laver

steaks, rainbow trout, pike, moose livers that filled the kitchen sink, and precious smoked salmon. I've relished each distinctive taste and texture.

The cold, clear waters surrounding Alaska's 34,000-mile coastline are among the world's most productive fishing grounds. Just how many kinds of Alaskan fish are there? Experts have cataloged 370 different species, including 24 types of crab, 22 shrimp, and 25 clams.

Fish was a staple food of Pacific Northwest Coast Indian, Eskimo, and Aleut peoples, whether they caught it themselves or traded for it. Tasty salmon, meaty halibut and cod, and oil-rich smelt, herring, and hooligan were prized. Each board-like dried fish was cached like an edible, odorous banknote. Clams, mussels, abalone, limpets, and sea urchins were also gathered, served up with side dishes of seasonal greens, willow buds, berries, and seaweed.

North of the Aleutian Islands lived Alaska's Eskimos. Fish, chiefly salmon and herring, has been the mainstay of the Yupik Eskimo diet in the Yukon-Kuskokwim area since man crossed the grassy tundra of the Bering Land Bridge at least 12,000 years ago. The Yukon and Kuskokwim rivers form a delta about the size of Kansas. This delta sustains the largest Native population of any Alaska region and that population is sustained with fish, chiefly salmon. Residents are able to catch and cure enough fish to tide them and their animals over the long, dark winter.

Alaska's seafood bounty is near-legendary. In 1900, L. H. French, a physician/prospector, sent home this glowing report of the Seward Peninsula's finny resources:

A majority of the rivers are so filled with fish, that . . . bucket, shovel and club supply the place of rod and line.

Some idea of the quantities of them running up the rivers may be gained from my experience in crossing the Solomon River on horseback, when the animal I was riding became so frightened by the salmon darting around his legs as to be nearly unmanageable.

Today, nearly a century after French prospected the area south of Nome, at Ambler and other villages, Inupiat Eskimos gut fresh salmon and halve each fish, expertly removing the backbone but leaving the tail intact, and drape the fish over racks for drying. Heads, left attached by a strip of skin, are considered a delicacy. A meal of dried fish heads—toasted or boiled—is as welcome as beans in Boston.

While the salmon are running, women will labor 12 hours at a stretch, day after day, "cutting fish."

When herring migrate upriver in schools, they stay around only three or four days, and the Eskimos must be ready. As the people mend their nets, they watch for the sign that announces that the herring have arrived: flocks of screeching gulls skimming low over the water. It's a moment of great joy.

To preserve this valuable food, residents drape the silvery herring on huge outdoor driftwood drying racks built in the shape of pup tents or tepees: First, the gutted herring are carefully twined into braids with grass. Then the ponderous braids are looped around and around the tepees, forming arrangements resembling multitiered grass skirts.

Traditionally, Native calendars of Alaska, whether Aleut, Indian, or Eskimo, have been organized around subsistence hunting and gathering, around the cycles of various plants, birds, mammals, and fish. For example, in the spring in Alaska's Panhandle and along the contiguous coast of British Columbia, hooligan and herring spawned in tremendous schools, some miles across. During the summer, bottom-fishing for halibut on shallow offshore banks was the rule. In the fall, the people would move to traditional fishing sites—fish camps—situated along rivers and streams known to host substantial runs of pink or chum salmon.

Though salmon has always held the dominant position in Alaska's fisheries, halibut has also been very important.

Alaska's early peoples caught halibut with large wooden hooks that were as intricately carved as ceremonial rattles. Among Southeast Alaska's tribes, hooks were formed from strong hemlock knots, steamed until flexible inside the bulbs of giant kelp. A bone barb was lashed to the hook with strips of spruce bark or wild cherry bark. Bait was tied on with whale sinew.

The abundance of seafood available to Pacific Northwest Coast peoples in Southeast allowed them periods of leisure and time to develop elaborate cultural traditions. They created monumental works of art such as tall carved totem poles and painted housefronts. Thanks to the moderate climate of the region and the edible bounty supplied by warmer waters, the life of the Northwest Coast Indians was not that of unceasing daily pursuit of food typical of so many hunting and gathering cultures. However, farther north, Eskimo and Athabascan peoples often waged an almost daily struggle against malnutrition and starvation in a less bountiful, harsher climate.

Namely Fish

Place-names in Alaska bear witness to the importance of fish to the residents. In Anchorage, for example, street names include Chinook Avenue, King Circle, Spring Street, and King Street. The Wrangell–Saint Elias National Park and Preserve contains both a Silver Lake and a Sculpin Lake. The Kenai National Wildlife Refuge has a Rainbow Lake, a Dolly Varden Lake, and a Trout Lake.

Tlingit halibut hook

Water, Water, Everywhere

Eighty percent of Alaska's population lives within 10 miles of the ocean or a river.

Salmon purse seiner

For at least 12,000 years, the traditional fisheries of the Northland flourished. In these Native fisheries, the catch was laboriously dipnetted fish by fish, enticed with elegant hooks, or directed into intricate weirs and traps. The experiences and memories of elders sorted out the best methods and the best places to catch fish. This traditional lifestyle is still very much alive in bush Native villages of Alaska today.

Modern Alaskans, too, eat lots of fish. The average American eats about 15 pounds of seafood a year—chiefly shrimp and tuna—but the average Alaskan consumes 86 pounds, and for that reason has developed bulging files of seafood recipes and recommendations.

Fishing is one of the state's most constant sources of revenue, rivaled only by mining, timber, and oil. Since 1950, the fishing industry has represented a "bank account" totaling about $100 million annually. Salmon is the main product of Alaska fisheries.

At the eastern end of the Aleutian Chain, Dutch Harbor is one of the world's top five ports for fish volume and dollar value. In 1993, it was the foremost U.S. port, bringing in a catch worth $161 million.

Salmon was the first Alaska fish to be commercially harvested, but soon other species were being hauled aboard. In the late 1880s, several Gloucester fishing schooners sailed around from New England to try open-sea seal hunting and to fish for halibut. They did most of their fishing off Cape Flattery in Washington or near the Queen Charlotte Islands in British Columbia. But the *Oscar and Hattie*, under the command of Captain C. Johansen, sailed north to the Gulf of Alaska, and in the fall of 1887 hauled in 100,000 pounds of halibut. These huge, flat fish were shipped on ice by rail to eastern states, creating a new market. (See photograph on pages 22–23.)

In the period from 1911 to 1915, Alaska recorded an annual average landing of nearly 10 million pounds of halibut (measured in cleaned, heads-off pounds). The peak came in 1946–1950, when the haul was over 23 million pounds. Since 1988, waters contiguous to Alaska have produced over 75 percent of the Pacific Coast's halibut catch.

Since the 1890s, the economies of Alaska communities such as Ketchikan, Petersburg, Wrangell, Sitka, Juneau, Yakutat, Seward, Kodiak, and Cordova have all been closely connected to the halibut catch. Today, Cordova fishermen have added to halibut these commercial catches: Dungeness, king, and snow crab; herring; king, sockeye, coho, chum, and pink salmon; herring roe on kelp; and clams.

The 1976 Magnuson Act declared a 200-mile zone off the coast would henceforth be considered part of U.S. territory. The Alaska seafood industry expanded to embrace that new harvest area. Meanwhile, as the public's appetite for a variety of seafood species grows, arrowtooth flounder and yellowfin sole have come to glisten under the bright lights of supermarkets, and specialty products such as arctic char, lingcod, Pacific Ocean perch, sheefish, and silver smelt surface seasonally.

But let's disembark from the fishing schooner and take shore leave in the kitchen.

Lillian Akootchook hanging arctic char to dry, 1993

Century upon century, Alaska's indigenous cooking remained largely unchanged. It was Eskimo and Indian food—basic and sustaining, cyclical and seasonal.

Then, in the 1700s, European explorers began to cruise the coast—seeking a Northwest Passage as well as natural resources like gold, coal, and tall timber for masts. The passage turned out to be a pipe dream, but resources were here in abundance, plus that most wondrous discovery: "soft gold," the luxurious pelts of sea otters.

Each new expedition had its effect on Alaskan cuisine. The Russians introduced rye flour and bricks of compressed China tea. The British shipped out with limes, rice, potatoes, and sugar. The Spanish and French stocked the larder with tomatoes and cheese. Each vessel carried the tastes of home to sustain its crew in this strange land.

HAMMERED WATER

The word "Klondike," after 1896 one of the most famous place-names in the history of the Northland, comes from tron-diuck, *which means "hammered water."*

It refers to stakes hammered into the bed of the Klondike River at its mouth, where Han Athabascan people annually set their salmon traps and nets.

The nets and weirs would be anchored to stakes laboriously driven into the bed of the river. Tron *refers to the hefty hammer stones used to pound in the stakes. There are fewer than two dozen Han speakers living today, but this word of theirs, "Klondike," lives on in history because of its association with the lure of northern gold.*

Homestead Lemons and Canned Cows

While cooks in the "Lower 48" may be tracking down fresh herbs and radicchio, Alaskans are still relying on A-1 Sauce, chili powder, and vegetables from a can, still tracking down moose, and still whitening their coffee with "canned cow."

Even in the big city of Anchorage, where half the state's population resides, supermarkets can run out of fresh milk and cream is not dependable. Habituated to shortages, many cooks shun cream entirely—reaching for the evaporated milk (locally called canned cow) whenever a recipe calls for light cream.

Those who spent their prime on traplines and have now moved closer to streetlights, even if they currently have access to fresh milk, find it difficult to rid themselves of the taste for evaporated in their coffee. The canned cow maintains its position of honor on the table, cheek by jowl with the salt and pepper ☞

Even during a century of contact with explorers, change came slowly. When the United States purchased the territory from Russia in 1867, there were only a few hundred Westerners in residence, only a few plots of cabbage and root vegetables soaking up summer's generous daylight.

Foreign influences continued. After whalers from New England skimmed the shore near Barrow and Nome, Eskimos began frying doughnuts in whale oil. During the Klondike and Nome gold rushes of the late 1800s, stampeders came from all over America as well as Australia, New Zealand, and Europe, toting condiments such as catsup and molasses, recipes for Irish stew and white bread.

As gold fever cooled, many "cheechakos" (newcomers) stayed on, settling down as storekeepers, fox farmers, trappers, or fishermen.

The waves of immigration to the Last Frontier were largely a trickle of the bubbling stream of newcomers flowing into the "Lower 48." Epidemics, tyranny, overpopulation, poverty, greed—all this and more drove men and women to cross land and sea seeking new homes and new lives. Between 1880 and 1914, for instance, nearly 4 million Italian farmers fled to America, bringing with them a love of olive oil, wine, tomatoes, and pasta. In a twinkling of time's eye, macaroni was being used to thicken Inupiat whitefish soup.

Because of Sweden's nationwide harvest failure in the 1860s, starving Swedes also immigrated en masse, first to the Midwest, especially Minnesota and Wisconsin. Growing homesick for fjords and mountains, they moved farther—to the Dakotas, Nebraska, and eventually Puget Sound. Later, gritty, adventurous Swedes were among those making major strikes on Eldorado Creek in the Klondike and at Anvil Creek near Nome.

Portuguese arriving in the States at the turn of the century were typically teenage boys fleeing military conscription. For centuries, the Portuguese had been known as brave sailors and fishermen, and some joined the fishing fleets of San Francisco Bay and voyaged north to the Gulf of Alaska, bringing with them coconut, peanuts, tapioca, and a wealth of salt fish dishes.

Japanese cooks had ventured north to the Klondike to open restaurants during the gold rush. More Japanese, as well as Filipino laborers, arrived in the first decades of the 1900s to work in canneries in Southeast Alaska during the summers. Some stayed; their soy sauce, stir-frying, and sweet-and-sour dishes, too, put down roots.

Scottish preachers, Moravian missionaries, Mexican fishing fleets, and soldiers constructing the Alaska Highway in the early 1940s all added their own "seasoning" to the communal pot.

During the 20th century, thousands of Americans have come north seeking employment in Alaska's boom industries, such as railroad-building and logging. Skilled technicians from the "oil patches" of Oklahoma and Texas were attracted by the high wages of the 1970s to the construction of the trans-Alaska oil pipeline, packing an appetite for barbecued ribs and crispy corn fritters.

Influence from without continues today, as the lure of Alaska attracts to its restaurants and hotels bakers apprenticed in Bavaria and chocolatiers from Holland. This dynamic process of fusion and reinvigoration keeps Alaska's cuisine varied and creative.

Much of what we know of Alaska's indigenous foodways is recorded in the journals of early explorers, sailors, and surveyors. For example, in October 1778, British explorer Captain James Cook anchored at Unalaska in the Aleutians. Cook's journal gives this account of Aleut cookery:

> They dry large quantities of fish in the summer, lay it up in small huts for winter use. . . . They eat almost everything raw; boiling and broiling were the only Methods of Cooking I saw them use. . . . I was once present when the Chief of Oonalashka dined on the raw head of a large halibut but just caught. Before any was given to the chief two of his servants eat the gills without any other dressing. . . . This done one of them cut off the head of the fish, took it to the sea and washed it, then came with it and sat down by the chief; first pulling up some grass a part of which he laid the head upon and the rest before the chief. He then cut large mouthfulls of meat off the Cheeks and laid [them] down before the Chief who [ate] it with the same satisfaction as we would do a raw oyster.

A few days after Cook made this entry, a member of his crew, Thomas Edgar, went ashore. Edgar climbed hills, forded rivers, and came to the Russian outpost, where he and his dripping companions were afforded dry clothes and refreshment. Edgar wrote:

> About seven a table was brought for supper on which in a short time after was serv'd up in a very rough kind of trough some boil'd Halibut; round the bowl on the table was laid thick slices of boild whale, two bowls of the Juice of the large blue berry's & a wooden spoon to each person. The whale & halibut are eat together and with every two or three mouthfulls they take a

shakers and the sugar bowl. Similarly, when a single lemon costs 65 cents, a homestead lemon (bottled lemon juice) can be a regular staple of the refrigerator.

Tlingit grease dish

spoonful of the berry juice; . . . we found [the halibut] very agreeable eating & made a very hearty supper.

As Britons, Russians, and other Westerners came into the country, cooks relied on supplies being shipped north once a year. It was necessary to calculate how many sacks of flour, cases of canned corn, and gallons of molasses would be gobbled up in the next 1,100 meals. Short growing seasons in Alaska limited gardens to root vegetables like potatoes, turnips, and carrots, or cool-weather crops like cabbage. Limited provender meant not only that menu selections changed little, but also that the cook's creativity was repeatedly challenged.

This firmly rooted make-do feature of Alaska's cuisine is echoed in the modern experiences of homesteader Caroline Geisler-Schlentner. For 20 years in the mid-1900s, Geisler-Schlentner lived in a 16- by 18-foot cabin far from big-city comforts. Of her family's typical holiday menu she writes:

We usually ate what was on hand—moose meat, snowshoe hare, grouse, salmon, cranberries, turnips, potatoes, and cabbages. . . . We rarely had fresh eggs or enough vanilla or the correct spices, so I have always invented new recipes whenever ingredients were missing. One time the only oil or shortening for Christmas cookies was bacon grease.

Bog cranberries (*Oxycoccus sp.*)

But as railroads, highways, and airplanes crisscrossed the state, the trapper's pantry cupboard has become less bare. True, some Alaskans still choose to live in rural or wilderness situations such as Geisler-Schlentner describes, in cabins equipped with kerosene lamps and woodstoves, relying on canned goods and large supplies of dried comestibles like beans and barley. Fresh produce is simply not available to those folks unless homegrown or flown in by bush plane, because, when carried home by dogsled or snowmobile in winter, supplies like apples and lettuce freeze and spoil. After decades of such pragmatic approaches to cooking, some Alaskan cooks still dote on recipes based on bacon, powdered garlic, and canned mushroom soup.

On the other hand, half of Alaska's population resides in the metropolitan Anchorage area, where produce wings its way from Florida and California several times a week. There, supermarkets stock bananas and apples year-round, and juicy hothouse tomatoes (and lively cut flowers) from Holland have become commonplace. And Alaska's seafood cuisine has developed markedly since the days of Captain

Cook—the days of boiling, smoking, stick-roasting, and clay cooking. Today's dishes may be no more savory, but they are decidedly more elaborate and more various.

For example, chef Roberto Alfaro of the Crow's Nest, an award-winning restaurant perched atop Anchorage's Hotel Captain Cook, serves such seasonal specials as sautéed tiger prawns, sea scallops flambé, and salmon tartare. And he enriches his dishes with wild mushrooms from Oregon and black truffles from Europe.

Hundreds of miles to the west, in the spotless kitchens of the Grand Aleutian Hotel, executive chef David Wood strives to create a "Northern Pacific Rim cuisine," which he defines as "Southwest Alaskan products with Asian artistic interpretations." California-born Wood wielded spatula and whisk in two Salt Lake City hotels before moving to Alaska. He takes full advantage of the fresh seafood available in Dutch Harbor and also explores innovative ways to incorporate local produce. Aided by a hydroponic greenhouse that shelters tender vegetables from the unpredictable Aleutian weather, Wood offers Steak Calamari, grilled Alaskan Scallops with Mango Basil Salsa, and Grilled Shrimp and King Crab Salad drizzled with warm Brie Dressing.

Like the cuisine of any region, Alaska's seafood cookery began with simple dishes composed entirely of locally available ingredients (salmon steamed in skunk cabbage), absorbed the tastes, techniques, and ingredients of newcomers (Russian Fish Pie, or Pirog), and, in the 20th century, transcended seasons and cultures to reach a worldly blend.

Unalaska crabber/trawler night fishing, 1980

The recipes I have gathered in this collection derive from the many different lifestyles and personalities that make up Alaska. There are recipes from sophisticated chefs like Alfaro and Wood. There are recipes from nostalgic camp cooks who remember the glory days of salt fish. There are recipes from commercial fishermen, from housewives who maintain their own set net sites, from romance writers who enjoy ice fishing, from mountain climbers, bed-and-breakfast proprietors, bush pilots, schoolteachers, and meter readers.

These recipes come from the real, diverse Alaska, past and present. Alaska's seafood cookery embraces the tastes of Inupiat Eskimos, transplanted Cajuns, adventurous Japanese, and hearty Norwegians. Its heritage is Pacific Rim, Continental, Tex-Mex, and beyond. It's a complex and many-flavored kettle of fish, sloshing over its brim with aromatic and delicious pleasures.

FISH AND SHELLFISH RECIPES

Unloading halibut for rail shipment to the east, 1888

FRESHWATER FISH

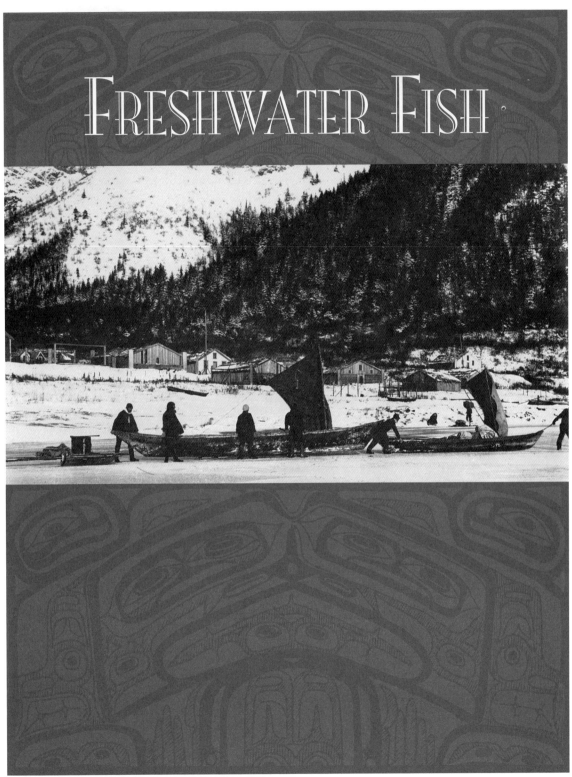

Canoes by Yindastuki, Tlingit village on the Chilkat River, 1895

ARCTIC CHAR

Delicious kissing cousins, arctic char and Dolly Varden are trout-like fish superficially as alike as two plump peas in a pod.

From Greenland's icy mountains to Baffin Island to Nome, cooks who dislike the mess of scaling give a cheer for char: arctic char's scales are so tiny the fish seems scaleless, with a silvery belly and sides spotted with large pink dots.

Char has been the subject of aquaculture experiments for at least 30 years in Canada, Iceland, and Norway. These farmed fish stock American markets. But landlocked wild char are still sought after by sportfishermen.

Delicate arctic char flesh may be white, pink, or deep salmon in color. In texture, the flesh is salmon-like, but creamier than salmon. This delectable fish can be baked, deep-fried, stuffed and baked, broiled, or steamed.

Char's rising star picked up a tailwind early in 1994 when the Clinton White House served grilled char with lobster sausage at a state dinner for Japanese Emperor Akihito and Empress Michiko.

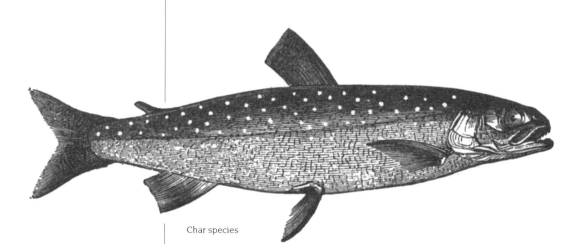

Char species

Nick's Stir-Fried Char

Writer Nick Jans lives and teaches school in Ambler, an Eskimo village of 350 on the western edge of the Brooks Range, reached only by airplane or boat. "I think arctic char is the best eating fish in Alaska," Nick says, "but you have to treat it gently. You can put your thumb right through it when cleaning it if you aren't careful."

Nick Jans with arctic char in the Brooks Range, 1992

2 tablespoons olive oil, more if needed
2 cloves garlic, finely chopped
2 medium onions, finely chopped
1½ pounds arctic char, cut in 3½-inch by 1-inch strips
1 bell pepper, cut in thin strips
3 carrots, cut in thin strips
4 to 6 cups cooked rice (white or brown)
1 tablespoon soy sauce
1 tablespoon oyster sauce
Cayenne pepper (optional)
Lime wedges

Heat the olive oil in a skillet or wok over medium-high heat. Add the garlic and onion and cook, stirring often, until just beginning to brown, 3 to 4 minutes. Transfer to a large bowl and set aside.

Return the pan to the heat, and let it get very hot. Film the bottom with more oil, if necessary. Lay the strips of char in the pan, placing them away from you so that the oil does not spatter. Leave at least ½ inch between the strips. Do not crowd the fish or it will steam instead of forming a crust. When one side is browned, turn and sear the other side. Remove the fish from the pan when it feels springy, with a slight resistance.

When all the fish has been cooked and removed from the pan, add more oil to the pan if needed, and reheat. Add the bell pepper and carrot strips, and stir-fry until crisp-tender, about 3 minutes. Add the rice to the pan and stir-fry for 4 or 5 minutes more, or until the rice is heated through and beginning to brown. Add the soy sauce and oyster sauce and stir to mix evenly. Return the fish, onion, and garlic to the pan, stir-frying gently until heated through. Season to taste with cayenne, if desired.

Spoon the char onto warmed plates, and serve with lime wedges.

Garlic

MAKES 4 TO 6 SERVINGS.

BLACKFISH

Raw Fish

Although scarcely known in commercial markets, blackfish is a significant subsistence catch in small Alaskan Eskimo communities. Traditionally, blackfish is eaten by Alaska's Eskimos as coq *or* quak*—raw, frozen fish, cut into thin, bite-sized slices and dipped into seal oil before being popped into the mouth. Eskimos traditionally eat much of their food raw—whale skin and caribou included. This practice preserves nutrients that would be reduced by cooking, and also saves fuel.*

Blackfish are small, lively brown fish with black splotches, flowing fins and tail, and big lips. Because they are hardy as well as attractive, blackfish appear both in Alaskans' freshwater aquariums and on their dinner plates. Blackfish are a notable example of adaptation to the rigors of the Northern winter. When ponds freeze solid, blackfish survive by coating their skin with mucus, lacing their blood with a chemical antifreeze, burrowing into the mud of the bottom, and going dormant.

The naturalist Lucien M. Turner wrote in the 1870s: "The vitality of these fish is astounding. They will remain [outdoors, frozen] in . . . grass-baskets for weeks, and when brought into the house and thawed out will be as lively as ever."

Or, as an Eskimo ice fisherman on Delong Lake (behind my house in Anchorage) told my husband one February day, "They all die in January—and then they come back." The patient fisherman had pulled in a bucket of these tasty little fish. When I arrived home from work that evening, my husband had a 7-inch specimen gulping air in the kitchen sink. We kept the blackfish for two days, admiring its delicate fins—then (in the interest of research) fried it. To me, it tasted even better than the fingerling trout annually stocked in Delong.

Blackfish have delicate, slightly oily, white flesh. Pan-frying is one of the best ways to prepare them.

Children at Portmann Fish Factory, Loring, Alaska, ca. 1910

Blackfish á la Chef Alan

Providence Alaska Medical Center in Anchorage sponsors an annual sampling of heart-healthy recipes created by local chefs, an event called the Elegance of Good Nutrition. On this festive occasion, recipes are supplied for all the dishes, like this one created by Alan Lorimer. The genial Lorimer spent many years developing top-of-the-line dishes for Carr Gottstein Foods. In 1994, however, he took charge of the new Cafe of the Lyons Family in Indian, a small town south of Anchorage. Lorimer's dill-scented, low-calorie recipe, originally created for halibut, has here been adapted to blackfish.

1 large onion, thinly sliced
6 blackfish fillets, 6 ounces each
¼ cup lemon juice
⅓ cup white zinfandel
1 tablespoon coarsely chopped fresh dill
1 lime, thinly sliced

Preheat the oven to 350°F.

Arrange the onion in the bottom of a shallow baking dish. Cut the blackfish fillets into serving portions. Place the fillets on the onions and pour the lemon juice and wine over the top. Sprinkle with the dill. Cover each fillet with 2 or 3 lime slices. Cover the dish with foil and bake for 18 to 20 minutes, until the fish is opaque in the center.

MAKES 6 SERVINGS.

Dill

Haida design from
painted spruce-root mat

BURBOT

Burbot is a secretive bottom-dweller distinguished by a bulbous head and a snaky, eel-like body. Its skin is mottled, greenish, or brownish, and it may grow to 3½ feet in length. The burbot bears two small fleshy protrusions on its nose and a third on its chin.

Widely distributed in Europe, Asia, and North America, the burbot is the only member of the cod family found in freshwater. In Alaska it is widespread in lakes and rivers, including the Chisana, the Nabesna, the Chena (which flows through Fairbanks), and the Tanana.

Spencer De Vito served as a Bureau of Indian Affairs teacher in the village of Northway in 1968. In his leisure time, De Vito caught many record burbot through the ice of the Chisana River, using pieces of fresh rabbit meat as bait on homemade treble hooks. "Wonderful eating fish that they are, burbot became part of our diet in Northway," De Vito recalled more than 25 years later in a recent Homer *Dispatch* column entitled "Nothing is a fish story if you can prove it!" "We also traded additional burbot catches for mukluks, beaver gloves, and even a pair of caribou socks."

Romance writer Ted Leonard of Salcha notes that a favorite spot for burbot winter ice-fishing sets is off the Chena Pump Campground on the Tanana. "But any place you can find a deep hole along the Tanana is a likely spot for a burbot set line," Leonard says, "especially in back eddies by cliffs or at the confluence of a tributary."

The burbot's tender, flaky flesh is delectable in chowder or deep-fried.

May 30, 1968. After breakfast I checked the trotline. The pulley heavy with a tugging now and then on the way in. Two burbot . . . fifteen inches and a nineteen-incher. A burbot is ugly, all mottled and big-headed . . . looks like the result of an eel getting mixed up with a codfish. It tastes a whole lot better than it looks.

—*Dick Proenneke*, One Man's Wilderness
(Alaska Northwest Books, 1973)

Burbot in Beer Batter

Soft-spoken Ted Leonard and his statuesque, gun-totin' wife, Dottie, recommend burbot either coated with beer batter and deep-fried or broiled and served with melted butter. The Leonards fairly drool at the thought of fresh burbot, adding that "cheechakos [new-comers to Alaska], repelled by its ugliness, have been known to release it back into the river. What a mistake!"

Beer Batter:
1⅓ cups flour
1 teaspoon salt
¼ teaspoon freshly ground black pepper
1 tablespoon corn oil
2 eggs, beaten
¾ cup flat beer
2 egg whites

4 cups oil, for deep-frying
2 pounds burbot fillets

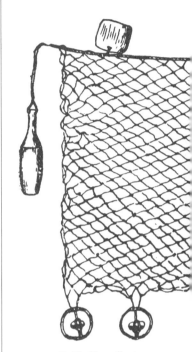

Nettle-fiber gillnet

To make the Beer Batter, in a medium bowl, beat together the flour, salt, pepper, oil, eggs, and beer. Allow the batter to rest, covered and refrigerated, for 3 hours or overnight.

Just before using, stir the batter energetically. Beat the egg whites until they form stiff peaks. Then gently fold the egg whites into the batter.

In a deep-fat fryer or deep saucepan, heat the oil to 350°F.

Cut the burbot fillets into serving pieces no larger than 3 inches square. Pat the fish dry with paper towels. Dip the fish in the batter. Place several of the fish pieces in the hot oil, being careful not to crowd them. Fry for 3 to 4 minutes, or until golden. Repeat with the remaining pieces. Serve piping hot.

MAKES 4 SERVINGS.

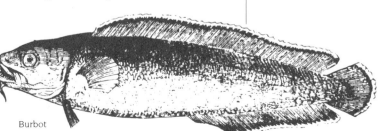

Burbot

DOLLY VARDEN

Fish Watching In and Around Anchorage

Anchorage is an intriguing blend of wilderness and sophistication, where you can see bear and moose in the backyard as well as at the zoo.

For those who want to watch fish instead of mammals, there are many possibilities:

■ Elmendorf State Hatchery, corner of Reeve Boulevard and Post Road. A visitor viewing area is located within the compound. The best viewing of kings is from the last week of June through mid-August, 8 a.m. to 10 p.m.

■ Chugach State Park is one of the nation's largest, with 495,000 acres of forests and meadows, peaks and pinnacles. It surrounds Anchorage on the east and south. Lakes and streams boast resident populations or spawning fish of many species, including hooligan, Dolly Varden, ☞

Often classed as a trout and sometimes called a "salmon trout," the elegant Dolly Varden is a close relative of the arctic char. It grows 18 to 36 inches long. As subtle in coloration as a Monet canvas of water lilies, Dolly derives its name from the cherry-colored mantle and hat worn by a pretty, lively miss with the same name in Charles Dickens's novel *Barnaby Rudge.* Dickens described this young lady as "the very pink and pattern of good looks."

The name was suggested in 1876 by Elda McCloud, landlady of Friday Springs, a California resort, as she exclaimed over the beauty of a sample fish being sent to an expert for classification.

The Dolly or "golden fin" can be a loyal freshwater fish, in which case they are more slender and may reach only 6 to 8 inches long. Most Dolly Varden, however, are anadromous; they spend a few years in freshwater after hatching, then go to sea for a couple of years. After maturing sufficiently to be ready for spawning, the fish return to freshwater streams to spawn. Although the post-spawning mortality of Dolly Vardens is high, some hardy females survive to spawn as many as four times. Their lives can span 12 years.

The Dolly is dark blue above, silver on the sides, and white below. The body sports cream-colored spots with attractive yellow to red and pink spots gracing the back and sides. This auroral exterior clothes pink, firm, flavorful flesh—not as beefy as cod or halibut, but perfection for melting in the mouth. The Dolly is my favorite Alaskan fish.

Dolly Varden are versatile in the kitchen, suitable for boiling, steaming, frying, or baking, as well as smoking. To my taste, the French preparation *à la meunière* is a perfect match for this fish.

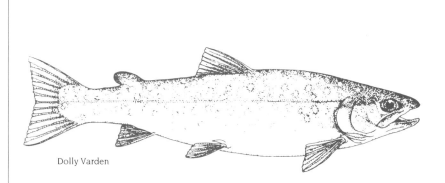

Dolly Varden

Dolly Varden à la Meunière

Cooking in Alaska and on other American frontiers was repeatedly influenced by European methods, especially among the upwardly mobile. The French influence on American cuisine got a boost when Thomas Jefferson installed the first French chef in the White House. Fish cooked *à la meunière* is seasoned, lightly floured, fried, and then drizzled with browned butter and fresh lemon juice. Simple recipes like this French preparation allow the true, pristine flavor of the fish to predominate. Serve with boiled potatoes.

1 Dolly Varden, 2 to 3 pounds
2 tablespoons flour
½ teaspoon salt
Pinch of freshly ground black pepper
1 teaspoon paprika
⅓ cup Clarified Butter (see page 232)
2 tablespoons chopped fresh parsley
½ lemon

Scale the fish, if necessary. Gut and rinse. Remove the head and skin if you wish. Pat the fish dry with paper towels.

With a sharp knife, make ½-inch-deep incisions across the thick part of the whole fish on each side, spacing the cuts about 1 inch apart.

Combine the flour, salt, pepper, and paprika, and use this mixture to coat the fish well. Heat the butter in a large, heavy frying pan over medium-high heat, and sauté the fish until it is golden and cooked through, 5 to 6 minutes per side or a total of about 10 minutes per inch of thickness.

Place the fish on a warm serving dish, sprinkle with the parsley, and squeeze the juice of the lemon half over it. Heat the butter remaining in the pan until it is brown, and pour it, sizzling, over the fish. Serve at once.

Makes 4 to 6 servings.

grayling, and all five Alaska species of salmon.

■ *At the Ship Creek Salmon Overlook, near the Alaska Railroad Station downtown, you can get a closeup view of kings shouldering one another for a prime spot to try to leap a falls to get to upstream spawning areas. You can see locals angling for dinner, or you can purchase a license, don hip boots, and join them. This is the approximate site of a pre-1915 Tanaina Athabascan fish camp.*

Parsley

GRAYLING

The arctic grayling is the Marlene Dietrich of fish, famed for its sleek beauty, crowned with a sail-like dorsal fin. The grayling's slate gray skin dazzles with aurora-like shadings ranging from rainbow trout pink to walleye bronze. The distinctive dorsal fin, covered with tiny circles of iridescent turquoise, is much larger on the male than the female. When grayling spawn, the male genteelly drapes his fin over the female's back as if to shield their intimacy from public view.

Feeding chiefly on insects, the elusive grayling is highly territorial, vigorously defending its home waters from other fish. Its fighting spirit earns accolades from sportfishermen and subsistence fishermen alike.

The grayling derives its genus name, *Thymallus,* from the fact that the freshly caught fish smells like thyme. The average grayling weighs a pound, making it an ideal single-serving fish. The trout-like flesh, pan-fried over a campfire, is hard to equal.

Grayling

Lemon-Herb Campfire Grayling

This recipe comes from Kieran O'Farrell, owner of Celebrations Catering in Auke Bay near Juneau. O'Farrell specializes in "Pacific Northwest cuisine with a unique flair." O'Farrell explains, "I started my own catering company after 12 years in the restaurant-food industry, because I wanted to further explore my passion for cooking—and to offset my slow winter season." O'Farrell is a commercial floatplane pilot for Wings of Alaska during the summer, flying throughout Alaska's Panhandle. "Cooking and flying are remarkably compatible," she adds.

1 lemon, halved
4 pan-ready grayling, 10 to 16 ounces each
Lemon pepper to taste
Cajun seasoning to taste (see Note)
4 tablespoons butter, cut into small pieces
8 slices bacon
1 tomato, thinly sliced
½ red onion, sliced and separated into strips
1 lemon, thinly sliced
2 fresh basil leaves, chopped
2 tablespoons chardonnay or other dry white wine

Light campfire or start barbecue coals. Squeeze the juice of ½ lemon inside the cavities of the grayling. Season the cavities with lemon pepper and Cajun seasoning, and dot with the butter.

Inside each fish, place 1 slice of bacon. Divide among the cavities the tomato slices, red onion strips, lemon slices, and basil.

Rub the outsides of the fish with the other lemon half and sprinkle with the wine. Wrap each fish with one of the remaining bacon slices, and secure with toothpicks.

Place the fish on a grill over the campfire. Cover with a sheet of foil. Grill for 20 minutes. Turn the fish and replace the foil, which helps to hold in the heat. Cook for another 10 to 20 minutes, or until the fish is done. (The fish will flame up when done.)

MAKES 4 SERVINGS.

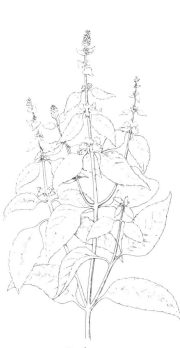

Basil

NOTE: Cajun seasoning is a bottled blend available in most supermarkets. The cook's own mixture (to taste) of cayenne pepper, garlic, bay leaf, black pepper, and thyme may be substituted.

Grayling en Gelée

A sophisticated dish for a summer luncheon, cold grayling in aspic, like Dolly Varden *à la Meunière,* has Continental roots. This elegant entrée can be decorated to a fare-thee-well with fresh herbs, wildflower blossoms, and nasturtium flowers—or with herb and egg "blossoms" as described below. This particular recipe comes from apprentice taxidermist Janice Worthington of Peters Creek, who occasionally has the challenge of mounting trophy marlin caught Outside (that is, outside Alaska) by Alaska sportfishermen. Cracked-wheat sourdough rolls nicely complement this dish.

4 cups Court Bouillon (see page 38)
6 pan-ready grayling, 8 to 12 ounces each
1 egg white, lightly beaten
4 eggshells, crushed
1½ envelopes (1½ tablespoons) unflavored gelatin
⅓ cup water
Green onion, leek, or chive stems, for decoration
Tarragon, thyme, or sage leaves, for decoration
3 hard-boiled eggs, sliced, for decoration
1½ cups Homemade Mayonnaise (see page 233)

Wild chives

In a large, shallow sauté pan or frying pan, bring the Court Bouillon to a boil. Add the grayling in a single layer (do this in several batches if necessary), and poach the fish, simmering it gently until it is cooked through, 8 to 12 minutes, depending on the size of the fish. Remove the cooked fish to a platter.

Bring the Court Bouillon to a boil, add the egg white and crushed eggshells, and boil for about 10 minutes, until the bouillon is clear and reduced to 3 cups. Push any foam that forms to the side of the pot. Allow the bouillon to cool to room temperature, then strain. Place the bouillon in a clean pot, and bring it back to a boil.

Soften the gelatin in the water for 5 minutes; then add to the boiling bouillon, stirring until the gelatin granules are dissolved. Allow the broth to cool, then chill until thick and syrupy.

If you like, decorate each fish as follows: Remove the skin from the upper side of each fish. Make a floral design with green onion "stems," tarragon "leaves," and "petals" of egg slices. The fish may be placed on individual fish plates, or all may be arranged on one large platter.

After decorating the fish, if desired, gently spoon enough of the syrupy aspic over each fish to cover it thoroughly. Place the plates and the remaining aspic in the refrigerator to chill for 3 to 4 hours (it will set like gelatin).

Just before serving, chop the remaining aspic very fine and garnish the plates/platter with it. Serve the mayonnaise on the side.

MAKES 6 SERVINGS.

Ahtna Indian fish camp, early 1900s

SUBSISTENCE

Subsistence is the contemporary term for the old hunter-gatherer way of stocking the larder. Subsistence has special meaning in bush communities of Alaska, where there may be electricity and personal computers, but where households still rely on walrus, whale, or caribou as a renewable resource.

In the subsistence lifestyle, dinner depends on the vagaries of weather, of fish runs, and of the resources of tundra or taiga itself. Along the Kuskokwim, for example, the river offers king, silver, sockeye, and chum salmon as well as whitefish, pike, grayling, Dolly Varden, sheefish, and eel.

At Scammon Bay, the available fish are salmon, whitefish, blackfish, smelt, needlefish, herring, and tomcod. Fish supplements prey like beluga whale, walrus, seal, and waterfowl.

At Eek, families dine on bear, beaver, salmon, pike, grayling, smelt, moose, caribou, rabbit, and seal. This may sound like quite a plentiful supply of food, but these items are not always available. Dining habits must be adapted to the wanderings of migratory caribou herds, to the nesting of birds, the sprouting of wild greens.

And subsistence also means sharing. When a small percentage of families in one village catches a large supply of fish, the catch is generally shared with their neighbors. In turn, those neighbors will share their fish on another day.

In the subsistence way, nothing is taken for granted, nothing is wasted. The turning earth and its seasonal resources are respected and honored.

Court Bouillon (Basic Poaching Liquid)

This is a very simple stock made with water, aromatic vegetables, and other seasonings—like a fish stock without the fish bones. The flavorful liquid produced is used to cook seafoods or as a soup base.

If you are making Court Bouillon for a recipe that involves reduction, *do not* add salt and pepper. If seasoned before reduction, it may be too salty when reduced.

As a variation, you can use a dry white wine low in alcohol, such as Vouvray, sauvignon blanc, or riesling, in place of 3 cups of the water. See also Bobby Alfaro's Fish Stock, part of the Alaskan Seafood Chowder recipe (page 190).

4 cups cold water
1 onion, quartered
1 stalk celery, with leaves, coarsely chopped
1 carrot, scrubbed and coarsely chopped
2 parsley sprigs
2 tablespoons white vinegar
3 lemon slices
1 bay leaf
6 peppercorns
4 whole cloves (optional)
Salt and pepper to taste

Combine all the ingredients in a large pot and bring just to a boil. Reduce heat to simmer and cook 20 to 30 minutes. (Cooked too long, the stock may become bitter.) Strain and let cool before using. If not used right away, refrigerate covered, or freeze until needed.

MAKES ABOUT 1 QUART.

Celery

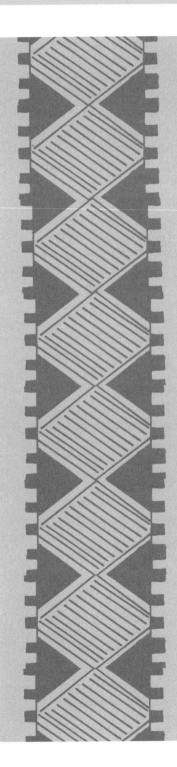

THE ULU

ULUS MUST BE CHECKED
—*Sign at security checkpoint in
Anchorage International Airport*

The ulu *is a traditional Alaskan knife with a crescent- or fan-shaped blade. For thousands of years, the ulu's curved blade was fashioned of stone such as slate, while the rectangular handle was made of bone or wood. Its complete name is* uluaq, *an Eskimo term still used in the Kwethluk area. Remains of ulus 11,000 years old have been found in arctic archaeological sites.*

Today's ulus are often made from recycled saw blades, with handles from walnut wood, moose or caribou antler, ivory, cultured ivory, or jade. Engraved ulus with their own slotted wooden stands are a unique form of award "plaque" peculiar to Alaska—as are engraved gold pans.

The ulu (pronounced OO-loo*) is a woman's tool, used for filleting, skinning, splitting sinew, chopping, or sewing. A typical woman's sewing kit contained awls, needles—and a dainty ulu that never touched messy fish and game.*

The ulu's basic design improves dexterity and increases leverage for fine slicing or heavy chopping. Many Alaskans find its convex shape ideal for chopping foods in a concave wooden bowl.

Ulu

PIKE

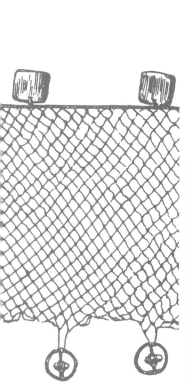

Nettle-fiber gillnet

Muscular carnivores, northern pike are the bouncers of Alaska's freshwater. As formidable as film villains, pike have a large mouth rimmed with vicious teeth, with a streamlined body and dorsal fins set close to the tail that make darting around in the water a breeze. The head and back are dark green with bean-shaped spots; the belly is paler green to tan. The razor-sharp, pointed teeth angle toward the back of the mouth like an alligator's—making escape difficult.

Compared to the Midwestern pike, the northern or arctic pike grows slowly in its colder, less fertile habitat. An arctic pike tipping the scales at 15 pounds is an impressive 30 years of age, while its Great Lakes counterpart might require only 10 or 15 years to reach the same weight. Alaska's most widely distributed sportfish, pike, when hooked, head for the depths and put up a mighty tug-of-war, making them thrilling quarry for anglers.

Like the proverbial billy goat, the omnivorous pike will snack on almost anything it can nab. It is not unusual to find small waterfowl and even careless muskrats in its stomach.

Delicate, lean, and flaky, pike flesh is perfect for classic Continental treatments such as *quenelles* (feather-light dumplings) and mousses. It is also delicious grilled, poached, or baked. The sweet meat tends to dry out, so cook it covered or wrapped in foil or bacon. Pike is coated with large scales and heavy mucus, so the skin is usually removed before cooking. The flesh harbors many bones, so filleting is a challenge. The most tender pike are under 5 or 6 pounds. Pike liver is considered a delicacy; use it in stuffing or add it to sauces.

KOYUKON ATHABASCAN USES OF PIKE

As Plains Indians had uses for every part of the buffalo, the Koyukon Athabascans of Alaska used every scrap of the northern pike. The meat, head, liver, eggs, intestines, and air bladder were all eaten. The pike stomach was cured and used as a container for storing fish grease. Pike jawbones were encased in moosehide and worn as bracelets by young boys to make them good hunters (because pike are skillful at catching prey). Dried pike heads were nailed on the doors of cabins to protect the inhabitants against dangerous spirits.

Shan's Baked Pike Fillets

Shan and Eric Johnson live year-round at Northwoods Lodge, their remote fishing lodge in Skwentna, renowned in March as a cozy front-row seat from which to view the passing parade of the Iditarod Trail Sled Dog Race. Tourists, including songbirds like Neil Diamond and movie stars like Clint Eastwood, flock to Alaska's secluded lodges to fish and to get away from it all.

The Johnsons were Eagle River contractors before founding their lodge in 1984. "Construction went belly-up in Alaska's economic downturn of the mid-'80s," Shan explains, "and we decided to run the lodge full-time. In the summer we're so busy, but in the winter we can enjoy ourselves."

When Eric lands a nice pike, Shan prepares it with this easy recipe, using Italian-style bread crumbs, which she favors for their built-in savory seasoning. You can substitute snapper or rockfish for the pike.

Marjoram

2 teaspoons butter, softened
½ cup chopped onion or green onions
5 small mushrooms, sliced (about ⅓ cup)
2 pounds skinned pike fillets
1 teaspoon dried marjoram
Salt and pepper to taste
2 tablespoons dry white wine
2 teaspoons lemon juice
¼ cup grated Monterey Jack cheese
¼ cup dry bread crumbs
½ cup butter, melted

Pike

Preheat the oven to 400°F.

With the softened butter, lightly coat a baking dish just large enough to hold the pike fillets in 1 even layer. Distribute the onions and mushrooms over the bottom of the dish. Arrange the fillets on top, slightly overlapping the thin (tail) portions so the fish will cook evenly.

Sprinkle the marjoram over the fish, and season sparingly with salt and pepper. Drizzle the wine and lemon juice over all.

Top the fillets with the cheese and bread crumbs. Pour the melted butter over all. Bake for 7 to 12 minutes, or until the fillets are opaque.

MAKES 6 SERVINGS.

SHEEFISH

Stewart's Treat

Every February since 1958, during the Anchorage winter festival of Fur Rendezvous, Oro Stewart of Stewart's Photo Shop has hosted a free Wild Game Barbecue. Folks wait in line to taste such Alaskan delicacies as sheefish, buffalo, venison, elk, seal, and muktuk (a fatty whale-skin and flesh snack).

Sheefish are whitefish, a valuable subsistence catch in cold northern lakes in both Alaska and Canada's Northern Territories. They are freshwater relatives of salmon. Sheefish, however, also swim in the salt water of Russia's White Sea and the Bering Sea.

In Alaska, sheefish or "Eskimo tarpon" frequent the waters of the Bethel and Kotzebue areas. They range generally from 7 to 10 pounds, have large scales, and are silvery and shiny, giving them a ghostly look under water. Sheefish in excess of 50 pounds have been taken in the Yukon and Kuskokwim drainages, where they migrate in fall. Recreational anglers consider this acrobatic fish at its best during winter months.

The odd name "shee" stems from terms in several of the 11 different Athabascan Indian languages of Alaska, including the Gwichin and Tanaina.

Sheefish's rich flesh takes to roasting, poaching, and broiling, and it is also excellent smoked. Alaska's Japanese cooks covet sheefish for soup and sashimi. Eskimos ferment sheefish into a delicacy known by the unprepossessing name of "stink fish."

Ahtna Indians at a summer camp, 1898

Nick Jans's Seared Sheefish

ALASKA magazine columnist Nick Jans has fished the rivers of the Western Brooks Range for more than a decade, hooking lunker sheefish. On the trail, Nick and his knowledgeable Inupiat friend Clarence Wood will divide a 5-pound fish between them and make a meal of it. Nick uses margarine or olive oil on the trail. Home cooks may want to substitute peanut oil, which has a higher scorching point. Lemon juice can be substituted for the lime juice.

1 sheefish, about 5 pounds
¼ cup oil, more if needed, for frying
1 lime
Freshly ground black pepper or lemon pepper to taste

Fillet the sheefish, and cut it into pieces that will fit in a large cast-iron skillet. Place the oil in the skillet and heat until smoking hot. Lay the fish in the skillet with the skin side down. Sear (brown well) over high heat. While the fish is cooking, squeeze juice from the lime over it and sprinkle with black pepper or lemon pepper to taste. Add more oil if necessary to keep the fish from sticking.

Turn the fillets and sear the other side.

Reduce the heat and flip the fish over again, cooking it once more on each side. Remove the fish from the heat as soon as it flakes and turns opaque within. The heat already in the flesh will finish the cooking.

MAKES 2 SERVINGS FOR HUNGRY CARIBOU HUNTERS, 8 FOR ORDINARY MORTALS.

As we skimmed upstream toward home, the sun filtered through the fog, casting the world in silver light. "What time is it?" one of my friends asked. I looked down at the boat bottom, bright with fish. The light, diffused and timeless, seemed to flow from them. Sheefish time, I whispered to myself.

—*Nick Jans,* The Last Light Breaking *(Alaska Northwest Books, 1993)*

Nettle-fiber dipnet

STEELHEAD

teelhead is a freshwater game fish, a delectable descendant of the common ancestor to salmon and char. It is an *anadromous* rainbow trout; that is, it hatches in freshwater rivers but subsequently migrates to salt water to feed and mature, eventually returning to freshwater to spawn. However, unlike most salmon—which spawn once and then die—the scrappy steelhead often survives the rigors of ascending spawning streams. Biologists estimate that at least 10 percent of all steelhead spawn twice, some three times.

Once hatched, young steelhead linger in streams 10 to 12 months before migrating to the rich feeding grounds at the river mouth where fresh and salt water mix. Here they fatten while developing a saltwater tolerance. Finally, they ease into the sea, where they wander and feed for a year or two or three. In the ocean they dine on krill, shrimp, and small fish.

Mature steelhead range from 6 to 40 pounds. Sleek, silvery creatures, they gleam dark blue along the back, with polished chrome sides and cream-colored bellies. Their color darkens when they are spawning, with the bright silver returning as they again near the ocean.

Female steelhead are called "hens," and males are "bucks." Lean, spawned-out adults headed back to sea are "kelts."

Alaska sportfishermen consider steelhead prime in October, when their runs peak in the Situk, Thorne, and Karta river systems, and the Karluk and Ayakulik rivers on Kodiak Island. Because their smaller scales are weaker armor than the scales of trout, steelhead tend to spoil more quickly and should be cooked promptly. Steelhead flesh is white, delicate, and moist, good for barbecuing or smoking, pan-frying, broiling, steaming, poaching, or baking. You can prepare steelhead using any recipe for trout or Dolly Varden.

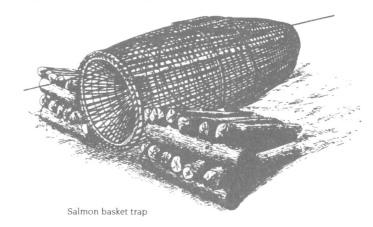

Salmon basket trap

Chinese-Style Steamed Steelhead

More than 300,000 Chinese immigrants entered the United States between 1850 and 1882, the majority coming from the province of Canton. Wherever they settled, they opened Chinese restaurants. By the 1920s, Cantonese cooking could be found in the Klondike, in Alaska—all over North America.

In Chinese cuisine, a whole fish represents bounty and abundance, partially because in Chinese the word for "fish" sounds like the word for "surplus." A fish cooked whole is central to birthday and wedding celebrations as well as for the multicourse banquet typical of Chinese New Year's Eve. The fish is cleaned through the gills, leaving head and body intact. The head of the cooked fish faces the guest of honor.

Fragrant and tender, steamed fish is a specialty of Dori Blaser, former owner of the Little Fisherman fish market in Anchorage. Sea bass, rockfish, or porgy may be substituted for steelhead in this recipe.

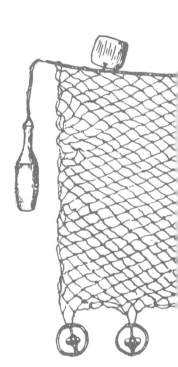

Nettle-fiber gillnet

1 steelhead, 3 to 4 pounds, cleaned
4 ounces slab bacon, ¼ inch thick, diced
1½ tablespoons diced fresh ginger
5 green onions, cut in 1-inch pieces
¼ cup dry sherry, Court Bouillon (see page 38), or rice wine
2 tablespoons soy sauce
1 teaspoon sugar
½ teaspoon salt
¾ cup chicken stock
½ cup water

Rinse the fish under cold running water, and shake dry. Remove the fins, which can give an off taste. Cut slashes ½ inch deep across both sides, at 1-inch intervals, and place on paper towels to dry.

To steam the fish on the stovetop: In a heavy 2- to 3-quart saucepan or wok, cook the bacon until sizzling. Add the ginger and green onions. Stir-fry for 1½ minutes. Add the sherry, soy sauce, sugar, salt, stock, and water, and mix thoroughly. Remove from heat.

Put the fish on a heatproof plate, and place the plate on a steamer rack wide enough to hold it comfortably. Pour the bacon-ginger sauce over the fish, using a long wooden spoon to poke bits of bacon, ginger, and onion off the fish and position them around it. ☞

Pour 2 or 3 inches of water into the bottom of the steamer. Bring the water to a boil over high heat. Set the steamer rack (with the fish on it) in the steamer and cover tightly. Reduce the heat to medium-low and steam for 30 minutes, uncovering the steamer once after 12 minutes to turn the fish over.

To steam the fish in the oven: Preheat the oven to 375°F. Place the fish on 2 sheets of heavy foil large enough to enclose the fish. Turn up the edges of the foil to form a dish shape. Pour the bacon, ginger, green onions, sherry, and soy sauce over the fish. Bring the ends of the foil together and fold securely, sealing the fish in the package but leaving a bit of room for expansion. Place on a baking sheet and bake for 20 to 25 minutes, or until the fish can be pierced easily by a toothpick, right through the foil.

Serve the fish whole with the seasonings arranged around it.

MAKES 6 TO 8 SERVINGS.

Haida argillite platter design

Alaska's splendid trout include the rainbow trout, the coastal cutthroat, and the steelhead (see page 44). Monster lake trout (actually a char, as is the brook trout) are potentially the state's biggest freshwater fish—even bigger than sheefish; lakers up to 65 pounds have been taken with rod and reel.

The rainbow sports a reddish pink stripe that runs along the lateral line. The olive green back is spotted, as is the tail. Flesh varies from pale pink to red, depending on the diet.

The lake trout is a finicky creature that requires deep, cold (no warmer than 50°F), clean, well-oxygenated habitats. Known for loitering languidly on the bottom until hooked, and then for battling like a prizefighter, the lovely "laker" is blue-gray or bronze-green to nearly black, with pale spots on the sides and back continuing into the fins.

Like arctic pike, cutthroats have a slug-slow growth rate. The average 8-inch Southeast cutthroat is 4 years old; a 3-pound, 20-inch fish—considered trophy size—is about 12 years old.

None of Alaska's native trout are retailed. The trout retailed in Alaska are raised on trout farms outside of Alaska; they are available year-round and are of consistent quality. (Many Alaskans rely on fly-fishing and ice fishing for the trout they put into the skillet and onto the table.) Farmed trout are marketed head-on, dressed; as skin-on fillets; and as butterfly fillets. Value-added products such as frozen, stuffed trout are more and more common. Farmed trout have flesh that is invariably pale, while the flesh of wild trout can vary from alabaster to deep pink.

Delicate trout meat tends to crumble when cooked. To maintain its shape when frying, leave the skin on, roll the fish in flour or cornmeal, and brown in butter or bacon drippings, turning gently with a large spatula.

TROUT

Family Salmonidae

Trout and salmon are members of the same family, Salmonidae. Salmon live an anadromous life cycle—meaning they hatch in freshwater and spend their prime in salt water. In general, trout remain in freshwater for their entire lives. However, anadromous trout forms, like steelhead, tend to grow much larger than their freshwater equivalents, like rainbows. The larger size is due to a more varied and plentiful diet.

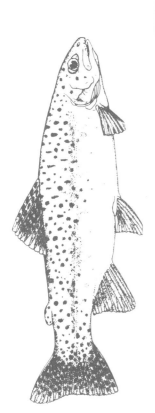

Rainbow trout

Bacon-Grilled Trout

Familiar to many Alaskans who own hip boots and cook over a campfire, this recipe can also be prepared under the home broiler. For grilling fish outdoors, hinged, fish-shaped wire racks help make cooking a breeze.

The recipe was shared by Gil Whitman, a Nenana resident who earns his living by creating relief carvings from caribou antlers and moose racks. (Caribou and moose both shed their heavy appendages once a year, and craftspeople gather them from the tundra or forest floor.)

As side dishes, consider Bannock (see page 217), corn on the cob, foil-wrapped potatoes baked in the coals, potato salad with fresh dill, or watermelon from the cooler.

1 can (8 ounces) tomato sauce
½ cup beer
1 tablespoon Worcestershire sauce
1 teaspoon onion salt
1 teaspoon lemon juice
6 whole pan-dressed trout, about 8 ounces each
12 slices bacon, partially cooked

In a small saucepan, combine the tomato sauce, beer, Worcestershire sauce, onion salt, and lemon juice. Simmer the sauce for 2 minutes, then let cool. (This mixture can be prepared at home and transported in a plastic container.)

Light the coals or preheat the broiler. Brush the inside of the fish with part of the sauce. Wrap 2 slices of bacon around each trout. Grill over low coals in a wire rack or broil under a broiler, basting frequently with the remaining sauce and turning occasionally, until the bacon and trout skin are crisp, 13 to 16 minutes.

MAKES 6 SERVINGS.

Minted Rainbows

In Homer, Alaska's "banana belt," wild mint grows 5 feet tall. Many Homer cooks harvest the wild mint to stuff fresh trout. The creator of this recipe is perky Jacqueline "Jaqui" Soule of Homer, a college student and waitress who never tires of trying new trout dishes.

6 whole pan-dressed trout, 6 to 8 ounces each
1 tablespoon plus ¾ cup corn oil
3 cups lightly packed fresh mint leaves (or ¾ cup crushed dried mint)
1 tablespoon salt
6 strips turkey bacon

Light the coals or preheat the broiler.

Dry the trout with paper towels. Brush them with 1 tablespoon of the oil. Mash the fresh mint with the salt to release the flavor; add the remaining ¾ cup oil. (If using dried mint, mix it with the salt and oil.)

Fill the cavities of the trout with the mint mixture; wrap each trout with 1 strip of bacon, securing with toothpicks. Grill over hot coals or broil under a broiler, 4 to 6 inches from the heat, for 4 to 5 minutes. Turn and cook for about 5 minutes longer, or until the trout flakes when tested with a fork.

MAKES 6 SERVINGS.

Field mint

A PROSPECTOR'S DIET

Rigging up a fishing pole with string and a hook baited with bear meat, I sat on the edge of the creek to have some fun, but try as I would with fat meat and lean, the fish only came close to the hook, then scooted off again. After an hour or so I was almost ready to give up. Then in exasperation, I tied a small piece of red flannel from my shirt onto the hook. That did the trick. . . . Every time the hook hit the water I had another fish, until by late afternoon I counted 34 wriggling on the gravel bank. . . . In the spirit of celebration, I made a few pancakes to go with the fish. Pancakes were a delicacy I hadn't tasted for more than a month. I had lived entirely on meat or an occasional fish and a few blueberries picked along the way.

—Harald Eide, describing his adventures prospecting outside Nome
in 1914, in The Norwegian (Alaska Northwest Books, 1975)

Trout with Anchovy Sauce

Salty and addictive, anchovies lend their essence to this exuberant recipe from Stacy Andrews. An oil-field worker who labors three weeks on, two weeks off at Prudhoe Bay, Stacy likes "something a little different from steak and fries" for his dinners back home. With the golden trout, he serves crisp potato pancakes and steamed broccoli, finishing with halves of ripe papaya filled with lemon yogurt.

½ cup water
2 eggs, beaten
1 cup flour
½ teaspoon baking powder
1½ teaspoons salt
¾ cup dry bread crumbs
¼ teaspoon freshly ground white pepper
2 tablespoons butter
2 tablespoons olive oil
4 whole pan-dressed trout, 8 to 12 ounces each

Anchovy Sauce:
2 tablespoons anchovy paste
¾ cup heavy cream
Juice of 1 medium lemon

Whisk the water and eggs together. Combine the flour, baking powder, and 1 teaspoon of the salt, and slowly whisk into the egg mixture. Allow the batter to sit for 30 minutes before using. Whisk briefly before using.

Mix the bread crumbs with the remaining ½ teaspoon salt and the pepper. In a heavy skillet, heat the butter and olive oil over medium heat. Dip each trout into the egg batter, then roll in the bread crumbs. Fry the trout until golden on both sides. Keep hot.

To make the Anchovy Sauce: In a small saucepan, whisk together the anchovy paste and cream. Simmer over very low heat for 3 minutes. Add the lemon juice and remove at once from the heat.

Serve the hot trout on 4 warmed plates, with the Anchovy Sauce divided evenly among them.

MAKES 4 SERVINGS.

Eskimo transformation mask

The silvery, deep-bodied whitefish is a northern cold-water dweller, a member of the salmon family averaging 1 to 6 pounds. Whitefish flourish throughout Alaska and Canada, as well as in the lakes of Maine and in the Great Lakes.

"Whitefish" (or "white fish") is a confusing term, sometimes used to market white-fleshed saltwater species such as cod, hake, and cusk. True whitefish are freshwater fish like cisco and the oily-fleshed sheefish (see page 42).

Whitefish flesh is white, delicate, and sweet. No wonder Fairbanks author and angler Chris Batin calls it the "king of food fish." A 4- to 5-pound whitefish is delicious stuffed and baked. Dione Lucas, the first recognized American teacher of French cooking, favors a blend of parsley, chives, flowery marjoram, and delicate chervil for seasoning baked and poached whitefish, as well as fried fish of all varieties.

Whitefish roe—"golden caviar"—makes a gleaming garnish. For a glistening, lavish appetizer, coat a brick of cream cheese with a thick layer of this golden roe and serve with crackers.

You can prepare whitefish much as you would trout, pike, or rockfish.

WHITEFISH

IDITAFISH

The Iditarod Trail Sled Dog Race, a 1,000-mile mush from Anchorage to Nome that takes place in March, requires a good deal of fuel to keep both dogs and mushers going.

Top dogs are often fueled with fatty mutton or beaver to keep them warm in cold temperatures, and nutritious fish to keep their muscles humming over snowy trails. The frozen fish is hacked into dog-sized chunks with an axe when the dogs are "snacked." Other foods may be cooked up in a kettle to produce a rich gruel that provides both hydrating water and nutrition.

The mushers themselves get fancier fare such as barbecue, smoked salmon, pizza, and ice cream bars.

In 1993, a top musher included among his dog provisions: 336 pounds of sausage, 155 pounds of salmon, and 125 pounds of whitefish. (The 58 Häagen Dazs bars and 200 sticks of gum were for him.)

—From musher Rick Swenson's newsletter,
"Pawprint News" (1993)

Native Alaskan Delicacies

The roe of whitefish, sheefish, salmon, lingcod, and pike is a prized Eskimo food. Roe is stirred or whipped with wild cranberries, or seal or whitefish oil, and a little sugar to make a fluffy mixture called kapuktuk, *eaten immediately because it does not hold well. A favorite early fall delicacy among the Koyukon Athabascan people is raw, frozen whitefish dipped in bear grease.*

Parsley

Whitefish with Browned Butter Sauce

This recipe was developed by Kellsee Labridale of Gustavus, a college student majoring in international trade. Kellsee has earned her tuition by spending summers on fish-processing "slime lines"—smelly, scaly assembly lines where fish are gutted, headed, and readied for canning—but even that heady experience has not diminished her appetite for seafood dishes. The browned butter gives this dish a nutty flavor. Serve with sliced, steamed radishes, drizzled with a bit of butter and honey, and a crusty onion loaf.

> *1½ to 2 pounds whitefish fillets*
> *⅓ cup flour*
> *Freshly ground black pepper to taste*
> *¼ teaspoon salt*
> *¼ cup butter*
> *1 cup Court Bouillon prepared with dry white wine (see page 38)*
> *¼ cup lemon juice*
> *2 egg yolks*
> *⅓ cup heavy cream*
> *1 lemon, sliced and seeded, for garnish*
> *½ cup chopped parsley, for garnish*

Rinse the fillets and pat them dry with paper towels. Cut into 4 portions.

Mix the flour, pepper, and salt; toss the fish in the flour mixture, shaking off any excess. Reserve the remaining flour mixture.

Melt the butter in a large skillet over medium heat, letting it turn a golden brown. Do not allow it to burn or turn black. Add the floured fish fillets and sauté over medium-high heat for 1 minute on each side. Remove the fish from the pan and drain on paper towels.

Stir any remaining flour mixture into the pan juices. Add the Court Bouillon and lemon juice. Cook and stir until thickened. Add the fish and simmer, uncovered, until it flakes easily when tested with a fork, 5 to 10 minutes. Remove the fish from the skillet and keep warm.

In a small bowl, whisk the egg yolks with the cream. Add this mixture to the skillet. Cook and stir until thickened, but do not allow to boil. Serve the sauce over the fish. Garnish with lemon slices and parsley.

MAKES 4 SERVINGS.

Fish Pockets

Whitefish makes a tasty sandwich filling. The combination of tomatoes, cottage cheese, and sour cream in this recipe was inspired by a creamy dairy salad I ate at Child's in New York City in 1963.

Almost any leftover broiled or poached fish can be used in this recipe. I've made Fish Pockets with leftover fried halibut and taken them on hikes in the Chugach Range above Anchorage. The recipe also works with canned (drained) fish. Chopped parsley, mushrooms, cucumber slices, mayonnaise, and even tabbouleh may be added to taste.

1 tomato, chopped
2 tablespoons chopped red onion or other mild onion
1 pint alfalfa sprouts
1 cup cooked, flaked whitefish
⅓ cup low-fat cottage cheese or reduced-fat ricotta
¼ cup light sour cream or plain yogurt
4 spinach leaves, washed, dried, and shredded
1 small carrot, grated
Salt and pepper, as needed
4 whole-wheat pita pocket breads, slit open across top edge

In a bowl, combine the tomato, onion, sprouts, whitefish, cottage cheese, sour cream, spinach, and carrot, tossing lightly. Taste, and add salt and pepper if necessary. Stuff the fish mixture into the pita breads and serve at once.

MAKES 4 SERVINGS.

Carrots

SALTWATER FISH

Messrs. Smith, Stone, Penberthy, and Nicoli with a 300-pound halibut, Homer, 1904

COD

In the fall near Nome, tomcod often wash ashore in considerable numbers at night, and freeze on the beach. Nome Eskimos string them up to dry in the ocean breezes; they are considered tasty boiled when half dry. Fat tomcod livers are boiled slowly and stirred until the mixture coats the stirring stick. The liver paste is cooled, and mossberries are added before it is eaten.

Like herring, cod is one of the most important fish in the history of the world, both as food and as an item of trade. The Vikings relied on cod caught in the winter and dried in the air. The bounty of cod off the North Atlantic seaboard attracted Viking explorers, paving the "sea road" for the colonization of New England as well as the Canadian maritime provinces.

By the 1860s, the presence of cod off the coast of Alaska was well known. Together with gold and furs, cod was one of the tempting resources William Seward mentioned in his 3-hour speech to Congress urging the purchase of this Russian territory.

Four major members of the codfish family inhabit Pacific Northwest waters, but only two, the true cod and the pollock (see page 98), are important to commercial fishermen.

A swift swimmer, the cod has smooth gray skin, three dorsal fins, and a single chin barbel. The true cod (also called Pacific cod) is the largest of the Northwest cod, sometimes reaching 40 inches and 25 pounds.

True cod are most often caught during the winter spawning months, although the declared commercial season is year-round. A miniature relative, the tomcod, is a subsistence catch—little known to the public at large. In Barrow, though, Eskimo women can be seen jigging for it through holes in the pack ice just offshore on any fair October day.

The flesh of true cod is snowy white, firm, tender, and delicate, highly valued as food. People who say they "don't like fish" may down cod with pleasure. The moist flesh separates into large, attractive flakes when cooked. True cod is versatile: bake, microwave, pan-fry, poach, or broil it. Cod excels as fish and chips and in salads, casseroles, and chowders.

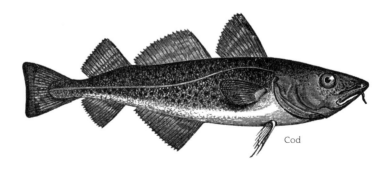

Cod

Parmesan Baked Cod

This entrée comes from the Alaska Seafood Marketing Institute in Juneau, a state office devoted to disseminating information about fish harvested in Alaska. It is a simple and savory way to cook fish, suitable for many species, including rockfish and orange roughy. When my sons were growing up, this comfort food was a favorite. I usually serve it with my garlic mashed potatoes: add diced onion and garlic to unpeeled potatoes for the final half of their cooking time. Mash energetically.

3 tablespoons flour
3 tablespoons yellow cornmeal
¼ teaspoon onion salt
⅛ teaspoon freshly ground black pepper
2 tablespoons butter or margarine
1½ pounds cod fillets
¼ cup freshly grated Parmesan cheese

Preheat the oven to 450°F.

Combine the flour, cornmeal, onion salt, and pepper. Melt the butter in a shallow baking dish. Dredge the cod in the flour mixture and place it in the baking dish. Turn the cod to coat it with butter, then sprinkle it with the Parmesan. Bake until the cod flakes easily when tested with a fork, about 10 to 12 minutes.

MAKES 4 SERVINGS.

SOUTHEAST'S BOUNTY

This part of Alaska [Southeast] abounds in food. Yesterday I bought four codfish for ten cents, and a string of bass for five cents. A silver salmon, weighing thirty-eight to forty pounds, is sold for fifteen or twenty cents.

—John G. Brady, in an 1878 letter printed in missionary Sheldon Jackson's Alaska, and Missions on the North Pacific Coast *(1880)*

Baby's First Fish

Tomcod livers were an important source of traditional baby food in the village of Unalakleet and other areas where this fish was caught. The livers were simmered with a little water, and the mixture cooled. The oil floating on top was skimmed off and fed to babies. The liver itself, prechewed by the baby's mother and given mouth to mouth, was often the first solid food fed to the infant.

Hair crab, 1981

Dutch Harbor Bouillabaisse

John Ziebro, a chef at UniSea Inn in the Aleutian port of Dutch Harbor, has been in the restaurant business since the tender age of 15. Ziebro has developed a bouillabaisse featuring ingredients indigenous to Dutch Harbor. "When all of the ingredients are at their peak of freshness, they complement each other extraordinarily," Ziebro says. "My customers say it's the best seafood stew they've ever eaten."

Shellfish Broth:
2 cups clam juice
1 cup tomato sauce
¾ cup white wine
¼ cup Pernod (anise liqueur, optional)
3 tablespoons fresh herbs to taste, such as thyme, oregano,
   parsley, and chives

2 pounds clams, scrubbed
2 pounds mussels, scrubbed and debearded
1 pound king crab legs, in the shell, cut into 3-inch pieces
3 Dungeness crabs, steamed, cleaned, and cut into 3-inch pieces
1 pound halibut fillets, cut into 1½-inch cubes
1 pound cod fillets, cut into 1½-inch cubes

To make the Shellfish Broth, place the clam juice, tomato sauce, wine, Pernod, and fresh herbs in a saucepan, and simmer for 30 minutes. Strain. (See Note.)

Layer clams, mussels, crab, halibut, and cod in a stockpot, putting the shellfish on the bottom and the fish over it. Pour the Shellfish Broth over the seafood.

Steam, covered, over medium heat until the clams and mussels have opened and the fish flakes when touched with a fork, 7 to 10 minutes. Do not overcook.

MAKES 8 TO 10 SERVINGS.

NOTE: Shellfish broth can be served alone as the first course of a lavish dinner.

Baked Cod with Yogurt

This recipe whispers of India, with its balance of sweet raisins, cool yogurt, and almonds against the spicy forces of coriander, garlic, and hot chile peppers. I was inspired to create this recipe after dining on the Chicken Tikki served at Maharaja's in Anchorage. Serve with steamed rice or couscous, pita bread with sesame seeds, spinach salad or coleslaw, and a little sitar music, please.

2 pounds cod fillets, ¾ inch thick
⅓ cup extra-virgin olive oil
1 medium onion, chopped
2 to 3 serrano or jalapeño peppers, minced
2 tablespoons minced fresh ginger
1 clove garlic, minced
1 teaspoon whole coriander, crushed in a mortar
Salt and freshly ground black pepper to taste
½ cup raisins
8 ounces plain yogurt
½ cup sliced almonds

Preheat the oven to 450°F.

Place the cod in a shallow baking pan and brush with 2 tablespoons of the olive oil.

Heat the remaining oil in a frying pan and sauté the onion, peppers, ginger, and garlic for about 1 minute; stir in the crushed coriander, salt, and pepper. Sprinkle this mixture over the cod. Bake until the fish turns opaque, 10 to 12 minutes. (If using frozen cod, do not thaw before baking. Bake 18 to 20 minutes.) While the fish is cooking, plump the raisins by soaking them in hot water for 15 to 20 minutes. Drain well.

Serve the fish topped with a dollop of plain yogurt and a sprinkling of raisins and almonds.

MAKES 4 TO 6 SERVINGS.

Onions

The side dish served with seafood at Simon & Seafort's is Pecan Wild Rice (see page 229). Rockfish and salmon (white or red king) also work well in this recipe.

Cod Baked with Sun-Dried Tomato-Thyme Butter

For years chef Darin Hudson delighted diners at Simon & Seafort's Saloon & Grill in Anchorage with his inventive flavorings for baked and broiled fish.

1 cup flour
1 teaspoon salt
1 teaspoon freshly ground black pepper
Pinch of granulated garlic or onion powder
2 eggs, lightly beaten
1 cup milk
2 pounds cod fillets
4 lemon wedges, for garnish
4 sprigs thyme, for garnish
4 tomato fans (see Note) or tomato wedges, for garnish

Sun-Dried Tomato-Thyme Butter:
½ cup sun-dried tomatoes packed in olive oil, drained
1 cup softened butter
1 tablespoon minced shallots
1 teaspoon minced garlic
1½ tablespoons chopped fresh thyme or 1 teaspoon dried thyme
1 tablespoon fresh lemon juice

To make the Sun-Dried Tomato-Thyme Butter, dice the tomatoes in ¼-inch pieces. Whip the butter until smooth. Blend together the butter, shallots, garlic, thyme, and lemon juice. When well combined, add the tomatoes and gently fold just until incorporated. Makes 1 cup.

Preheat the oven to 400°F.

Combine the flour with the salt, pepper, and granulated garlic, and place on a plate or in a shallow bowl. In a separate bowl, combine the eggs with the milk.

Dredge the cod fillets in the seasoned flour, then dip in the egg mixture. Place in a greased baking pan. Spread each fillet with 2 to 3 tablespoons of the Sun-Dried Tomato-Thyme Butter. Bake until the fish is cooked through, 6 to 12 minutes. Garnish each serving with a lemon wedge, a thyme sprig, and a tomato fan.

MAKES 4 SERVINGS.

NOTE: To make tomato fans, choose tomatoes no larger than 2 inches in diameter. Holding a tomato by the stem end, slice almost through the tomato at ¼- to ⅓-inch intervals, leaving the slices attached at the stem end. Fan out the resulting blades to resemble a fan.

DOGFISH

The dogfish is the most common shark in Alaska waters—from the Gulf of Alaska and Kodiak Island to British Columbia. It often tangles the set nets of salmon fishermen, eliciting their choicest vocabulary as they try to get it free, because the sharp spines located just ahead of its two dorsal fins can cause painful wounds.

A streamlined swimmer that evolved to its present form 200 million years ago, the dogfish is gray to brown on its back, white on its belly, with white spots along its sides. Ranging from 2 to 3 feet long, the compact dogfish tips the scales at 7 to 10 pounds.

Dogfish is one of the principal ocean fish traditionally caught by the Indians of the Pacific Northwest. Among the Tlingits, rough and tough dogfish skin was cut in rectangles, pulled off, dried flat, and then used as sandpaper for large carvings like totem poles. Oil in the skin gave a sheen to the wood at the same time.

Firm, white, moderately lean dogfish flesh is suitable for frying and smoking. You can also poach dogfish, allow it to cool in the stock, and serve cold with a cool yogurt sauce or Aïoli (see page 238).

Tlingit dogfish design on
woven spruce-root hat

Broiled Folkstone Beef with Berry Sauce

Tlingit dogfish design

Once upon a time, Sandy Burd of Gustavus worked on a long-liner that caught dogfish for an experimental marketing program. "I spent several weeks trying to find ways to serve it to a crew that was less than enthusiastic about eating the catch," Burd recalls. "In addition to developing some recipes that were worth keeping, I found it advantageous to employ some of its other names—grayfish, huss, or, my favorite, Folkstone beef."

Having had her fill of fish research, Sandy Burd now earns her keep as proprietor of the three-story, spruce-log Good Riverbed and Breakfast, within touring distance of Glacier Bay. At breakfast, guests chow down on homemade bread, locally smoked salmon, granola, and blueberry flapjacks with spruce-tip syrup. Ah, Alaska!

Dogfish flesh takes on an unpleasant odor as it ages. To neutralize any odor, Burd marinates fillets of questionable vintage in lemon juice or vinegar for at least 4 hours.

Sandy's recipe is an interesting modern descendant of the berry-and-fish dish served to Thomas Edgar at Unalaska in 1778 (see pages 19–20).

4 dogfish fillets, 4 to 6 ounces each
1 teaspoon plus 2 tablespoons lemon juice or white vinegar,
   more if needed
1 cup water, more if needed
¾ cup olive oil
½ onion, finely minced
Fresh parsley and thyme, finely minced
Salt, pepper, and paprika to taste
2 cups nagoonberries, raspberries, blueberries, gooseberries,
   red currants, or salmonberries
1 cup water
1 tablespoon flour, more if needed
Chopped fresh fennel, oregano, tarragon, or cilantro to taste
   (optional)

Soak the fillets overnight in a mixture of 1 teaspoon of the lemon juice to each cup of water, being sure the fish is covered by this liquid.

One hour before serving, drain the fillets. Combine ½ cup of the olive oil with the remaining lemon juice, onion, parsley, thyme, salt, pepper, and paprika, and marinate the fillets in this mixture. Turn the fillets every 15 minutes.

While the fillets marinate, heat the berries with the water just until soft. Do not overcook, or the flavor will dissipate. Put the mixture through a sieve to remove the seeds. Set aside. You should have 1½ cups of berry juice.

Preheat the broiler.

In a small saucepan, heat the remaining ¼ cup olive oil and whisk in enough flour to form a paste. Add the berry juice to the mixture and stir over low heat until thick. Add fresh herbs to taste, if desired. Do not boil the sauce.

Drain the fish and broil until cooked through, about 5 minutes per side. Serve the sauce with the fillets.

MAKES 4 SERVINGS.

Salmonberries

FISH AS CLAN CRESTS

Both the dogfish and the sculpin were frequently carved by the Tlingit as clan crests on totem poles.

The dogfish can be recognized by its high, domed forehead, gill slits, and pointed teeth. A tongue sometimes protrudes from the dogfish's mouth downward over the lower row of teeth, or a labret may ornament the fish's lower lip. Other conventions in carving dogfish include asymmetrical tail flukes, sharp spines, and small dorsal fins.

The sculpin, on the other hand, is carved with an outsize head and a number of sharp spines. The spines are portrayed by cedar boards attached as horizontal projections, often several feet long.

FLOUNDER AND SOLE

School Days

Juneau's newest school, which opened in September 1994, was named by the school board after the Tlingit name for Juneau, Dzant K'heeni. *The name translates "where the flounder gather."*

Plaice

Flounder and sole—along with halibut (page 72) and turbot—are known as flatfish because of their distinctive broad, thin configuration. These bottom-dwelling fish are marine chameleons, able to alter their exterior to blend with a change in surroundings. Triggered by visual stimuli, the skin cells concentrate or dissipate minute granules of red, orange, yellow, and black, creating hues to match the sand or rock on which they rest. Another singular characteristic of adult flatfish is that both eyes are on one side of the body, rather than one on each side as is the case for other fish.

Alaskan species include Alaska plaice or "lemon sole," arrowtooth flounder or "turbot," blackback flounder, Dover sole (not the same as the true Dover sole of Britain), which tend to be quite large in deep water off Alaska, flathead sole from the Gulf of Alaska, Greenland turbot, rex sole, and rock sole. Rock sole, one of the most highly regarded North Pacific flatfish, is particularly abundant in the Gulf of Alaska. Rock sole roe is a valuable food exported to Asia.

The predominant market form is as skinless fillets, boneless with the "frill" (band of small fin bones) trimmed away. On the West Coast, small flounder such as Pacific sand dabs and rex sole are sometimes marketed whole as "skinners." In this form, both tail and head are removed, and the dark side skinned. Large flounder may be cut across into steaks—as halibut often is.

Because flatfish are thin, with a high ratio of surface area to weight, their flesh is susceptible to dehydration and spoilage. Buying these fish fresh, recently cut, and properly chilled is crucial.

The flesh of flounder is light and delicate. "No fish lends itself more to such a variety of imaginative dishes," writes Albert Jules McClane in his highly regarded *Encyclopedia of Fish Cookery*. Sole tends to be more delicate than flounder, but the two are generally interchangeable in recipes. In fact, what's labeled in the market as "sole" may well be fillets from small flounder.

Recipes that preserve flounder's moisture are best: poach, steam, sauté, microwave, and pan-fry.

Flounder with Apricots and Green Pepper

Rockfish, skate, steelhead, weakfish, Alaska pollock, or orange roughy may be substituted for the flounder in this recipe. And when fresh apricots are available, use half a pound of them instead of the canned fruit, with apricot nectar or orange juice for the canned liquid. Serve with steamed basmati rice.

1 pound flounder fillets
1 teaspoon paprika
1 teaspoon fennel seed
3 tablespoons olive oil
½ to 1 cup finely chopped onion
3 cloves garlic, finely minced
1 green pepper, cored, seeded, and cut in strips
1 can (8¼ ounces) apricot halves in juice (drain juice and reserve)
2 teaspoons cider vinegar or lemon juice
1 tablespoon cornstarch
Salt and freshly ground black pepper to taste
Soy sauce, fish sauce, or curry powder to taste
2 teaspoons grated lemon zest

Peppers

Cut the fillets across their width into ½-inch strips. Toss in a plastic bag with the paprika and fennel seed. Heat 2 tablespoons of the olive oil in a large cast-iron skillet. Fry the fish over medium heat, turning once, until well browned and cooked through, about 5 minutes. Remove the fish to a warm pan. Clean the skillet and return it to the burner. Add the remaining 1 tablespoon oil. Sauté the onion over medium-high heat until it begins to brown, 2 to 4 minutes. Add the garlic and green pepper, and stir-fry for an additional 2 minutes.

Pour the reserved apricot juice into a measuring cup. Add the cider vinegar and cornstarch, and stir well. If needed, add more water to make ¾ cup. Pour this mixture into the skillet and stir over low heat until thickened. Add the fish and warm for about 30 seconds, stirring carefully so that the strips of fish do not break up. Add salt and pepper to taste, then season with soy sauce, fish sauce, or curry power to taste.

Top the fish with the apricots and lemon zest, and allow the mixture to warm for 30 seconds.

MAKES 4 SERVINGS.

Philippine Escabeche

The recipe for this escabeche is handed out on cards by New Sagaya, a supermarket in Anchorage where cooks can find everything from rice cookers to herring roe on kelp. The original Sagaya, tucked away on winding Spenard Road, was opened in 1973 by Paul Reid and his mother, Hiroko Nito.

Escabeche is a convenient buffet dish because it can be made the day before and served at room temperature. Bass, butterfish, mackerel, mahimahi, grouper, sole, red snapper, swordfish—any firm, meaty fish—may be substituted for the flounder. For Caribbean escabeche, add allspice berries, chile peppers, and sliced Spanish olives to the marinade. Serve this dish with crusty bread and steamed new red potatoes tossed with parsley butter.

½ teaspoon salt
¼ teaspoon freshly ground black pepper
¼ cup flour
2 pounds flounder fillets or steaks
¼ cup corn or olive oil
1 small onion, sliced
1 red bell pepper, cored, seeded, and sliced
1 green or yellow bell pepper, cored, seeded, and sliced
⅓ cup sugar
¼ cup lime juice
¼ cup water
1 tablespoon rice vinegar or white wine vinegar
1 tablespoon cornstarch
2 tablespoons soy sauce
2 medium tomatoes, cut into wedges, for garnish
1 cucumber, sliced, for garnish
Sliced green onions, for garnish

Combine the salt, pepper, and flour. Coat the flounder with this mixture. Heat a skillet and add 2 tablespoons of the oil. Fry the fish over medium heat until golden on both sides. Set the skillet, with the fish still in it, aside.

In a clean skillet, heat the remaining 2 tablespoons oil. Sauté the onion and the red and green peppers over medium-high heat until browned. Arrange the browned vegetables over the fish in the other skillet.

Wild onion

In the same skillet used to brown the onion and peppers, combine the sugar, lime juice, water, and vinegar, and bring to a boil. Pour this mixture over the fish. Return the fish to the heat and simmer for 10 minutes. Combine the cornstarch and soy sauce, add to the skillet, and cook until the sauce is thickened. Serve hot, or cool to room temperature before serving. Garnish with the tomato wedges, cucumber slices, and green onions.

MAKES 4 SERVINGS.

THE FLOUNDER MAN

Once upon a time there lived a rich man with a beautiful daughter. The girl had many suitors, and even her grandma was jealous of all the attention she got.

The wily grandma scattered berries over a little mossy point and undermined the moss with her ulu, and when the daughter went to pick the juicy berries, the point dropped away into the river and was swept to sea.

Through the night, the girl floated and floated, until the little mossy point was in danger of being broken apart on rocks. So she jumped into a cave on a cliff face. But there was no way out.

The next evening a man paddling by in his kayak heard the rich man's daughter weeping. "Come home with me," he offered, adding, "Hurry! I must be home by midnight." The girl was afraid, but her fear was lessened by the stranger's deep voice and his wonderful perfume, distilled from a rare mountain plant. So she went home with him.

The girl lived with the man and his grandma, but she didn't care for their food—raw seal lungs—and they were mean to her. Life was odd, because the only time she could go outside was when the man came home at midnight.

One morning the girl awoke early and saw her husband in full daylight. He was ugly, with one eye right in the middle of his face. The eye drained odorous pus, which collected in a basket hung on his cheek. He was a flounder-man.

One afternoon while the flounder was hunting and grandma napped, the girl escaped. She fled next door to his handsome masters, who were real men—and rich, too. They escorted her home, and gave many gifts to her parents. After two months of feasting, the handsome men went home— taking the pretty girl as wife.

—A legend told by the Tanaina Athabascan Indians, adapted from "The Flounder Story," in Tanaina Tales from Alaska *by Bill Vaudrin (University of Oklahoma Press, 1969)*

Sole Basquaise

Growing up in Algiers, Rabah "Randy" Chettfour little dreamed of being a chef in faraway Alaska. But after working for seven and a half years at the Anchorage Hilton as director of catering, Chettfour graduated to preside as chef of his own restaurant, Aladdin's. Here diners may recline on carpets on the floor if they wish, and dine on lamb, couscous, or Sole Basquaise.

"I use rockfish, sole, marlin—almost any fish will do for this dish," Chettfour says. "Sometimes I use half large shrimp or cod, and half red snapper, and call it 'Seafood Basquaise.'" He serves his spicy ragout with rice and lemon wedges.

If the sole fillets you choose are small, you may have enough to serve more than one per person. Larger fillets may need to be cut to make four equal serving pieces.

> ⅓ cup flour
> Salt and freshly ground black pepper to taste
> 2 pounds sole fillets
> 2 tablespoons butter

Ragout:
> 2 tablespoons olive oil
> 1 medium onion, cut in ¼-inch julienne
> 3 cloves garlic, finely chopped
> 1 eggplant, cut in 1-inch dice
> 1 bell pepper, cored, seeded, and cut in ¼-inch julienne
> 10 mushrooms, quartered
> 2 tablespoons sliced black olives
> 2 tablespoons sliced green olives
> 1 tablespoon paprika
> Pinch of cayenne pepper
> 1 tablespoon ground cumin
> 2 tablespoons tomato paste
> 2 teaspoons dried oregano

To make the Ragout, heat the olive oil in a large saucepan and sauté the onion and garlic for about 4 minutes. Add the eggplant, bell pepper, mushrooms, black and green olives, paprika, cayenne, cumin, tomato paste, and oregano. Add sufficient water to cover. Bring to a

Eggplant

boil, reduce the heat, and simmer until the eggplant and bell peppers are crisp-tender, about 10 minutes. Taste and adjust the seasonings if necessary.

To prepare the fish, mix the flour with salt and pepper to taste. Coat the sole fillets in flour, patting to remove excess. Heat the butter in a sauté pan. Sauté the floured fillets until golden. Add a cup or so of the Ragout, and simmer over low heat just until the fish is cooked through, 4 to 5 minutes.

For each serving, ladle one-fourth of the Ragout onto a warm plate and place a fish fillet on top.

MAKES 4 SERVINGS.

Haida design from painted spruce-root mat

Tlingit woman in Chilkat blanket, ca. 1900

GREENLING

The primary greenling species swimming in the emerald green, plankton-rich waters of Alaska include the kelp greenling, masked greenling, and rock greenling, as well as the lingcod (not actually a cod; see page 92) and the Atka mackerel (not a true mackerel). The lingcod is the only greenling caught commercially; the others are primarily sportfish.

A hardy fighter, the kelp greenling is a good catch on surf tackle near kelp and eelgrass beds or rock breakwaters. It grows to 2 feet long and can tip the scales at 5 pounds. The Atka mackerel, named for one of the two largest islands in the Aleutian Chain, is abundant in the Bering Sea and off the Aleutians.

All members of the greenling family are distinguished by a long, continuous dorsal fin, notched slightly at the midpoint. They sport verdigris to bronze exteriors.

Raw greenling flesh tends to pale blue or blue-green in color. Cooked, it becomes white.

Bull kelp

Naomi's Baked Greenling

Anchorage fiction writer Naomi Warren Klouda was teaching college in Kodiak when she first ate kelp greenling that had been caught from a Kodiak beach. For the occasion she developed this tasty preparation, which met the exacting standards of her young son and daughter. "It's a pretty fish," Klouda says, "with so many colors it almost looks tropical." Serve with cornbread.

1 cup plain yogurt
1 cup salsa
1 medium onion, thinly sliced
1 greenling, about 5 pounds, gutted and head removed

Mix the yogurt and salsa in a small bowl.

Preheat the oven to 375°F.

In the bottom of a roasting pan place a sheet of heavy foil large enough to enclose the fish. Spread one-third of the sliced onion on the foil. Dollop one-third of the yogurt-salsa mixture over the onion. Place the greenling on top. Put another third of the onion and yogurt-salsa mixture inside the fish, and the remaining third of each on top. Fold and seal the foil around the fish.

Bake until the fish flakes easily, about 30 to 40 minutes. Serve hot.

MAKES 6 SERVINGS.

A 300-pound halibut, 1904

The halibut starts life swimming in an upright position. Gradually, however, it assumes the typical oddities of a flatfish. One eye begins to migrate closer to the other. The dorsal fin creeps forward and the fish swims drunkenly. Eventually—looking like a serving platter with fins—the halibut swims on its side, both eyes facing up. The back skin changes color, darkening to blend in with the bottom; the belly lightens.

Halibut is a member of the flounder family, cousin to a great many other flatfish—such as the plaice, turbot, and rex sole—that share the same odd metamorphosis as they mature. The transformation of distinctive skin to a natural camouflage has proven a good evolutionary move, because there are nearly 200 members of the flatfish family (see also Flounder and Sole, page 64), halibut being among the largest.

Alaska's halibut is the Pacific halibut, dark gray or brown on its top side (the side to which the eyes have migrated), with the bottom or "blind" side porcelain white. When it lies quietly on the bottom, it blends into the sand, thus avoiding predators.

Halibut grow slowly, requiring about 5 years to reach 20 inches. Males may reach 4 feet and 40 pounds. But females can grow to 8 feet and tip the scales at 500 pounds after 15 years. Females are the trophies that tourists love to haul in off Homer and Cordova and with which they proudly pose for Polaroids.

Small halibut are called "chickens" or "Ping-Pong paddles." Large trophy females are known as "barn doors" or "whales." Large halibut are capable of breaking legs and tipping over small craft while thrashing about. Among Native peoples, halibut traditionally were dispatched with clubs; today a revolver may be used to quiet a lively catch.

A fish with a notably meaty texture, halibut is delicious baked, broiled, grilled, in casseroles, in chowder, poached, or steamed. When cooked, the flesh is mild flavored, lean, very white, and firm textured yet tender.

Roast Halibut with Figs

This dish may also be cooled to room temperature and served as an appetizer.

What distinguishes this fish dish is the gift wrap: halibut with orange sections and fresh figs, enveloped in a grape leaf. The method is simplicity itself, but the Mediterranean effect is exotic and mouth-watering. This recipe is the bright idea of John Lowry, chef for Carrs Specialty Meats in Anchorage. Lowry designed it as a low-cal entrée, but, to wow gourmet guests, you might present it as the fish course in a splendiferous summer feast.

2 seedless oranges
1¼ pounds skinless halibut fillets
2½ tablespoons olive oil
Juice of 1 lemon
1 jar drained whole grape leaves (net weight 8 ounces) (see Note)
10 fresh figs, stemmed and halved
¼ teaspoon coarse salt
Freshly ground black pepper to taste

Preheat the oven to 450°F.

Using a vegetable peeler, remove the zest from the oranges in strips from stem to stern. Place strips in a shallow baking dish and bake for 5 minutes, or until the strips begin to color and release their essential oils. Remove zist (white material inside the zest) from the oranges, and discard. Separate oranges into sections. (You need 20 sections.)

Cut the halibut into 20 fingers about 1 inch by 1 inch by 3 inches. (Equality is not crucial, because the grape leaves will present a variety of covering abilities, so smaller fingers can be wrapped in smaller leaves.)

Heat 1½ tablespoons of the olive oil in a frying pan and sauté the halibut fingers until the flesh is firm and beginning to brown—about 1 minute each, top and bottom. Drizzle fingers with lemon juice.

Place each finger on a grape leaf with 1 fig half and 1 orange section. Roll each leaf around its stuffing, and place in an ovenproof serving dish. Pour the pan drippings over the stuffed leaves.

Reduce oven heat to 375°F. Bake the stuffed leaves for 10 to 12 minutes. Drizzle with the remaining tablespoon of olive oil. Sprinkle with salt and pepper. Garnish with orange zest strips, and serve at once.

MAKES 4 MAIN DISH SERVINGS, OR 20 APPETIZER SERVINGS.

Figs

NOTE: Grape leaves are sold in jars of about 2 dozen on the gourmet shelves of major supermarkets.

Unloading halibut, 1888

Halibut hook with wolf figure

Stuffed Halibut in Phyllo

Raim "Randy" Douti, chef/owner of Anchorage's Mama Mia Restaurante, began offering halibut stuffed and wrapped in tissue-thin phyllo pastry as a weekly special and soon added it to his permanent menu. Born in Albania of an Albanian father and Italian mother, Douti grew up eating "all fresh, homemade cooking," and he still prefers that kind of cuisine. He trained at Sorento's in Anchorage, then purchased Mama Mia in 1993. "I *love* to play with sauces," he says. "When I can taste the flavor I'm looking for, I stop experimenting."

3 tablespoons olive oil
1 large onion, finely chopped
½ pound mushrooms, chopped
½ pound scallops, diced
½ pound shrimp, diced
½ pound king crabmeat, diced
½ teaspoon dried oregano
¼ teaspoon dried basil
1 teaspoon granulated garlic
Salt and freshly ground black pepper to taste
½ cup (about) dry bread crumbs
12 boneless halibut slices, 4 ounces each, cut ¼ to ½ inch thick and
  as square as possible
12 sheets (about ⅜ pound) phyllo dough (see Note)
½ cup melted butter

Onion Cream Sauce:
1 medium onion, finely chopped
1 clove garlic, chopped
1 bay leaf
5 black peppercorns
1 cup water
2 tablespoons Chablis wine
1 tablespoon white vinegar
¼ cup butter
¼ cup flour
1 cup heavy cream
⅔ cup freshly grated Parmesan cheese
Salt and white pepper to taste

To make the Onion Cream Sauce, place the onion, garlic, bay leaf, peppercorns, and water in a small saucepan. Boil for 5 minutes. Strain. Measure 1 cup. Add the Chablis and vinegar.

Melt the butter in a heavy saucepan over low heat; do not allow it to brown. Slowly blend in the flour until a thick paste is formed, and cook 3 minutes, stirring constantly. Slowly stir in the cream and the onion mixture. Continue to stir until the sauce is thick, but still thin enough that it can be drizzled. Stir in the cheese. Season to taste with salt and white pepper. Keep the sauce warm in the top of a double boiler.

Tsimshian sea monster
halibut hook

To prepare the stuffing, heat the olive oil in a large frying pan and sauté the onion and mushrooms until brown, about 5 minutes. Add the scallops, shrimp, and crabmeat, and sauté until barely cooked through, 3 to 4 minutes. Add the oregano, basil, and garlic. Taste, and adjust the seasoning with salt and pepper.

Stir in the bread crumbs and allow to rest 5 minutes off the heat. There should be enough bread crumbs to soak up all the liquid released by the seafood, but no more; add a few more bread crumbs if needed.

On a cutting board, line up half of the halibut slices. Top each with some of the stuffing, dividing it evenly among them. Top with the remaining halibut.

Preheat the oven to 450°F.

Lay out the phyllo dough and cover it with clear plastic wrap. Using a clean pastry brush, butter the top of 1 sheet of phyllo. Place another sheet on top, and brush with butter. Wrap the buttered sheets around 1 halibut "sandwich." Repeat with the remaining phyllo and halibut.

Place the filled packets seam side down on a buttered baking sheet and brush with melted butter.

Place in the oven and bake for 8 to 11 minutes. Watch carefully. When the pastry begins to turn golden, cover it with foil. When the halibut can be pierced easily with a metal skewer or the point of a knife, brush the packets again with butter. (This increases the tenderness of the pastry.) Bake for another 30 seconds. Serve hot on warmed plates that have been drizzled with Onion Cream Sauce. Drizzle a little more sauce on top.

MAKES 6 SERVINGS.

NOTE: If phyllo dough is purchased frozen, thaw very slowly, still wrapped (overnight in the refrigerator will do); plan to use all exposed sheets immediately.

Barbara's Halibut Dip

Because Homer is famed for its trophy halibut, the *Homer News* holds an annual Fish, Photos & Fibs contest. In the summer of 1993, Barbara J. Springer won the Fish category. Barbara's rich and creamy dip is an excellent destination for leftover cooked halibut. Other fish, such as leftover grilled or poached salmon or trout, or smoked halibut or trout, would be tasty in this great make-ahead party dish, too. Serve this dip with crudités, chips, bagel chips, crackers, or toast points.

2 cups cooked, flaked halibut
2 teaspoons sweet-hot mustard
½ teaspoon celery seed
½ cup mayonnaise
½ to ¾ cup sour cream
2 tablespoons Worcestershire sauce
1 teaspoon lemon juice
2 cloves garlic, finely minced
½ teaspoon dried dill
Dash of Tabasco sauce
Dash of nutmeg

Mix the halibut, mustard, celery seed, mayonnaise, sour cream, Worcestershire sauce, lemon juice, garlic, dill, Tabasco sauce, and nutmeg, adjusting the seasoning to taste. Chill, covered, for at least 1 hour.

MAKES 6 TO 8 SERVINGS.

Haida halibut club

THE HALIBUT CLUB

The phrase "hooked on art" takes on fresh meaning when admiring halibut hooks and halibut clubs. This Pacific Northwest fishing gear often took the form of highly decorated, carved works of art.

Among the Tlingit and Haida particularly, the hardwood fish clubs often bore the intricate designs usually associated with screens, grease bowls, and totems. Averaging 40 centimeters in length, the clubs were made of hardwood—difficult to carve, but design and painstaking craftsmanship were considered propitious for good fishing.

Sailing in the territorial waters of the northern Tlingit in 1787, Captain George Dixon wrote of their halibut fishing:

They bait their hooks with a kind of fish . . . or squid . . . and having sunk it to the bottom they fix a [seal] bladder to the end of the line as a buoy. . . . One man is sufficient to look after five or six of these buoys; when he perceives a fish bite he is in no great hurry to haul up his line, but gives him time to be well hooked, and when he has hauled the fish up to the surface of the water he knocks him on the head with a short club.

Clubbing subdued the struggling halibut, which, if very large, was capable of breaking legs and damaging or even upsetting the canoe in its final struggle.

Today, the blunt object that is the halibut club is prized by art collectors.

Halibut Scaloppine à la Marsala

Karan Dersham of Anchor Point dishes up the home cooking at Dersham's Outlook Lodge, a log structure with a panoramic view, used as a base for Cook Inlet fishing charters. One of Karan's specialties is an inspired halibut version of a veal standard, served with pasta. Guests applaud.

1½ pounds boneless halibut fillets
¼ cup flour
Salt and freshly ground black pepper to taste
Garlic powder to taste
2 tablespoons butter
2 tablespoons olive oil
½ pound mushrooms, sliced
¼ cup Marsala wine
½ cup chicken stock or clam liquor
Juice of ½ lemon
1 tablespoon chopped fresh parsley

Cut the halibut fillets into ¼-inch slices. Season the flour with salt, pepper, and a dash of garlic powder, and dredge the slices in the flour mixture. Set the remaining flour aside for the sauce. Heat the butter and olive oil in a large skillet, and briefly fry the floured halibut slices, being careful not to overcook them. Keep the browned halibut warm in the oven on low heat.

Add the mushrooms to the same skillet and sauté briefly, adding more butter if necessary. Stir in the leftover seasoned flour to make a paste and cook, stirring, until the mushrooms have released their liquid and are nearly tender. Add the Marsala, and stir in just enough chicken stock to make a light sauce. Stir in the lemon juice. Pour the sauce over the browned halibut. Sprinkle with the fresh parsley and serve at once.

Makes 4 servings.

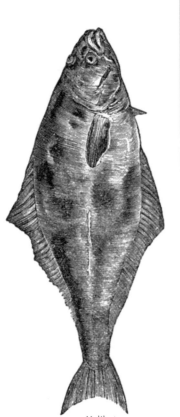

Halibut

Halibut Cheek and Wild Rice Soup

During the spring and summer, Kathie Mears of Seward labors on the processing line at Icicle Seafoods. Cheeking halibut heads is an employment benefit that she and her coworkers on the line gleefully anticipate, as halibut cheeks are delicious boneless chunks ranging in size from as small as a sea scallop to as large as one's palm.

One year, Mears says, "I filled my freezer with over 100 pounds of this treat. I've been gradually trying to eat my way to the back of my freezer—trying out new and unconventional recipes." She serves her cheeky soup with Scandinavian rye crackers.

2 tablespoons oil or Clarified Butter (see page 232)
1 cup broccoli florets
1 cup sliced carrots
1 teaspoon finely chopped fresh ginger
1 teaspoon freshly ground black pepper
3 tablespoons flour
1½ cups water
1½ cups cooked wild rice
1 cup raw halibut cheeks or boneless fillets, cut into bite-sized pieces
1¼ cups light cream or half-and-half
½ cup toasted slivered almonds
1 tablespoon herbes de Provence (see Note)

Tlingit halibut hook

Heat the oil in a 4-quart saucepan. Add the broccoli, carrots, ginger, and pepper, and sauté for 3 minutes. Gradually add the flour, stirring. The mixture will be sticky.

Add the water and stir until the flour is thoroughly incorporated. Then stir in the wild rice and halibut. Bring to a boil. Reduce the heat, cover, and simmer for 10 minutes, stirring occasionally. Then add the cream, almonds, and herbes de Provence. Serve at once.

MAKES 4 TO 6 SERVINGS.

NOTE: Herbes de Provence is a traditional French blend of dried marjoram, rosemary, sage, thyme, aniseed, and savory, often marketed in a small crock.

Praline Halibut

Legal whiz A. Isabel Lee of Anchorage smacks her lips when talking about this exuberantly buttery entrée, which she first encountered in Florida restaurants. No counting calories here! The dish was originally made with grouper; now that she's settled in Alaska, Lee uses halibut. Serve with individual loaves of sourdough bread, pasta, or small red potatoes—something to soak up the drippings.

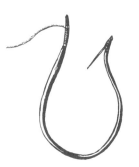

Tlingit halibut hook

½ cup butter, softened
½ cup light brown sugar
½ cup finely ground pecans
3 pounds halibut fillets
Juice of 2 lemons
Salt and white pepper to taste
½ cup flour
¼ cup Clarified Butter (see page 232)
Chopped fresh parsley, for garnish

Combine the Softened Butter, brown sugar, and pecans. Mix well and set aside.

Sprinkle the fish with the lemon juice, salt, and pepper. Dust lightly with the flour.

Heat the Clarified Butter over medium-high heat in a sauté pan. When hot, add the fish. Cook until the fish is golden brown on one side, 4 to 6 minutes. Turn, cover, and continue cooking on low heat until the fish is cooked through (about 4 more minutes).

Remove the fish to a warm serving dish. Pour off the excess clarified butter. Add the pecan butter to the pan. When the butter begins to foam, pour it over the fillets. Sprinkle with the parsley. Serve immediately.

Makes 6 servings.

Halibut Olympia Simmons

During the winter, helicopter pilot Chet Simmons of Valdez whisks adventurers visiting from Scotland, Austria, Japan, and Korea high into the Chugach Range for "extreme skiing" on steep unmarked powder slopes.

Simmons comments, "It's great flying here. I couldn't fly in America. It's too taxi-driving, too constructed out there. Alaska's the place to do what I do."

After flying into Anchorage to stock up on his favorite ingredients, Simmons cooks for diversion. A favorite menu choice is his personal take on one of Alaska's ubiquitous seafood entrées, Halibut Olympia—halibut baked under a coating of mayonnaise. He serves Spanish Artichokes (see page 224) on the side.

Unloading halibut, 1888

6 tablespoons mayonnaise, more if needed
6 tablespoons butter, softened
½ cup slivered almonds
2 white or yellow onions, thinly sliced
1 pound mushrooms, thickly sliced
2 pounds halibut fillets, sliced across the grain into 1-inch strips
¼ cup fresh lemon juice
Black pepper to taste
Salt to taste (optional)
Coarsely chopped parsley, for garnish

Preheat the oven to 375°F.

Coat the bottom of a glass baking pan with 2 tablespoons of the mayonnaise and 2 tablespoons of the butter. Sprinkle with one third of the almonds. Over that, put a layer of half of the onions, separated into rings. Add a layer of half of the mushrooms, then half of the halibut. Sprinkle 2 tablespoons of the lemon juice over the top. Repeat the butter and mayonnaise layer. Then sprinkle with black pepper and salt. Top with another third of the almonds. Layer the remaining onions, mushrooms, and halibut on top, sprinkle with the remaining 2 tablespoons lemon juice, and top with a final layer of mayonnaise and butter and the remaining almonds.

Bake for 30 minutes. As soon as the almonds are toasted, remove the dish from the oven. Sprinkle with parsley and serve.

MAKES 6 SERVINGS.

RAVEN BRINGS MAN HALIBUT

In the beginning, man lacked access to halibut. So Raven went to see Chief Cormorant as he sat in his fine canoe pulling in halibut after halibut.

Invited aboard, Raven sat for a long time looking hungrily at the gleaming catch at his feet. "Chief, I'm starving! May I have just one small halibut for my supper?"

"No way!" grumbled Cormorant.

But while Cormorant attended to his line, Raven slyly stuck a biting bug on the back of his neck. "Get that off!" protested Cormorant.

"Sure," said Raven, "just open your mouth."

"Are you nuts?" protested Cormorant.

"It's delicious," Raven wheedled. "Stick out your tongue."

"Oh, all right," agreed greedy Cormorant, "give it here."

As Cormorant opened his great beak, Raven seized his vulnerable tongue and tore it out by the roots. Screaming in pain, Cormorant grappled with Raven, the canoe rocking and rolling. Finally, Cormorant fainted. When he came to, all he could say was, "Gogogo!"

"If you want your tongue, Chief, the deal is that I get all the fish I want for my supper, and my people can catch halibut any time."

"Gogogo!" agreed Cormorant.

Cormorant's tongue never did grow back properly. To this day, Cormorant can cry only, "Gogogo!"

—A legend told by Southeast Alaska Natives

Macadamia Nut-Crusted Halibut

Some Alaska lodges are rustic; some aren't. In the latter class is Tutka Bay Lodge on Kachemak Bay, profiled in 1992 by both Florence Fabricant in the *New York Times*'s Sunday travel section and by Giselle Smith in *Alaska Airlines* magazine. A 25-minute motorboat ride from Homer, Tutka Bay Lodge is owned by Jon and Nelda Osgood. A helicopter pilot in Vietnam, Jon offers "extras" such as helicopter viewing of and landings on Harding Glacier, complete with chilled champagne. Nelda, a naturalist, oversees menus showcasing local seafood—salmon, halibut, scallops, and crab. The dredged, coated fillets in this nutty main dish can be prepared an hour or two ahead and refrigerated. Almonds can be substituted for the macadamia nuts.

Serve with Oscar's Tartar Sauce (see page 234) and lemon wedges.

1 cup flour
1 tablespoon paprika
½ tablespoon garlic powder
½ teaspoon salt
½ teaspoon white pepper
2 eggs, well beaten
⅓ cup water or milk
½ cup dry bread crumbs
½ cup coarsely chopped macadamia nuts
2 pounds halibut fillets, cut into serving-sized pieces
1 cup peanut oil, more as needed

Raven

Combine the flour, paprika, garlic powder, salt, and pepper in a shallow bowl. Combine the eggs and water in a second shallow bowl. Combine the bread crumbs and macadamia nuts in a third shallow bowl.

Dredge the fillets in the seasoned flour. Dip the floured pieces in the egg mixture. Coat with the nut mixture, pressing the nuts onto the fish. Lay the fillets on waxed paper or plastic wrap.

Pour peanut oil into a large skillet to a depth of ¼ to ½ inch. Heat the oil to 375°F. Fry the coated fish pieces for 2 to 4 minutes per side, or until golden. Cook just until the fish is golden on both sides and opaque in the center. Drain on paper towels. Serve hot.

MAKES 4 SERVINGS.

HERRING

As fall comes on in Petersburg, Alaska, it's time to prepare herring for winter. Herring are caught, gutted ("gibbed"), and salted. Some old-timers recommend you skip the gibbing—claiming innards give the food a more robust flavor!

Herring are small fish related to the shad, alewife, and sardine, as well as to the freshwater or lake herring, the "cisco." They are a migratory species, spending most of their lives in deep waters offshore. In the spring they swim to beaches in schools that may be miles wide, to spawn. For pre-freezer cooks, foods that handily congregated at the same beaches or estuaries at the same time each year were valuable harvests indeed.

At 6 to 12 inches long, the Pacific herring is slightly smaller than the Atlantic; it is distinguished by a single, short dorsal fin and large scales. The sleek Pacific herring is dark green to silvery blue on the back, with silver-blue sides and bellies. They can live up to 19 years.

Alaskans find a variety of uses for herring, from bait in crab pots to an important export commodity. Most herring commercially harvested in Alaskan waters are sought for their roe, which is exported to Japan. The herring used in Alaskan kitchens are generally from recreational catches, seldom from the market.

Herring's dark, rich flesh cooks up moist and ivory. It is especially delicious grilled, smoked, or pickled.

Because of its high fat content, herring turns rancid quicker than leaner fish. Fresh herring should be cooked right away. Salt-brined herring keeps in the refrigerator up to a week. Smoking increases the refrigerator life of herring to 2 to 3 weeks.

Herring

RAVEN LEARNS TO COOK HERRING

One spring, Raven and his wife, Bright-Cloud Woman, went fishing far from shore. They netted 40 canoeloads of slippery herring. But as they paddled home, they became lost. Exhausted, they landed on a strange beach. Oil Woman, a sorceress, invited them in to rest. A tempting perfume awakened Raven. Following his pointed nose, he found Oil Woman cooking herring. "How do you do that wonderful thing?" he asked, his stomach rumbling.

"Who cares if I'm a good cook," moaned Oil Woman, "for I am alone in all the world." Raven stroked her hair and kissed her, but Oil Woman would not reveal her secret.

"You beast!" stormed Bright-Cloud that evening. "How could you hug and kiss that person?" Raven just hid his face in his bowl of raw fish. Bright-Cloud paddled home by herself.

Days passed. Oil Woman and Raven braided and dried his catch. She cooked even more delicious meals, but never offered him any. "What's the matter, my dear?" she asked. "Why so glum?"

My people are hungry," sighed Raven. "How can I get these dry fish home?"

"That's easy, my love; we'll just hitch up my magic elderberry canoe, and it will tow your cargo to your camp."

Finally, sick with desire for Raven, Oil Woman taught him how to heat stones to cook herring and how to render oil. Soon, shaking off her influence, Raven escaped. The people were so pleased to see him—and to dine on hot herring for the very first time.

—A legend told by Southeast Alaska Natives,
adapted from The Box of Daylight by
William Hurd Hillyer (Alfred A. Knopf, 1931)

SCANDINAVIAN FUSION

Gravad lax, lutefisk, pickled herring, fattigmand! *How did Alaska's cuisine come to embrace so many Scandinavian dishes?*

The tale begins with a famine. Because of a nationwide harvest failure in Sweden in the late 1860s, massive waves of Scandinavian emigrants took ship for the U.S. In the throes of hunger, nothing looked more appetizing than the Homestead Act of 1862, which offered 160 acres free.

Families who migrated to the Midwest began to yearn for the mountains of home, and their children boarded the new railroads to the Northwest. From fishing in the Columbia, it was but a hop and a skip to the Klondike and adjoining Alaskan territory.

Midway between Juneau and Ketchikan lies Petersburg, founded by Peter Buschmann in 1897 as the site for a salmon cannery and sawmill. It became the heart of Alaska's Scandinavian heritage, from rosemaling *(painted designs) to* sylta flesk *(pressed pork).*

Other Norwegian-Americans followed Buschmann's lead, naming the main street Nordic Drive and building a Sons of Norway Hall (1912) on pilings over Hammer Slough.

Every May, on the weekend closest to Norwegian Independence Day, the Little Norway Festival spruces up the town with fashion shows, dancing, and feasting. The Norwegian "fish feed" draws visitors from all over. Typical dishes served include gravad lax (laved with a mustard sauce from Oslo's Grand Hotel), poached salmon, Norwegian fish pudding, baked black cod, Swede Wasvick's pickled herring (see next page), and lutefisk (made in 600-pound batches). And the feast is topped off with fattigmand *(fried cardamom pastries) and* krumkaker *(crisp wafers baked on a special iron).*

Petersburg is not the only Alaskan settlement that celebrates its Scandinavian roots. Both Anchorage and Fairbanks host annual lutefisk dinners, complete with lefse and savory meatballs. In Anchorage, the lutefisk is made from rockfish, and wild cranberries (lingonberries) round out the feast.

Swede's Pickled Herring

This recipe is a specialty of retired fisherman and camp cook Swede Wasvick of Petersburg. Both Swede's Pickled Herring and his lutefisk (made ahead in 600-pound batches and then frozen) are regular features of Petersburg's Little Norway Festival. His lutefisk recipe was brought from Norway by his father; this Scandinavian staple is traditionally made with cod prepared with lye, but Swede uses rockfish and sal soda (crystallized sodium carbonate).

For a more bracing flavor, use 3 cloves of garlic instead of the orange and lemon slices. Fresh herring may be substituted. If you use fresh fish, freeze it for 3 or 4 days before making this recipe, to kill any parasites (see pages 282–83 for details). Serve the pickled herring with sliced ripe tomatoes and crusty dark Russian rye.

> 12 salted herring, skinned and filleted
> ¼ cup sugar
> ½ cup water
> 1½ cups white vinegar
> About 2 tablespoons whole mixed pickling spices (see Note)
> 3 medium onions, sliced
> 3 orange slices
> 3 lemon slices

Soak the herring in cold water for 6 hours. (Skip this step if you are using fresh herring.)

Mix the sugar, water, vinegar, and pickling spices in a saucepan. Bring to a boil and simmer for 5 minutes, then cool.

In a nonreactive glass or crockery container, alternate layers of herring pieces, onion, and citrus slices. Pour the cooled pickling liquid over the contents, covering them entirely. Allow the flavors to meld, refrigerated, for 1 or 2 days before serving.

MAKES 12 SERVINGS.

Once the Gods Smiled

Herring roe on kelp is a Tlingit and Athabascan Indian delicacy that must be tasted to be appreciated.

The small white "pearls" of herring roe are deposited on kelp, fucus (popweed), and laminaria. Once the gods smiled; I was invited to a potluck where this treat had been flown in from the Athabascan hostess's childhood home on Bristol Bay. When eaten absolutely fresh, the delicious, crunchy raw snack is delectable.

NOTE: Mixed pickling spices are a commercial blend that can be found on the spice shelves of most supermarkets

HOOLIGAN

A Hooligan Amulet

A young Inupiat girl was traditionally given an amulet to carry—the dried stomach of a tiny hooligan—to help insure that the girl would be healthy even if she had very little to eat. It was also to remind her to eat just a small amount after she had gone without food for a long time, to prevent illness. Throughout Alaska, clever girls with small appetites were considered the best marriage prospects.

NOTE: Hooligan's ivory flesh is delicate and oily. Extremely perishable, it should be cooked the same day it is caught. Pickled with bay leaf and pickling spices, hooligan will keep, refrigerated, for several days. Anchorage anglers typically bread and deep-fry hooligan.

When is a fish a candle? When it's a hooligan. Hooligan or "candle fish" are so oily that they can be used as a source of light. The clever Tlingit dried them, inserted a wick of twisted spruce bark, and voilà! A fish became a candle.

Both rich and thin, hooligan (also known as eulachon or Columbia River smelt) grow to 9 inches in length. They are related to both the Atlantic smelt and the capelin or grunion. In coloration, hooligan are a shimmering brown to dark blue above, with fine black flecks on the back and silver toward the belly.

Hooligan are the spring crocus, the Capistrano swallow, of Alaska fish—the first to run up the rivers after the winter's ice breaks up. Hooligan, which spawn at age 3, begin to enter the rivers west of Glacier Bay in late February or early March, and Cook Inlet in May before the runs of other fish. In early times, this made them most welcome, often rescuing indigenous peoples from near starvation, when their stores of food for winter were nearly exhausted.

Tlingits caught hooligan in great numbers, ripened them for several days to speed the release of the oil from the flesh, and then rendered their oil in baskets, in bentwood cooking boxes, or by using their dugout canoes as impromptu cooking pots (see pages 271–72). The flavor and color of the oil or "grease" were determined by the length of time the fish ripened. Expert rendering could produce a clear, colorless, mild grease suitable for consuming with fruit.

The oil was stored in bulb kelp "jars" corked with wooden plugs or in bentwood boxes. Some of the oil was traded with Interior peoples by packing it up over time-worn paths through the Coast Range, which became known as "grease trails." Native groups who did not have natural access to hooligan fishing sites traveled long distances to barter their own treasured harvests for the precious oil.

The Tlingit considered hooligan oil vital to their diet. The Gitksan, a Tsimshian people, address hooligan as "the little friend to all the world," and say hooligan grease is *ha la mootxw,* or "for curing humanity."

Gallons and gallons of grease were consumed during the winter as a nutritious condiment or "dip" for dried fish, dried herring eggs, and roasted roots. The dip helped reconstitute dried staples while contributing its own high-anchovy flavor, iodine, and oil-soluble vitamins.

Hooligan are a subsistence or sport catch only. They can be netted in quantities during spring spawning. A favorite hooligan destination for Anchorage residents is Twentymile River on Turnagain Arm. Dipnetters annually scoop up 100,000 hooligan in the vicinity of the Twentymile.

Pan-Fried Hooligan with Caper Sauce

Sportfisherman Calvin Donnelly of Hope anoints his hooligan with a caper sauce that adds lively bursts of flavor. Calvin says the recipe tastes best when made with hooligan that has been out of the water for less than 24 hours. For "can-venience," Calvin, 3 hours from the nearest supermarket, may substitute evaporated milk for whole milk.

2 pounds hooligan, gutted and heads removed
⅓ cup whole milk
⅓ cup flour
⅓ cup yellow cornmeal
2 teaspoons salt
⅛ teaspoon freshly ground black pepper
Oil or shortening for frying

Caper Sauce:
¼ cup butter
Juice of ½ lemon
1 tablespoon drained capers
1 tablespoon minced fresh parsley

To make the Caper Sauce, melt the butter in a small saucepan. Add the lemon juice, capers, and parsley. Set aside.

Wipe the fish dry with paper towels. Pour the milk into a soup plate. On another plate, combine the flour, cornmeal, salt, and pepper. Dip the fish into the milk, and then roll it in the flour mixture. Heat enough oil or shortening to cover the bottom of a skillet. Pan-fry the fish for about 5 minutes on each side, or until it is well browned and cooked through. Pour the Caper Sauce over the hot fish, or pass it in a warmed gravy boat.

MAKES 4 SERVINGS.

Canoes Light as Leaves

On one of his trips to climb Mount McKinley in the early 1900s, writer/artist/mountaineer Belmore Browne passed through the Tanaina Athabascan settlement at Susitna Station on the Susitna River north of Cook Inlet. "There were many Indians around," he wrote, "and scaffolds lined the banks weighted down with long fringes of dried hooligans. The Susitna birch-bark canoes were everywhere, flitting light as leaves through the swift water."

Haida hooligan grease dish

IRISH LORD

Bagging Herring

Apparently the Northwest Coast Indians did not invent their ingenious bag net—to supplement dip nets and rakes for fishing—until shortly before European explorers appeared. Tradition has it that the net was invented by a girl who was inspired by watching an Irish lord swallowing tiny fish in its path. Like the Irish lord, the bag net has a wide mouth and a narrow body. In use, the net is staked so that the mouth faces downstream. The body, woven of nettle fibers, has its "tail" tied shut. When enough herring cram themselves into the bag, the wide end is closed, and the narrow end is hauled into a dugout and opened to release the catch.

The Irish lord is counted among the large family of sculpins—magnificently ugly, swelled-headed, bottom-dwelling fish that scoot about among the rocks. The name derives from the ethnic enmity between Englishmen and Irishmen. It was first applied to a British sculpin, emigrated even before the Colonial period to become the name for a sculpin in the Bay of Maine, and later set sail for Alaska.

The red Irish lord (also called "spotted Irish lord" or "bullhead") is one of the largest Pacific Coast members of this family, ranging from the Kamchatka Peninsula in Russia to Puffin Bay, Alaska. The red grows to 20 inches and bears white and purplish red spots on its olive green body.

Because sculpin are among the most abundant fish in Alaska, fishermen often catch them when seeking other prey. Taking valuable space in their hauls, Irish lord tends to be considered a "trash fish" of no use.

Neither do sportfishermen think very highly of the Irish lord. The typical Alaska fishing derby concentrates on sought-after trophies like king salmon, but residents of Seldovia obviously have a sense of humor. From May 15 to September 5 each year, the Seldovia Sportfishing Derby offers prizes for the largest halibut, salmon—and Irish lord.

Irish lord has a white, flaky, flounder-like flesh. Despite what commercial fishermen think of them, these fish are great baked, poached, or fried; they really don't deserve their dubious standing. For example, master chef Julia Child recommends Irish lord for bouillabaisse. I first enjoyed Irish lord on my honeymoon on the coast of Maine in 1966; my husband speared them while snorkeling.

WHAT IRISH LORD EAT

Irish lords are said to bite on almost any bait—as long as it is fished on or near the bottom. According to the Homer News, *Irish lords have been caught with herring, shrimp, spinners, banana peels, cigar butts, bologna sandwiches, and potato salad. "One locally caught Irish lord had a package of cigarettes in its stomach still in the cellophane. . . ."*

—1995 Homer Tourist & Recreation Guide

Herbed Irish Lord in White Wine

This silky preparation was shared with me a decade ago by Trudy Townes, a Nome high school science teacher who had inherited many of her recipes from her British-born mother. The shallots and herbs set off the fish perfectly. Serve over buttered egg noodles. As a side dish, try steamed spinach in raw radicchio cups.

Quagluk with Irish lord, ca. 1938

¼ cup butter
3 tablespoons minced shallots
1 teaspoon minced parsley
1 teaspoon dried chervil, crumbled (see Note)
1 teaspoon dried thyme, crumbled (see Note)
1 teaspoon dried tarragon, crumbled (see Note)
1 teaspoon salt
½ teaspoon freshly ground black pepper
1½ cups dry white wine
1½ pounds Irish lord fillets, cut into serving portions
1 cup heavy cream

In a large skillet in which the fish will fit in one layer, melt the butter over low heat and sauté the shallots until soft. Add the parsley, chervil, thyme, tarragon, salt, pepper, and wine. Remove from the heat. Arrange the fish over the herb mixture. Cover, return to the heat, and simmer until the fish flakes with a fork, about 5 minutes. Remove the fish to a heated platter and keep warm.

Boil the liquid remaining in the skillet until it is reduced to a thin film. Add the cream; cook and stir until the sauce is reduced to the desired consistency. Serve at once over the fish.

Note: If using fresh herbs, triple the amount.

MAKES 4 SERVINGS.

All Spines and Dagger Points

"... [There are] seemingly endless species of sculpins that abound in Alaska's seas and bays. Enormously wide of mouth are these 'Irish lords,' all head and spines and dagger-sharp points. No two of them are colored alike, varying from gray and yellow to flaming orange and scarlet—garishly-daubed, plug-ugly comics of the deep."

—Frank Dufresne, Alaska's Animals & Fishes (A. S. Barnes, 1946)

LINGCOD

The lingcod's large liver is considered a delicacy in the Arctic, where locals fry it in lard, then grind and mix it with ground gizzard of ptarmigan (Alaska's grouse-like state bird) for an energizing spread. Serve on pilot bread or other crackers.

A voracious and predatory bottom fish, the lingcod is not counted among the cod family but is considered a greenling. A large mouth of sharp canines nabs unsuspecting fish and crabs, a rich diet that helps the lingcod attain lengths up to 60 inches. Lingcod's color is variable, usually greenish brown with dark brown or copper spots arranged in clusters.

Because this piscine cat burglar frequents kelp beds in intertidal zones and enjoys lurking in the nooks and crannies of shipwrecks, it is difficult to catch intentionally and is not a quarry of commercial fishermen. As an "incidental catch," however, it fetches an excellent price. The lingcod is also a popular game fish.

Lingcod flesh bears a slight bluish tinge when raw, but turns an appetizing white when cooked. Firm and flaky, it lends itself to deep-frying, particularly as fish and chips. Some Alaskan cooks consider lingcod cheeks even more of a delicacy than halibut cheeks, seasoned to taste and broiled or fried. Lingcod may be substituted for sablefish, halibut, or cod.

Tlingit ceremonial dress

Alaska Creole Ya-Ya

This incendiary Alaska variation on a New Orleans classic comes from Glenn Denkler, an instructor at Anchorage's King Career Center. Denkler's warming stew contains only 208 calories per serving—low enough to quality for inclusion in the Providence Heart Diet. Because the Creole Seasoning and Shrimp Stock are made from scratch, the stew's flavors are enticingly fresh and deep. Note that you will have some of each left over after preparing this recipe. As a shortcut, prepared Creole or Cajun spice mix can be used. Scallops or halibut may be substituted for the lingcod. Serve this stew with white rice.

Haida design from painted spruce-root mat

3 bay leaves
1 15-ounce can tomato sauce
¼ cup olive oil
1½ cups diced onion (medium dice)
1 cup sliced celery (¼ inch thick)
1 cup diced green bell pepper (medium dice)
2 teaspoons minced fresh garlic
2 cups peeled, seeded, and diced fresh tomatoes, about 3 medium
¼ cup minced parsley
½ pound lingcod fillets, cut into bite-sized pieces
¾ pound medium-sized spot shrimp, shelled and halved
   (reserve shells for Shrimp Stock)

Creole Seasoning:

1 teaspoon cayenne pepper
1 teaspoon white pepper
1 teaspoon black pepper
1 teaspoon paprika
1 teaspoon pulverized dried basil
1 teaspoon dried thyme
1 teaspoon dried oregano

Shrimp Stock:

1 tablespoon butter
½ cup very thinly sliced onion
¼ cup very thinly sliced celery
¼ cup thinly sliced leek, white and green parts
Shells from ¾ pound shrimp ☞

Fish and Breathing

A recent Australian study reports that a diet high in high-fat fish (such as mackerel, cod, and salmon) appears to reduce markedly the incidence of childhood asthma.

Another study, involving 12,000 men in several countries over a 25-year period, found that the more fish (and fruit) the men ate, the less likely they were to die of emphysema and chronic bronchitis.

—from Simply Seafood *magazine, Summer 1995*

Fish basket

½ *cup dry white wine*
½ *bay leaf*
5 cups cold water

To make the Creole Seasoning, mix together the cayenne, white, and black peppers, paprika, basil, thyme, and oregano. Store in a bottle in a cool place. Makes 7 teaspoons; you will need 2 teaspoons for this recipe.

To make the Shrimp Stock, melt the butter over medium heat in a large saucepan. Add the onion, celery, and leek; stir until wilted. Add the shrimp shells and stir until they turn bright orange-pink, about 5 minutes. Add the wine. Increase the heat and stir until most of the liquid has evaporated. Add the bay leaf and water. Simmer for 45 minutes. Strain. The stock may be made several hours ahead. Leftover stock can be frozen. Makes 5 cups; you will need 2 cups for this recipe.

Place the bay leaves in the tomato sauce to rehydrate them.

In a large, heavy saucepan, heat the oil over high heat until it shimmers. Add the onion, celery, and green pepper. Stir constantly until the mixture starts to brown, about 4 minutes. Stir in the garlic, then immediately add the tomatoes and the 2 cups of Shrimp Stock. Reduce the heat. Add the tomato sauce and bay leaves; simmer for 30 minutes. Remove the bay leaves and add the 2 teaspoons of Creole Seasoning and the parsley. Diners unaccustomed to the heat of Creole food should experiment, starting cautiously with ¼ teaspoon of the seasoning, and increasing as tolerated.

Add the lingcod and shrimp, and cook until just done, about 5 minutes. Serve immediately.

MAKES 6 SERVINGS.

C lose relatives of the delectable tuna, mackerel thrive in salt water all over the world. Alaska's chub mackerel can be found from Alaska to Baja. The common Pacific or true mackerel is not a fish native to Alaska.

Mackerel is characterized by a symmetrical, streamlined body with double dorsal fins. The lovely striped pattern adorning the mackerel's back gives its name to the rippled cloud moiré called "mackerel sky."

Mackerel's delicate, oily flesh harbors a sultry flavor unlike any other—a flavor that quickly wins converts, especially when accented with a fresh fruit garnish. This fish lends itself to steaming and stews, salting, drying, canning, and smoking. The high oil content of mackerel causes it to spoil quickly, so fresh mackerel should be cooked right away.

MACKEREL

Fish wheel on the Tanana River west of Nenana, 1988

Mackerel Baked with Fennel Seed

With its Asian seasonings, this recipe has been handed down among good cooks in Yakutat and other cannery-based towns along the Inside Passage for several generations. Variations abound. Accented with the licorice-like warmth of fennel, this main dish is usually served over steamed rice.

4 mackerel, ½ pound each, or 2 mackerel, 1 pound each
2 tablespoons butter
1 cup thinly sliced onion
2 stalks celery, chopped
1 clove garlic, crushed
2 tablespoons grated or finely minced fresh ginger
2 tablespoons fennel seed

If the mackerel are whole, clean them: Remove the heads and cut off the gill covers. Cut the fish open along the ventral side and gut them, leaving the backbone intact.

Preheat the oven to 350°F.

Melt the butter in a frying pan and sauté the onion and celery until transparent, about 5 minutes. Add the garlic, ginger, and fennel seed, and sauté for 2 minutes more, stirring.

With a sharp knife, cut deep, diagonal slits from head to tail on both sides of the mackerel, 1 inch apart. Spoon the onion and fennel seed mixture into these slits.

Lay the fish in a baking dish. Bake for 15 minutes for small fish, 25 minutes for larger fish, or until the fish is cooked through (check the center of the fish to make sure it is done). Serve piping hot.

MAKES 4 SERVINGS.

Onions

Broiled Split Mackerel

When mackerel is in season, this dish is a favorite in kitchens throughout Southeast Alaska. Alaskan cooks with British ancestors serve mackerel with Gooseberry Sauce. Gooseberries grow well in Anchorage and environs south. This recipe comes from storekeeper and noted skeet shooter Dennis Ludvigson of Haines.

4 mackerel, about 12 ounces each
Salt and freshly ground black pepper to taste
1 tablespoon corn oil, more if needed
1½ cups Gooseberry Sauce (see page 240)

If the mackerel are whole, clean them: Remove the heads and cut off the gill covers. Cut the fish open along the ventral side and gut them, leaving the backbone intact.

Open the fish and press the backbone down to make them lie flat (like a butterfly). Pat the fish dry. Sprinkle the flesh side with salt and pepper and brush with a bit of oil. Let the fish reach room temperature. Warm the Gooseberry Sauce.

Preheat the broiler and oil the broiler rack. Place the mackerel on the rack, skin side down, and broil 5 inches from the heat source for 6 to 8 minutes. Turn carefully with a wide spatula and broil on the skin side for 6 minutes, or until the flesh flakes readily. Serve with the warm sauce.

MAKES 4 SERVINGS.

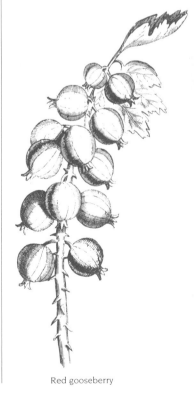

Red gooseberry

POLLOCK

The slender Alaska pollock is one of the region's most abundant resources. In terms of weight alone, Alaska pollock is the most important single market species in the world; it has made up almost 10 percent of the world's finfish catch in recent years. A member of the cod family, Alaska pollock is smaller than true cod and has a slightly sweeter flavor; commercially caught pollock average 16 inches in length and weigh about 1 pound.

Alaska pollock is a plentiful, inexpensive alternative to more pricey species such as true cod. It is marketed fresh or frozen year-round, usually in fillets ranging from 3 to 10 ounces.

Often compared to Atlantic haddock, Alaska pollock offers white flesh and a mild flavor. It is lean and firm and forms attractive flakes when cooked. Much of the pollock harvest is ground into a paste and used in the production of surimi, or imitation crabmeat (see page 152), a typical ingredient in sushi. Alaska pollock is popular with fish-and-chips franchises and Southern California taco restaurants, too.

Use versatile pollock in Fish and Chips (see page 148), baked under a tasty sauce, poached, steamed, or sautéed. Its firmness makes it a natural for Fish Tacos Pudwill (see page 110), chowder, or stew. Pollock can be used in recipes calling for cod.

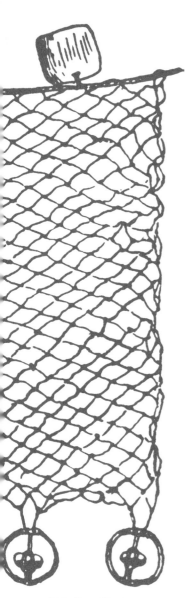

Nettle-fiber gillnet

Pollock being unloaded on deck from a net, 1987

Polynesian Pollock

This easy, lean entrée often surfaces at potlucks sponsored by Anchorage's small but active Samoan community. (Many Samoans first venture to Alaska to attend the multiethnic Alaska Pacific University.) The amount of garlic in the recipe can be increased if you wish. Fresh pineapple spears, tender boiled taro leaves, pale violet poi, and fried plantains are typical side dishes.

⅓ cup soy sauce
1 tablespoon brown sugar
½ teaspoon ground ginger or 1½ teaspoons finely diced fresh ginger
1 clove garlic, crushed
1 tablespoon cider vinegar
2 tablespoons corn oil
1½ pounds pollock fillets

Combine the soy sauce, brown sugar, ginger, garlic, vinegar, and oil in a 9- by 13-inch glass baking dish. Lay the fillets in this marinade. Marinate the fish for 20 minutes at room temperature, turning once.

Preheat the oven to 400°F.

Bake the fish, still in the marinade, for 20 minutes, or until cooked through.

MAKES 4 SERVINGS.

Garlic

SUSHI

The Alaska Roll

Sushi is so popular with Alaskans that Asian sushi chefs are on staff at most of the locations of the locally owned supermarket chain, Carrs Quality Centers. One of Carrs's specialties is the Alaska Roll, a variant of the Philly Roll. The Alaska Roll centers on a stick of smoked salmon, some cream cheese, and two flanking, smaller sticks of cucumber.

A sheet of yakinori *(toasted seaweed) wraps the outside of the Alaska Roll and many other rolled sushi variants. Green-brown in color and shiny,* yakinori *lends a distinctively pleasant, high-tide flavor and aroma to sushi preparations.*

A Primer of Alaska's Sushi

In the early 1980s, the Japanese dish called sushi began to take Alaska by storm. There seems no end to its appeal, either as a snack or as a light meal. In Anchorage, for example, a growing number of eateries offer sushi bars or menus featuring sushi.

Sushi actually means simply "vinegared rice," although it is rarely served alone as such, but is invariably paired with seafood or vegetables. The rice is seasoned with a special syrup that is poured over it, then made glossy by fanning while it cools. Next the rice is generally formed into a cylinder around strips of contrasting ingredients—tuna, cucumber, avocado, and/or watercress for example—wrapped in a sheet of dried seaweed, and then cut in bite-sized pieces. Sometimes the rice is hand-formed into ovals and topped with a gleaming slice of sashimi (raw fish). The whole glorious package may be garnished with roe and served with "vinegared things" such as marinated string beans.

Sushi is at its best when absolutely fresh—prepared by specially trained chefs as the diner looks on. This is why sushi bars have become so popular, combining delicious things to eat with the theater of watching them be prepared to order.

Different types of sushi are usually named after their main seafood ingredient. *Ama ebi* sushi features tender, sweet shrimp; *hirame* features flounder. *Chu toro* is topped with melt-in-your-mouth raw tuna, while *sawara* sushi is topped with mackerel. Luckily for the diner, restaurants generally use a pictorial menu of sushi options, simplifying the choice.

The best-known sushi in Alaska is the popular California Roll—sushi stuffed with tender steamed crab and meltingly ripe avocado. The exterior may be accented by rolling in paprika. J's Cafe in Anchorage serves a California Roll stuffed with surimi, avocado, flying fish eggs, and cucumber.

Another popular sushi is the Philly Roll, the invention of Hiro Kurotsu, chef/owner of Philadelphia's Kawabata restaurant. This refreshing combo marries Philadelphia cream cheese, crab, and cucumber.

Fish used in sushi is generally raw, but it can also be poached in *dashi* (a prepared soup base made from kelp and fish flakes) before it's paired with the rice. Opalescent raw scallops are popular at the sushi bar of Tempura Kitchen in Anchorage. When shopping for raw seafood, be sure it is impeccably fresh and of the highest quality (see Seafood Safety, page 282).

Basic Sushi Rice

Takeo Okamoto, manager of Japanese cuisine at the Alyeska Prince Hotel in Girdwood, uses this basic recipe. Okamoto oversees both Takanawa (the hotel's sushi bar) and Katsura (the intimate *teppanyaki* restaurant, where chefs cook to order as you watch). He holds a Professional Sushi Chef certification from Aoyama in Tokyo. Prior to joining the Alyeska resort, Okamoto earned a reputation at Anchorage's Tempura Kitchen, for crafting some of Alaska's finest sushi.

3⅓ cups short-grain rice
4 cups water
5 tablespoons plus 1 teaspoon rice vinegar
5 tablespoons sugar
2 tablespoons salt

Wash the rice in cold water until the water runs clear. Drain in a colander for 1 hour (30 minutes in warm weather).

Place the rice in a rice cooker or in a heavy pot with a close-fitting lid, and add the water. The rice cooker will take care of itself. If using a heavy pot, cover and bring to a boil over medium heat. Boil the rice over high heat for 2 minutes. Then reduce the heat to medium and boil for an additional 5 minutes. Over low heat, cook the rice for 15 minutes, or until all of the water has been absorbed. Remove the rice from the heat. Remove the lid, spread a clean kitchen towel over the top of the pot, replace the lid, and allow the rice to stand for 10 to 15 minutes.

While the rice is cooking, combine the vinegar, sugar, and salt in a nonreactive pot. Heat slowly until the sugar has dissolved, stirring constantly. Remove from the heat. (To cool the mixture quickly, put the pot into a bowl of ice cubes.) Empty the rice into a big tub (15 to 20 inches in diameter), and spread it evenly over the bottom with a large wooden spoon or paddle. Run the paddle through the rice in right and left slicing motions to separate the grains. As you do this, slowly dribble the cool vinegar mixture over the rice. Avoid adding too much; the rice must not be mushy.

Continue the slicing motions while a helper fans the rice with a piece of cardboard or an Oriental fan. The rice will become glossy. Fan and mix about 10 minutes, or until the rice reaches room temperature.

MAKES ENOUGH RICE FOR 10 SERVINGS.

Do not refrigerate cooked Basic Sushi Rice. Keep it in the tub, covered with a clean cloth, until you are ready to form the basic sushi. Sushi rice should be used the same day it is made, because its flavor declines on standing.

Sea lettuce (*Ulva sp.*)

A Dog Named Sushi

Libby Riddles, the first woman to win the Iditarod Trail Sled Dog Race, in 1985, by braving a blizzard when everyone else was sleeping, owns a sled dog named Sushi—not to mention her others named Flounder, Sockeye, Grayling, Trout, and Miss Minnow.

Nori, or laver
(*Porphyra sp.*),
seaweed used to
wrap sushi

Basic Sushi

Serve with small bowls of Chinese mustard and wasabi. *Wasabi* (green horseradish) is prepared from a tinned powder. Experiment with the tiniest dab initially, because this condiment possesses theatrical sinus-clearing properties.

My favorite side dish with sushi—and with many other seafood dishes—is a daikon salad, made of equal parts of grated daikon (giant white "icicle" radish) and carrot, dressed with drizzles of vinegar and honey.

8 sheets yakinori *(toasted seaweed)*
1 recipe Basic Sushi Rice (see page 101)
12 ounces seafood: surimi *(imitation crabmeat), bass, mackerel, sablefish, tuna, scallops, smoked salmon, king crab, etc.*
1 cup julienned bamboo shoots
1 cup julienned carrots
Sea urchin roe or fresh salmon caviar, for garnish

Just before serving, form the sushi. Take a sushi mat (a *makisu*, a flexible mat of bamboo splints). Lay a sheet of *yakinori* on it. Spread with an even layer (about ½ inch thick) of prepared rice, flattening gently with a wet hand. Near one edge, lay fillings of fish, bamboo shoots, and carrots.

Roll up the *yakinori*, enclosing the rice and fillings; use the mat to compress it, making a cylinder about 1½ inches across. Cut this cylinder into slices about 1 inch thick and serve at once at room temperature. If you will not be serving the sushi for a short time, cover it with waxed paper and then with a damp dish towel.

Garnish with sea urchin roe or fresh salmon caviar.

MAKES 8 CYLINDERS OF 5 TO 8 SLICES EACH,
ABOUT 10 APPETIZER SERVINGS.

Cone-Shaped Sushi

Takeo Okamoto's sushi at Takanawa showcases fresh Alaskan seafood, such as salmon, roe, halibut, shrimp, and rockfish. Depending on the day's catch, 50 different kinds of sushi may be available in a single evening. When he wishes to show off something special like salmon roe or sea urchin roe, Okamoto makes Cone-Shaped Sushi. If roe isn't available, kitchen manager Gabriel Herman of the Whole Earth Deli in Fairbanks recommends such fillings as hickory-smoked tofu, burdock root, *umiboshi* (plum) paste, and julienned raw beets.

20 sheets yakinori *(toasted seaweed)*
1 recipe Basic Sushi Rice (see next page)
Fillings such as salmon roe or sea urchin roe, about 1⅔ cups total

Cut the *yakinori* sheets in half. Hold a half-sheet diagonally in the left hand. Place about 2 tablespoons of sushi rice near the left side of the seaweed, from top to bottom. Center 2 teaspoons of the filling on the rice. Fold the lower left corner of the seaweed over, and keep rolling until you have a cone. It may take a little practice to do this skillfully.

MAKES 40 PIECES OF SUSHI, ABOUT 10 APPETIZER SERVINGS.

Ribbon kelp (*Alaria sp.*)

INTERTIDAL FOODS

The Native people of Kodiak and the Aleutians, the Alutiiq, call sea lettuce kapuustaaruaq, *a word of Russian origin meaning "something like cabbage." They traditionally gathered this thin, green, wide-bladed marine algae* (Ulva fenestrata) *for food, eating it raw dipped in oil, wrapping in it raw sea urchin eggs, octopus, and chitons—to create a traditional, seaside "sushi." Intertidal foods like this were very important in early spring when travel on both land and sea was difficult, hindering both hunting and fishing, and starvation stalked the villages.*

ROCKFISH

Alaska rockfish is a bottom-dwelling family of fish that includes over 40 tasty varieties; 12 to 15 species are marketed commercially. The primary Alaska species are the black rockfish, the yelloweye rockfish, the canary rockfish, the Pacific Ocean perch, the sharpchin rockfish, the shortraker rockfish, the thornyhead rockfish, and the quillback rockfish.

As a family, rockfish are as colorful as jungle parrots—striped, spotted, marbled, or speckled. Sharp spines in their fins repel predators. They resemble bass in appearance, with somewhat compressed bodies and large mouths. Rockfish have three unusual traits: they give birth to live young, few species reproduce before they are 20 years old, and they may live as long as 60 years. Rockfish are sought after by both commercial and sportfishermen alike.

The red-skinned varieties of rockfish are sometimes referred to as Alaska snapper or red snapper. However, true American red snapper is found only in the Gulf of Mexico and up the Atlantic Coast to North Carolina.

Raw rockfish flesh ranges from pearly pink to white with gray overtones, but it is always pearly white when cooked. Known for its mild, lean flesh, versatile rockfish can be baked, broiled, pan-fried, deep-fried, microwaved, poached, simmered in stew, or steamed.

Rockfish

Potlatch Plate

Rockfish comes into its own when prepared as tempura. This tasty Potlatch Plate of mixed tempura is a popular appetizer at Jeremiah's, a Ketchikan restaurant. Each plate serves several diners. A light dipping sauce sets off the crunchy, battered seafood.

Peanut, corn, or safflower oil, for deep-frying
¼ pound rockfish
¼ pound halibut, or squid fingers or rings (see Note)
½ pound shrimp
½ pound mushrooms
2 onions, peeled, sliced, and separated into rings

Tempura Dipping Sauce:
½ cup chicken stock
2 tablespoons soy sauce
1 tablespoon dry sherry, mirin (rice wine), or fresh orange juice
½ teaspoon vinegar

Tempura Batter:
1 cup ice water
1 egg
½ teaspoon salt
¾ cup flour

To make the Tempura Dipping Sauce, combine the stock, soy sauce, sherry, and vinegar, and stir to mix. Set aside.

Heat 4 inches of oil in a deep-fat fryer or heavy pan to 375°F.

While the oil is heating, prepare the Tempura Batter: Combine the ice water, egg, and salt in a small bowl; beat well. Add the flour, stirring only until combined. Set the batter in a larger bowl filled with ice water. (Cold batter is a key to a light, feathery coating.)

Cut the fish diagonally into 2-inch by 1-inch by ½-inch strips. Cut the mushrooms in half. Dip the seafood and vegetables, a few at a time, into the Tempura Batter. Gently add them to the hot oil and deep-fry for 2 to 3 minutes, or until lightly browned. Drain on paper towels. Serve hot with the Tempura Dipping Sauce.

MAKES 3 OR 4 SERVINGS.

NOTE: Squid fingers are about the size and shape of chunky french fries. Squid rings resemble small onion rings in appearance when cooked.

Rockfish with African Peanut Sauce

Cedar bark basket

Simon & Seafort's Saloon & Grill in Anchorage regularly offers this rockfish entrée on its lunch and dinner menus. Discriminating diners seem to welcome the contrast of the creamy peanut sauce with the bite of hot red chiles and lime. Serve with Pecan Wild Rice (see page 229) or baked potato. This recipe can easily be halved.

8 rockfish fillets, about 7 ounces each
2½ teaspoons seasoned steak salt of your choice
4 green onions, chopped
8 lemon slices or wedges

Hot Pepper Oil:
2 cups olive oil
2 teaspoons crushed red chile peppers
3 cloves garlic, minced
1 tablespoon kosher salt

Peanut Sauce:
¼ cup Clarified Butter (see page 232)
1 cup minced onion
2 teaspoons minced garlic
1 pound tomatoes, diced and drained
1 cup minced peanuts
4 cups chicken stock
2 teaspoons kosher salt
1 to 1½ teaspoons crushed red chile peppers
¼ cup fresh lime juice
1 cup heavy cream

To make the Hot Pepper Oil, heat the olive oil and peppers in a saucepan until hot. Let the peppers stand in the oil for 10 minutes. Strain. Purée the olive oil, garlic, and salt. Reserve in a cool place.

To make the Peanut Sauce, heat the clarified butter in a saucepan. Add the onion and garlic, and sauté until soft; do not brown. Add the tomatoes, peanuts, stock, salt, peppers, and lime juice. Simmer over medium heat until reduced by half. The sauce should be thick. Add the cream, and simmer for 10 minutes. Keep the sauce warm in the top of a double boiler.

Preheat a stovetop or gas grill, or light coals. Oil the grill rack.

Dip the fish in the Hot Pepper Oil. Remove any excess oil with your fingers.

Place the fish skin side up on the grill at a 45-degree angle with the tail end (the thinner section) on the cool side. Grill for 2 minutes, until marks form. Baste with Hot Pepper Oil, and season each fillet with ¼ teaspoon of the steak salt.

With a spatula, turn the fish 45 degrees in the other direction to form a diamond searing pattern. Press the spatula firmly against the grates to avoid tearing the surface of the fish. Grill for 2 minutes. Baste again with Hot Pepper Oil.

Turn the fish over. The diamond markings should be facing up. Baste with the Hot Pepper Oil, and grill for 2 or 3 more minutes, or until done. The fish should be soft and moist. Season with the remaining steak salt.

Place the fish on warmed plates, pouring about ⅓ cup of the Peanut Sauce over the center of each fillet. Leave the outer edges of the fish exposed, to show off the grill marks.

Sprinkle 1 teaspoon of chopped green onion over each fillet, and garnish with a lemon slice.

MAKES 8 SERVINGS.

The steamer *Admiral Sampson* at a Kodiak cannery, 1919

Grilled Rockfish Salad

This Polynesian-style salad adorned with an oniony green chive dressing is the creation of Thulani Saagal of Anchorage. Thulani, a jazz pianist, spent her formative years on the island of Maui. Thulani recommends "something with macadamia nuts—like brownies" for dessert.

Grilled Rockfish Salad is a dish you can prepare while entertaining friends on the patio. Sip a favorite wine, sample hors d'oeuvres, and let the guests prepare the papaya.

> *1 pound string beans, fresh or frozen, cut in 1-inch lengths*
> *¼ teaspoon salt*
> *2 tablespoons lemon juice*
> *3 tablespoons olive oil*
> *1 pound rockfish fillets*
> *1 pound scallops*
> *12 large shrimp (8 to 10 per pound), shelled and deveined*
> *4 cups shredded red cabbage*
> *Red lettuce leaves*
> *1 large ripe papaya, peeled and thinly sliced*

Green Chive Dressing:
> *⅓ cup balsamic vinegar*
> *⅔ cup extra-virgin olive oil*
> *3 shallots, finely chopped*
> *⅓ cup chopped parsley*
> *Salt and freshly ground black pepper to taste*
> *3 tablespoons chopped chives (½ inch in length)*

To make the Green Chive Dressing, combine the vinegar, olive oil, shallots, and parsley in a blender, and process until combined. Season to taste with salt and pepper. Sprinkle the chives on top, and set aside.

Bring a saucepan of water to a boil. Add the string beans and blanch for 2 to 3 minutes, keeping them crisp. Drain in a colander. Spritz with cold water to stop the cooking. Set aside.

Combine the salt, lemon juice, and olive oil in a zipper-top bag. Add the rockfish, scallops, and shrimp, and close the bag. Agitate gently to coat the seafood with the mixture. Marinate for 45 minutes at room temperature, or 2 hours in the refrigerator.

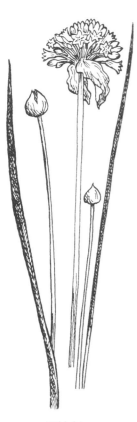

Wild chives

Start the barbecue coals about an hour before dinner, because it takes them about 45 minutes to get to the proper stage (or preheat the gas grill). Thread the scallops and shrimp onto skewers. Place the fillets and skewered seafood on the grill and cook until slightly underdone, about 6 minutes for the rockfish, 3 to 4 minutes for the shrimp and scallops.

Cut the rockfish into bite-sized pieces. Remove the scallops and shrimp from the skewers. Set the shrimp aside. Put the rockfish and scallops in a bowl and add just enough of the Green Chive Dressing to coat. Repeat with the green beans and red cabbage, keeping each separate.

Arrange the red lettuce leaves on a serving platter. Mound the rockfish and scallops in the center. Arrange the beans in a ring around the seafood. Arrange a ring of cabbage around the beans. Place slices of papaya at each corner. Pose the shrimp between the papaya slices. Serve immediately at room temperature.

MAKES 6 SERVINGS.

Ahtna man operating a fish wheel on the Copper River, ca. 1920

Fish Tacos Pudwill

Elizabeth "Liz" Pudwill operates Baja Taco Mexican restaurant in Cordova. "Fish Tacos are one of the house specialties—one of the things that my restaurant is famous for," Pudwill says. "The dish is traditional in coastal Mexico. Skeptics may balk at the idea of fish in tacos, especially with cabbage! But they all come around after one taste." The tacos are dressed with a tangy salsa of tomatillos or Mexican "green tomatoes." Red or king salmon, halibut, red snapper, or lingcod may be substituted for the rockfish. Serve with red beans and rice, and with condiments such as green onions, sour cream, and hot sauce.

Corn

¼ cup corn, safflower, or peanut oil, more if needed
2 pounds rockfish fillets, cut into 1-inch by 3-inch strips
Salt to taste
8 corn or flour tortillas
⅔ cup Homemade Mayonnaise, or as needed (see page 233)
3 cups finely shredded green cabbage

Deep-fry Batter:
1 egg
1 cup flour
6 to 12 ounces beer

Tomatillo Salsa:
2 cups fresh or canned tomatillos
½ large onion
2 cloves garlic
1 cup fresh or canned green chiles
¼ to ½ cup fresh or canned jalapeños (or to taste)
½ bunch fresh cilantro

To make the Tomatillo Salsa, blend the tomatillos, onion, garlic, green chiles, jalapeños, and cilantro in a food processor, stopping when the mixture is coarsely chopped. Pour the mixture into a small saucepan and bring to a boil, stirring constantly. Remove from the heat at once. Serve hot or cold. The salsa may be prepared the day before.

To make the Deep-fry Batter, blend the egg and flour. Slowly add enough beer, stirring, until the mixture is the consistency of thin pancake batter.

Heat the oil in a heavy frying pan. Dip the fish strips into the batter. Fry the battered fish strips until crisp and golden brown, turning once. Don't overcook. Sprinkle with salt to taste. Keep warm, but don't allow the fish to steam, or the crust will soften.

To assemble the tacos, heat the tortillas in a dry cast-iron skillet over low heat, turning frequently. Or steam them in a colander over simmering water.

Place the cooked fish strips on the warmed tortillas. Spread lightly with Homemade Mayonnaise, and mound with the shredded cabbage. Dollop with tomatillo salsa. Fold the tacos, and serve at once.

MAKES 4 SERVINGS.

Cabbage

ROCKFISH AND THE '64 EARTHQUAKE

Good Friday, March 27, 1964, began like any other late winter day in the port town of Valdez. But at 5:36 p.m., the ground began to shake and shimmy. For 4 full minutes, the ground heaved in rolling waves like swells on the open ocean. Ships at the waterfront rose 20 to 30 feet, then dropped. The dock broke in two; warehouses flipped forward and disappeared beneath the sea.

Irving Wedmore was aboard a fishing boat out in Prince William Sound. During the quake, he said later, his craft felt as if it were a toy sloshed about in a water bucket. Near Perry Island, other fishermen saw the water suddenly turn brilliant orange and red with the carcasses of yelloweye and canary rockfish killed by the sudden changes in pressure caused by the heaving of the ocean floor.

Citrus Rockfish

This snappy entrée cooks quickly in the microwave. The recipe comes from the computerized files of Darnell Burns of Haines, a busy tuba player who whistles Sousa marches as he cooks. Vary the seasonings as you wish, says Darnell. Sole can understudy for the rockfish.

2 pounds rockfish fillets
1 tablespoon fresh orange juice or lemon juice
Grated zest of 1 orange or lemon
Garlic powder to taste
Lemon pepper to taste
½ cup seasoned dry bread crumbs
2 tablespoons chopped parsley or onion

Cut the fillets into 4 serving portions. Place in 1 layer in a microwave-safe baking dish, and sprinkle with the orange juice and zest. Sprinkle garlic powder and lemon pepper over the fish to taste.

Combine the bread crumbs and parsley and sprinkle over the top. Cover the dish with plastic wrap. Cook in a microwave oven at high for 7 to 8 minutes, or until the fish flakes easily. (If the oven does not have a rotating rack, turn the dish once after 4 minutes.) Let the fish stand for 3 minutes before serving.

MAKES 4 SERVINGS.

Rockfish

Rockfish Piquant

Tangy with horseradish, this very model of a modern Alaskan entrée comes from Doris Shoemaker of Soldotna, a retired registered nurse who specialized in emergency medicine. Rainbow trout may be substituted for rockfish. Serve over egg noodles.

Lemon

2 tablespoons butter
2 tablespoons flour
1 cup sour cream
¼ cup prepared horseradish
1 teaspoon lemon juice
2 teaspoons white wine vinegar
1½ teaspoons sugar
¼ teaspoon dry mustard
Dash white pepper
4 rockfish fillets, 6 to 8 ounces each
¼ cup chopped fresh parsley

Preheat the oven to 425°F.

Melt the butter in a small saucepan; blend in the flour. Cook over low heat, stirring, for 1 to 2 minutes. Stir in the sour cream, horseradish, lemon juice, vinegar, sugar, mustard, and pepper. Cool. Spread half of this mixture in a 9-inch-square baking pan. Arrange the rockfish in the pan. Top with the remaining sauce, and cover tightly with foil.

Bake until the fish tests done, 15 to 25 minutes. Uncover and serve at once, sprinkled with the parsley.

MAKES 4 SERVINGS.

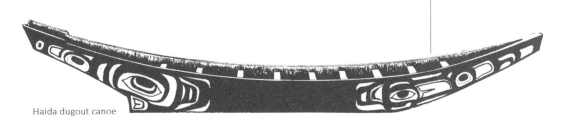

Haida dugout canoe

SABLEFISH

Tips

In Sitka, Tess Heyburn feels privileged if she has sablefish "tips" to cook. The tip is the pectoral fin flesh, part of the bony collar just behind the head—a part commercial processors discarded in the past as waste, but now save for the appreciative "tip" aficionado.

"You cut them out, marinate them, and barbecue 'em up, and let me tell you they are the best little things you ever tasted," Tess says. The collar is oilier than the rest of the fish, is firmer, and tastes a little like scallops, she adds.

The Alaska sablefish is a saltwater whitefish with a streamlined shape. Young fish are blue-green or copper brown; older, more mature individuals are black or dark gray. The distinctive furry texture of sablefish skin is what gave it its silky furbearer's name.

Growing to more than 3 feet in length, the sablefish—also known as black cod—is marketed year-round in various forms: as whole, dressed fish, ranging from 3 to 5 pounds; as fillets, ranging from 8 to 24 ounces; and as steaks. It is also sold smoked.

Because of its high fat content, sablefish is extremely fragile and perishable. The white flesh is velvety, soft to firm, and sweet, with large flakes. Versatile and succulent, with a rich, distinctive flavor, sablefish can be successfully baked, broiled, microwaved, stir-fried, poached, sautéed, or steamed. It is outstanding smoked or grilled.

Survivors of a wrecked cod-fishing schooner going aboard the SS *Dora*, 1912

Gingered Sablefish

Jim Meisis has fished Upper Cook Inlet for nearly two decades. Born in Vancouver, Washington, he spends his winters engaged in "secondary marketing"—smoking red salmon over alder and retailing this delicacy through his own Wild Alaska Salmon Company.

For years Jim has experimented with sablefish. "One of my friends calls it a pound of butter with fish bones in it, and doesn't think it worth bothering with. But my Japanese friends have taught me ways to deal with it."

Jim marinates sablefish in a mixture containing *mirin* and ginger, and then barbecues it. "It's phenomenal," Jim says. "People just keep nibbling; I seldom have leftovers, although the next day you can make sandwiches that are just killer!"

Tlingit design

½ cup soy sauce
2 tablespoons mirin *(rice wine)*
2 tablespoons whiskey
2 tablespoons grated fresh ginger
4 sablefish fillets, 6 to 8 ounces each

Combine the soy sauce, *mirin,* whiskey, and ginger. Marinate the sablefish fillets in this mixture for 6 to 8 hours, covered, in the refrigerator.

Cook according to Barbecuing directions (see pages 276–77).

MAKES 4 SERVINGS.

SALMON

Salmon-egg Cheese

Salmon-egg cheese is a traditional Haida dish, made from coho salmon roe. First the egg clusters are smoked on racks for three days, turned over each day. Then the eggs are put into a bowl and mashed. A special wooden box or form is prepared in the shape of a large brick about one foot square and lined with skunk cabbage leaves. The mashed eggs are added and the whole is wrapped in skunk cabbage, tied with cedar bark strips, and stored in a cool place to age. After aging, they are served in slices, like cheese, with baked potatoes. The Haida term for smoked and dried coho eggs is Taay Chaay tl'Skiidaas.

Salmon are the sleek, sought-after members of a fish family whose name stems from the Latin word for "leaper." They can attain velocities of 35 to 40 miles per hour when getting up speed to leap rapids and waterfalls with a single bound. Lovely visions of polished pewter and silver, the five glittering Pacific salmon species in Alaska—the king, chum, sockeye, pink, and silver—look as good as they taste.

The life of the anadromous salmon is one of travel and travail. Salmon eggs hatch in freshwater streams, but the "fry" (young) soon leave the streams to mature in salt water. Years later, grown to mature fish, salmon ascend freshwater streams again—often their specific natal streams, which they are believed to locate by an amazing sense of smell—to spawn. Adult Pacific salmon die soon after spawning.

The regal king or "Chinook" is the largest and most esteemed of the Pacific salmon. King salmon is dark blue-green above, silver below, with irregular black spots on upper back and tail. It is usually red-fleshed, but one in ten has white flesh. (Although different in color, the

Packing king salmon

flavor of white king is much the same as that of red king salmon.) Growing to over 75 pounds, the king is a fighting fish highly prized by anglers.

Firm and rich in fat, with an inimitable depth of flavor, the king is luscious whether grilled, poached, sautéed, baked, steamed, or smoked. Because of its legendary, distinctive flavor, this is one fish for which the simplest preparations can be among the best. It's also a favorite for sashimi preparations. Smaller kings are choice for barbecuing whole.

The sockeye or "red" salmon breaks the pattern of its cousins by loitering up to two years in freshwater before migrating to sea, where it spends two or three years. When they return to streams to spawn, sockeyes turn a conspicuous fire-engine red with mallard green heads. Although slightly leaner than king, sockeye salmon is still rich in oil and full-flavored. Its deep red flesh is prized by both cooks and commercial canners.

Blue lamé above and sterling below, the smaller silver salmon or "coho" is not as plentiful as the king and sockeye, but it is still a very tasty choice. Its attractive orange-red, firm flesh is as versatile as that of king salmon.

The chum salmon is an important subsistence fish in Alaska because it ranges farther north than other Pacific salmon—spawning hundreds of miles up the Yukon River, for example. Chum salmon are metallic blue above, gleaming silver below. They have a variety of nicknames, including "dog" (from the enlarged front teeth of spawning males), "calico" (because of the splotches it has when it leaves salt water and enters fresh), and "fall" (because it is the last salmon to return to the rivers in autumn—often not appearing until November). When spawning, these salmon become dark olive above, with reddish blotches on the sides. Chum flesh is pink with a medium fat content, adaptable to any salmon preparation and suitable for canning, drying, and smoking.

The pink salmon is metallic blue-green above, silver below, adorned with distinctive oval black spots on the tail and upper body. The spawning male develops a hump when he enters freshwater to spawn, thus the nickname "humpback" or "humpy." The pink is the smallest of Alaska's five Pacific salmon species, averaging 2 to 5 pounds. With its pale rose flesh and delicate flavor, the pink salmon is prized for canning and for barbecuing. Because they are quite lean, pinks are not as suitable as other salmon for smoking.

The peak availability of fresh salmon in Alaska is June through November, although seasons for individual species or local fisheries vary throughout the year.

Fish basket

NOTE: Certain seafoods, such as clams and halibut, can harbor parasites or harmful bacteria. Before preparing salmon, please read Seafood Safety, page 282.

Smoked Salmon Pâté

This smoked salmon pâté is an hors d'oeuvre specialty of Warren Coplin, formerly chef of the café at the Anchorage Museum of History and Art and currently executive chef at Jens' Restaurant in Anchorage.

Smoked halibut, smoked clams, smoked mussels, smoked oysters, or smoked shrimp may be substituted for the smoked salmon.

For my yummy Eggs Baranof, follow a basic Eggs Benedict recipe, but rather than Canadian bacon or deviled ham, spread Smoked Salmon Pâté on toasted English muffins.

¾ pound smoked salmon
1 pound cream cheese, softened
¼ cup lemon juice
2 tablespoons Worcestershire sauce
½ cup finely chopped parsley
2 cucumbers, thinly sliced
Dill sprigs

Place the smoked salmon in a food processor and mince. Slowly add chunks of cream cheese. Then add the lemon juice, Worcestershire sauce, and parsley. The pâté will be pink in color and firm in texture. This may be done a day ahead. Store, covered, in the refrigerator.

Just before serving, place the pâté in a pastry bag with a large star tip and gently squeeze mixture through tip to make florets on the cucumber slices. Garnish with dill.

MAKES 30 APPETIZERS.

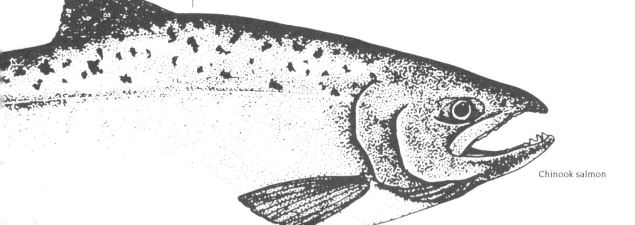

Chinook salmon

Steamed Salmon in Chinese Cabbage

While cooking for the Quarter Deck restaurant perched atop the Hotel Captain Cook, chef Dan Jacobsen of Anchorage was inspired to reinterpret this Tlingit classic through a Sichuan lens. A colorful sauce adds eye appeal.

4 salmon fillets, 6 ounces each
⅛ teaspoon sea salt or table salt
⅛ teaspoon coarsely ground Sichuan peppercorns
1 tablespoon finely minced fresh ginger
4 large Chinese (Napa) cabbage leaves

Orange-Shallot Sauce:
2 tablespoons rice wine
¼ cup fish stock
3 tablespoons orange juice
2 small shallots, finely chopped
2 teaspoons minced cilantro
2 teaspoons minced green onions
1 tablespoon minced red bell pepper
1 tablespoon cornstarch
1 tablespoon cold water

Prepare each salmon fillet by sprinkling it with the sea salt and Sichuan peppercorns. Then sprinkle with the ginger.

Wrap each fillet in a cabbage leaf, place on a steamer rack over simmering water, and steam until done, about 6 minutes.

To make the Orange-Shallot Sauce, in a saucepan, combine the rice wine, fish stock, orange juice, and shallots. Boil until reduced by half, then add the cilantro, green onion, and bell pepper. Mix the cornstarch with the cold water, add to the sauce, and stir over low heat until thickened. Serve warm over the salmon.

MAKES 4 SERVINGS.

Earth Ovens and Skunk Cabbage

When preparing a traditional luau, Hawaiians wrapped fish and pork in ti leaves and steamed these packages to succulent perfection in an imu or "earth oven." In the Tlingit version of this underground cooking method, salmon was wrapped in skunk cabbage leaves before being buried. The method is so ancient that one of the many Raven legends hinges on food cooked in skunk cabbage.

But the original wrapping is problematic because skunk cabbage leaves contain a high concentration of calcium oxalate crystals, which burn the human mouth and tongue (although deer forage on them). Fortunately, cuisine bends back upon itself like a Möbius strip as ingredients are discovered and rediscovered, mastered and remastered.

Koyukon Athabascan Amulets

The skins of silver and king salmon were traditionally sewn into children's vests to give protection from harmful spirits. This practice is no longer followed. But pieces of dried salmon skin are sometimes kept in pockets for good luck, or children are given dried salmon tails to carry on their persons as children in Wisconsin might carry rabbits' feet.

NOTE: For salmon of the proper thickness (¼ inch), have the fishmonger slice it for you, or purchase fillets and pound them to the proper thickness between two sheets of plastic wrap or waxed paper.

Salmon-Asparagus Bundles

Sushi Gardens, a Japanese restaurant in Anchorage, serves a fresh and artful first course combining steamed salmon and asparagus. Proprietor Kunsuchae Chang shared his recipe made memorable by a thick teriyaki sauce. Select asparagus with bright green, crisp, firm stalks. The scales (leaf buds at the tips) should be tightly closed.

At Sushi Gardens, the bundles are quickly grilled after they are steamed. Grilling results not only in decorative grill marks but also in intensified flavor. However, grilling is optional for the home cook.

> *16 stalks pencil-thin asparagus*
> *4 pieces boneless salmon, 3 inches by 4½ inches by ¼ inch thick*
>   *(see Note)*
> *½ cup commercial teriyaki sauce*

Thick Teriyaki Sauce:
> *1 cup soy sauce*
> *1 clove garlic, crushed*
> *1 tablespoon chopped fresh ginger*
> *4 teaspoons cornstarch*
> *2 tablespoons molasses*
> *¼ cup commercial teriyaki sauce*
> *2 tablespoons honey*
> *¼ teaspoon salt*
> *¼ teaspoon dark sesame oil (optional)*

To make the Thick Teriyaki Sauce, bring the soy sauce to a boil with the garlic and ginger. Boil for 1 minute. Mix the cornstarch with the molasses and add it to the hot liquid with the teriyaki sauce, honey, salt, and sesame oil. Simmer, stirring, until thick. Keep warm.

Snap off the tough, pale green or white portion at the base of the asparagus stalks. It will break off approximately at the point where the stalk turns tender. (The trimmings may be saved for stock or soup.) With asparagus stalks this slender and young, there is no need to peel them.

Divide the asparagus into 4 groups of 4 spears, and wrap each group of 4 with a piece of salmon, securing the salmon with white butcher's twine in two places. Marinate the bundles in the commercial teriyaki sauce in a nonreactive pan for 2 hours in the refrigerator. Turn every 30 minutes.

Cook the bundles by placing them upright in an asparagus steamer, with the bottoms of the stalks in ½ cup of boiling water. Cover and cook for 12 minutes, or until the asparagus is tender. Alternately, cook the bundles in an Asian rack-type steamer.

The bundles can be served hot or at room temperature. Remove the string before serving. Cut into slices about ¾ inch thick and serve with the Thick Teriyaki Sauce.

MAKES 4 SERVINGS.

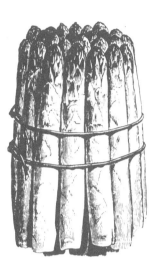

Asparagus

STINKY HEADS

One of the most notorious fish "dishes" of Alaska is Stinky Heads—fish heads soured or fermented underground.

Edna Wilder describes this traditional food in Once Upon an Eskimo Time *(Alaska Northwest Books, 1987), the fascinating tale of the early days and traditional ways of her mother, Nedercook. Nedercook (aka Minnie Tucker, ca. 1858–1979) refers to salmon heads buried in the ground as "a hole of the food we called rotten." This underground cache was opened and used when the village was short of food, usually in the late winter.*

The food was prepared by digging a hole 3 to 4½ feet deep and lining it with grass and/or bark. Fish heads were layered with grass, filling the hole to within 2 feet of the surface. The cache was finished off with more grass, a board or two, and then earth and a marker.

The cache of fish heads was always placed in a shady spot, so that the ground would not get overly hot. If not properly prepared, Stinky Heads can cause illness.

Both the Eskimo and Athabascans of Alaska prepared Stinky Heads. The popularity of this dish among Tanaina Athabascans is demonstrated by the presence of more than 1,000 fish-caching pits around Kijik on the north shore of Lake Clark. The Kijik fish-camp site was used until just after the turn of the 20th century.

The indigenous peoples of Alaska were never daunted by strong or pungent odors, because strong odors meant the presence of food. The Yupik and Inupiat also soured whale and beluga flippers, considering them "done" when the skin sloughed off.

Waking Up the Salmon

Eskimo elders along the Kuskokwim River believe to this day that if there is an early spring and lightning strikes the sea, "waking up the fish," there will be a generous salmon run.

Laurie's Grilled Salmon Fillets

"Summer" and "barbecued salmon" are synonymous for hordes of grill-happy Alaskans. Among these hordes is Laurie Johnson.

For more than six years, Johnson has cooked at Denali Center, a Fairbanks nursing home. Because many of Johnson's charges are Native Americans, she regularly receives donations of fish or game to prepare for the residents. Her grilled salmon is one of their favorites.

"I have a charcoal grill right on the deck outside the kitchen," Johnson says. "I do it year-round, even if it's 40 or 50 below. Of course, when it's cold, the fish *does* take longer to cook!" Vary the seasonings according to your whim.

> *½ cup butter, melted*
> *¾ cup finely chopped onion*
> *¼ cup Worcestershire sauce*
> *¼ teaspoon garlic powder, or fresh, pressed garlic to taste*
> *4 pounds salmon fillets, with skin left on*

Light the coals. In a small bowl, combine the butter, onion, Worcestershire sauce, and garlic powder. When the coals are at the proper state, place the filleted fish on the grill, skin side down, for 10 to 15 minutes. Cover fish with foil or the grill lid. Baste with the butter mixture as the fish cooks. Milky solids will coagulate on the fillets when they are cooked through. To check on cooking, cut into one fillet. If flesh is still raw in center, continue cooking.

MAKES 8 TO 12 SERVINGS.

Garlic

Tlingit fish camp, ca. 1920

Alaska Salmon with King Crab Ravioli and Fruit Salsa

Imaginative Roberto "Bobby" Alfaro, chef de cuisine at the Crow's Nest Restaurant of the Hotel Captain Cook in Anchorage, shares his favorite salmon dish—a symphony of fresh fish, fresh herbs, beurre blanc, ravioli, and fresh fruit. "It's a best-seller with summer tourists," Bobby says.

For a special occasion, this demanding recipe is well worth the trouble. If you prefer, you can save some time by substituting 40 *gyoza* (potsticker) wrappers for the Lemon-Egg Ravioli Pasta. These wrappers are available in Asian markets as well as in many large supermarkets.

6 salmon fillets, 8 ounces each
1 cup white wine
3 tablespoons melted butter
1 teaspoon minced fresh basil
1 teaspoon minced fresh tarragon
1 teaspoon minced chives
Salt and freshly ground black pepper to taste

Bobby's Fruit Salsa:
1 cup diced nectarine
1 cup diced fresh pineapple
1 cup peeled and diced kiwifruit
1 tablespoon minced mint leaves

Roasted Garlic Beurre Blanc:
1 whole head garlic
Olive oil for roasting garlic
¼ cup white wine
1 tablespoon heavy cream
1 tablespoon fresh lemon juice
¼ cup butter

King Crab Ravioli Filling:
1 cup minced king crabmeat
½ cup ricotta cheese
1 egg
1 tablespoon minced chives
1 tablespoon minced fresh basil ☞

Salmon Roe

Sometimes called "salmon caviar," salmon roe is a delectable by-product of the salmon, bright orange spheres about the size of small green peas. Chum salmon roe is the most popular. It can be used as garnish for poached salmon or other dishes, such as sushi or herb omelets. Fresh salmon roe—firm and rich, with a subtle yolky flavor—is best served within 24 hours of catching the fish. The roe is also harvested as a subsistence food by Eskimos, dried on racks slightly lower than those used for drying salmon flesh. Some salmon roe is preserved and sold as bait to be used by sportfishermen.

Pineapple

Labeling canned salmon, ca. 1907

Lemon-Egg Ravioli Pasta:
> *2 eggs*
> *1 teaspoon olive oil*
> *½ teaspoon salt*
> *1½ cups plus 1 tablespoon unbleached flour*
> *2 tablespoons finely grated lemon zest*
> *1 tablespoon water*
> *3 quarts boiling water*
> *Salt and olive oil to taste (for boiling water)*

To make Bobby's Fruit Salsa, combine the nectarine, pineapple, kiwifruit, and mint in a small bowl. Keep in a cool place until ready to serve.

To make the Roasted Garlic Beurre Blanc, first roast the garlic as follows: Preheat the oven to 350°F. Divide the head of garlic into cloves, but do not peel the cloves. Coat the cloves with olive oil. Place the garlic in a shallow baking pan and roast for 25 to 30 minutes, or until a knife can easily pierce a clove. Peel the roasted garlic cloves and purée them.

Combine the wine, cream, and lemon juice in a small saucepan. Add the roasted garlic purée and stir over medium heat until the liquid is reduced to ¼ cup. Cut the butter into small pieces and whisk it into the sauce, a piece at a time. Make sure that each piece is completely melted before adding the next. Do not boil. Remove the sauce from the heat and keep warm.

To make the King Crab Ravioli Filling, combine the crabmeat, ricotta, egg, chives, and basil in a small bowl. Set aside in a cool place.

To make the Lemon-Egg Ravioli Pasta, place the eggs, olive oil, salt, 1½ cups of the flour, and lemon zest in a food processor. Process for 30 seconds to 1 minute, or until the mixture forms pea-sized balls. With the motor running, slowly add the 1 tablespoon water, blending just until the mixture forms a ball.

Sprinkle the remaining 1 tablespoon of flour evenly over the work surface. Turn the dough out onto the floured surface. Knead until it is smooth and elastic, 10 to 15 minutes. Wrap the dough in plastic wrap and allow it to rest for 10 minutes.

Divide the dough in half. Working with one half at a time, pass the dough through the smooth rollers of a pasta machine on the widest setting. Continue moving the width gauge to narrower settings and roll the dough to the desired thinness, about ¹⁄₁₆ inch.

Partly score one of the pasta sheets to divide it into 2-inch squares.

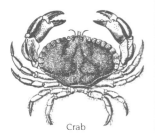
Crab

In the center of each square, place 2 to 3 teaspoons of the filling. Place the unscored sheet of dough over the scored sheet. Press with the fingertips to seal the dough on all 4 sides of each mound of filling. Then cut between and across the strips to separate the ravioli, using a crimped pastry cutter.

Typically, filled ravioli are allowed to dry for 1 or 2 hours before cooking. But chef Alfaro takes a shortcut: he freezes the filled ravioli for 25 minutes. Bring the water to a boil over high heat. Season with salt and olive oil. Cook the ravioli al dente, and set them aside. Keep warm.

Heat a stovetop or gas grill. (If you don't have one of these, skip the grilling step.) Preheat the oven to 400°F. Place the salmon fillets on the grill briefly, to mark both sides in a crisscross shape. Set aside on a baking sheet. Combine the wine, butter, basil, tarragon, and chives. Add salt and pepper to taste. Pour over the fillets. Bake for 12 to 15 minutes, until the fish flakes easily.

For each serving, center a salmon fillet on a warmed dinner plate. Garnish with a dollop of Roasted Garlic Beurre Blanc, a spoonful of drained fruit salsa, and a trio of hot king crab ravioli.

MAKES 6 SERVINGS.

Chinook salmon

NAMING THE CATCH

Indigenous peoples of the Pacific Northwest associated strict customs and taboos with fishing—protocols that would ensure the supply would not fail year after year.

One of the taboos concerned pronouncing the actual name of the prey. So as not to alarm, alert, or offend the fish, it was addressed by a ritual, often flattering, name.

During the First Salmon Ceremony of the Tsimshian, female shamans would address the salmon as it was being butchered with descriptive circumlocutions such as "Quartz Nose," "Two Gills on Back," "Lightning Follow One Another," and "Three Jumps." The fish was butchered on a new cedar-bark mat, specially plaited for the occasion.

Similarly, the Haida called the halibut "Great-One-Coming-Up-Against-the-Current."

Dill

NOTE: Traditionally, gravad lax was prepared with two whole sides of salmon, one laid evenly atop the other. However, whole sides can weigh many pounds—more suitable for Danish family reunions than family suppers. Shan Johnson has chosen to reduce the amount of fish to cut down on leftovers. When purchasing fish for this recipe, look for twin fillet pieces of equal size.

Shan's Gravad Lax

"Gravad lax" or "gravadlox" means grave-salmon or buried salmon—a Scandinavian cousin of Eskimo and Athabascan Stinky Heads (see page 121). In Europe gravad lax was originally prepared by coating salmon with seasonings such as ground white peppercorns, rolling it in seaweed, and burying it with pine twigs or dill. The fish was buried for up to a year and disinterred when it reached the desirable state of "falling-apart good." The texture and odor remind epicures of Gorgonzola cheese.

In the early 1900s, Scandinavian fishermen and cannery workers carried their recipes for gravad lax north to Alaska.

Eric and Shan Johnson dish up this version of gravad lax at Northwoods Lodge, 75 air miles northwest of Anchorage. The site of their lodge is famous for its huge runs of all of the salmon species plus resident populations of rainbow trout, grayling, and northern pike. Shan has mastered cooking all these finny favorites. Her Gravad Lax is served with a sweet Mustard Sauce.

Gravad lax is essentially raw salmon; please see Seafood Safety on page 282.

2 tablespoons salt
4 teaspoons sugar
1 teaspoon coarsely ground black peppercorns
1½ pounds salmon fillets, scaled, with skin on, bones removed
  (see Note)
1 tablespoon brandy (optional)
½ bunch fresh dill

Mustard Sauce:
½ cup dry mustard powder
½ cup olive or corn oil
⅓ cup sugar
¼ cup white vinegar
1 teaspoon sour cream
⅛ teaspoon salt
¼ cup chopped fresh dill

In a cup or small bowl, combine the salt, sugar, and peppercorns. Rub this mixture into all sides of the fish. Sprinkle with the brandy.

Place one-third of the dill in a shallow glass dish. Put 1 piece of fish, skin side down, on the dill, top with another one-third of the dill, add another piece of fish, skin side up, and top with the remaining dill.

Cover the dish with plastic wrap. Set a plate (larger than the salmon) on top. Place 2 heavy cans of food on top of the plate. Refrigerate for 24 to 36 hours.

To make the Mustard Sauce, combine the mustard powder, oil, sugar, vinegar, sour cream, and salt in a blender. Blend until smooth. Chill, covered. Stir in the dill just before serving.

Just before serving, scrape the dill and seasonings from the salmon. Place the salmon skin side down on a serving board. Slice the salmon thinly on the diagonal. Serve on crackers or rye cocktail loaf, accompanied by the Mustard Sauce.

Refrigerated, gravad lax keeps for a week. If it is frozen, the dill flavor fades; make only as much as can be consumed fresh.

MAKES 10 APPETIZER SERVINGS.

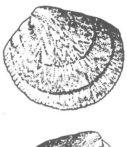

Littleneck clams

CLAMS AND SALMON

During the summer of 1880, Walter Pierce was prospecting for gold 160 miles from Sitka. As winter approached and the snow grew deeper, Pierce and his partners bought dried salmon from the Tlingit and began the long trip to town. But before they could launch their boats, wind and rough seas obliged them to lie low in camp. Pierce tried to make the best of it: "Here we could cook three meals a day, and have a change every meal. Thus, salmon and clams for breakfast, clams and salmon for dinner, and reverse it again for supper."

—*W. H. Pierce,* Thirteen Years of Travel and Exploration in Alaska, *(Alaska Northwest Books, 1977)*

THE LEGEND OF MOLDY END, OR, THE BOY WHO SWAM WITH SALMON

In the spruce forests of Southeast Alaska, it's hard to keep stored food from spoiling. During a rainy summer, no matter how faithfully the Native people fed the fires in the smoking sheds, no matter how often they rubbed down the salmon sides, mold formed.

Early one summer, a family set up their fish camp at the mouth of a spawning stream. A small boy snared gulls on the beach. When he became hungry, the only food left in the house were some moldy chunks of dog salmon. His mother gave him a little piece.

"Why do you always give me the moldy end?" the boy asked fretfully, throwing the food down.

Back he ran to his snares, where he found a gull in one. But when he waded into the water to grab it, the powerful bird pulled him out to sea. His family could find him nowhere, because he had been kidnapped by the Dog Salmon People, who took him to their camp.

The people held the boy captive and teased him, calling him "Moldy End" because he had had the bad manners to scorn food his mother had given him.

Gradually Moldy End realized he had offended the Dog Salmon People, and they instructed him how to treat food properly—how to set aside skin and bones and return them to the water.

After a whole year of lessons for the boy, the salmon chief guided his people to the very stream where Moldy End's family was again setting up camp. From shore, Moldy End's mother spotted a beautiful fish. "Spear that one!" she begged her husband. As the woman cut off the salmon's head with her shell ulu, she struck something hard. "What's this?" she exclaimed.

"It looks like our son's copper necklace!" the husband said.

The strange fish was placed on a new bark mat while the shaman sung him soothing songs. Slowly the boy regained his human form. And he told his family about respecting their catch—even the moldy ends.

—*A legend told by Southeast Alaska Natives, adapted from* The Box of Daylight *by Williams Hurd Hillyer (Alfred A. Knopf, 1931). Collected in Alaska ca. 1909.*

Bistro 401 Salmon

Reserved and self-deprecating, Anil Roy, executive chef at the Anchorage Sheraton, has cooked all over the world. A graduate of the Institute of Hotel Management in New Delhi, India, Roy has served as executive chef of the Elbow Beach Hotel in Bermuda and the Saint Louis Club in St. Louis, Missouri.

This salmon entrée from the Sheraton's Bistro 401 Restaurant is recommended by Roy for any festive table. It fits Roy's description of the Bistro's cuisine: "French country cooking"—tasty, but not overly demanding of the cook. "Customers like it," he adds.

Boy and king salmon, early 1920s

1 cup white wine
3 sprigs fresh dill
1 cup plus 1 tablespoon olive oil
½ cup honey
¼ cup lime juice
¼ teaspoon dry mustard powder
1 cup panko crumbs (see Note)
1 cup dry bread crumbs
4 salmon fillets, 7 ounces each
⅓ cup Dill Sauce (see page 239)

In a saucepan, combine the white wine and dill; bring to a boil and boil over medium heat until reduced by half.

Add 1 cup of the olive oil, the honey, lime juice, and dry mustard. Warm the mixture over medium heat, stirring constantly so that the honey will not scorch. Add the panko crumbs and bread crumbs. Mix evenly and allow to cool.

Preheat the oven to 350°F. Heat the remaining 1 tablespoon olive oil in a frying pan over high heat, and sear the salmon fillets quickly on both sides. Place fillets in a baking dish. Top each fillet with an even layer of the crumb mixture. Bake until the fish is opaque through, 12 to 15 minutes. Serve with Dill Sauce.

MAKES 4 SERVINGS.

NOTE: Panko is a prepared Asian breading for fried foods. Panko crumbs are available at Asian groceries and some large supermarkets.

Homeward Bound

There are over 10,000 streams in Alaska used by at least one species of salmon.

Mixed Hot Glacier (A Salmon Sausage Mixed Grill)

Earlier this year, Health Sea, Inc., of Juneau developed five flavors of salmon sausage from low-fat chum: dill, garlic, lemon pepper, Cajun, and original. An exclusive was quickly snapped up by Williams-Sonoma, which featured the sausages in its catalog.

The following mixed grill recipe was developed at the request of Health Sea by Nathan Schmidt of Hillsborough, California. The enthusiastic Schmidt, known as the "chef to celebrities" because of his clientele at Nathan's of Burlingame for the past 17 years, is now semiretired but still "working like a dog over the stove," he says.

8 ounces large sea scallops
8 ounces halibut fillets, cut in 4 pieces
¼ cup flour
1 to 2 tablespoons vegetable oil
8 ounces large spot shrimp, in the shell
3 shallots, chopped
2 cloves garlic, chopped
4 green onions, chopped
2 chile peppers, cored, seeded, and diced
1 red bell pepper, cored, seeded, and julienned or diced
2 tomatoes, peeled, seeded, and diced
1 tablespoon chopped fresh ginger
1 tablespoon chopped fresh dill or 1 teaspoon dried dill
8 ounces smoked salmon sausages, sliced 1 inch thick diagonally
2 tablespoons white wine or sherry
8 ounces cooked Dungeness or snow crab legs
½ teaspoon salt
¼ teaspoon freshly ground black pepper
3 tablespoons butter (optional)
1 pound dried pasta, cooked al dente, or 4 cups cooked rice
Cilantro sprigs, for garnish
Lemon slices, for garnish

Dredge the scallops and halibut in the flour. Heat 1 tablespoon of the vegetable oil in a skillet over high heat and sauté the scallops until browned, about 3 to 5 minutes. Remove from the pan. In the same skillet, cook the shrimp for 3 minutes. Remove from the pan.

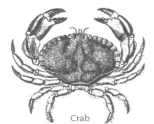

Crab

In the same pan, sauté the halibut until browned, about 3 to 5 minutes on each side. Remove from the pan.

Add the shallots to the pan, adding more oil if needed, and sauté until transparent. Add the garlic, green onions, chiles, red bell pepper, tomatoes, ginger, and dill. Sauté for 2 minutes, shaking or stirring frequently.

Add the smoked sausage and wine to the pan, and return the cooked seafood to the pan, along with the crab legs. Add the salt and pepper. Cook over medium heat until seafood is cooked and sausage and crab legs are warmed through. Add the butter, if desired, for a creamier texture.

Arrange the seafood and vegetables on a large platter, on a bed of cooked pasta or rice, putting the salmon sausages perpendicular to the crab to symbolize the craggy, icy peaks of an ocean-bound glacier face. Garnish with cilantro sprigs and lemon slices. Serve at once.

MAKES 6 SERVINGS.

Who's Who?

Caught in the ocean, king salmon can be distinguished by its dark tongue. But as salmon enter freshwater streams and cease eating, they change dramatically in color and shape. It's harder to distinguish among species.

Knowledgeable fishermen angling for a salmon dinner rely on tooth size and gum color to identify four salmon species.

The male chum's front teeth enlarge as it struggles upstream. The king or "blackmouth" sports gums that are sooty black at the base of its teeth. The silver can be distinguished by white gums, while the pink has pale gums.

Ketchikan fisherman Bo Smitt unloading king salmon, 1966

Salmon Ham

Lean, tasty salmon ham is one of Alaska's newest "value-added" seafood products. "Value added" indicates that a basic raw ingredient—a salmon, say—has been changed, re-formed, and/or combined with other materials to form a new product. Such products would typically be manu-factured with less prized species than king. Frozen salmon pot pie, salmon hot dogs, salmon pepperoni sticks, and canned salmon-sorrel soup are other examples of value-added products.

Salmon-Cheese Tartlets

Directions for this festive appetizer tartlet were furnished by Health Sea, Inc., of Juneau, makers of prizewinning Silver Bow Salmon Ham. If your local fishmonger doesn't carry salmon ham, any smoked fish or fish pepperoni may be used. (See also Fish by Mail, page 284.)

1 sheet (8 ounces) frozen puff pastry, thawed
½ cup grated smoked Gouda or crumbled chèvre (goat cheese)
2 eggs, beaten
⅓ cup milk
1 teaspoon Dijon mustard
2 green onions, minced
⅓ cup chopped sun-dried tomatoes
⅔ cup diced salmon ham
Salt and freshly ground black pepper to taste

Roll out the puff pastry on a floured board to an 11-inch by 14-inch rectangle. Cut the pastry into 12 squares and fit the squares into muffin tins. Sprinkle the cheese in the bottoms of the pastry cups.

Preheat the oven to 350°F.

Combine the eggs, milk, mustard, onions, tomatoes, salmon ham, salt, and pepper. Spoon this mixture over the cheese. Bake for 15 to 20 minutes, or until the tops are brown and the filling is set. Serve the tartlets whole or cut into quarters.

MAKES 12 TO 48 APPETIZERS.

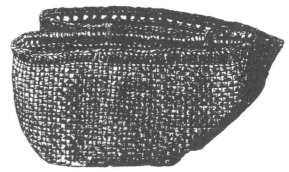

Folding cedar bark basket

Salmon Gravy on Biscuits

Joanne Nelson of Dillingham, a 40-year resident of Alaska, inherited her favorite canned salmon recipe from her mother. Joanne has been dishing up Salmon Gravy regularly since her marriage in 1953. This comfort food "can be served for breakfast or dinner, and is just as good reheated," she says.

Nelson spends her summers as a subsistence fisherman. "I have my set net site off Scandinavian Beach all summer, and I smoke fish, salt fish, can it, and freeze it," she says. "I put up several hundred fish a summer. My favorite fish are salmon, particularly kings. They're the greatest."

As a variant, ladle this milky gravy over polenta instead of biscuits. Leftover poached salmon can be substituted for the canned salmon.

10 slices bacon
¾ cup flour
5 cups milk, warmed
1 can (1 pound) or 1 jar (1 pint) king salmon, flaked, juice reserved
Salt and freshly ground black pepper to taste
10 biscuits

Dice the bacon and fry it until crisp. Remove the bacon from the skillet, leaving 3 tablespoons of the drippings in the skillet and reserving the rest. Add the flour to the skillet and fry until lightly browned, adding more bacon drippings as needed. Add the warm milk and cook over medium heat, stirring constantly, until thick and bubbly. Stir in the juice reserved from the salmon, followed by the flaked salmon, salt, pepper, and crisp bacon. Heat until warmed through. Serve over hot biscuits.

MAKES 5 GENEROUS SERVINGS.

Canned Salmon

Although fresh salmon gets more press, half of Alaska's annual salmon harvest is canned or "packed," numbering hundreds of millions of cans a year. All five species are canned, but reds and pinks predominate because they bring in lower prices as fresh fish.

In addition to the commercial Alaskan salmon pack, each summer thousands of Alaskans catch and can their own winter supply of salmon. Because so many Alaskans embrace this lifestyle, canned salmon figures in many dishes, like loaves and casseroles.

However, salmon in metal cans may soon go the way of the dodo; two Homer processors will soon be packaging pinks in foil pouches. The Marriott Corporation, which prepares more than 4 million meals a day, will be among the first to cook with pouched salmon.

Cannery Days

*There are three big
canneries at Ketchikan—
one has 110,000 cases of
canned salmon ready for
shipment, one has
82,000, and the third
80,000. . . . We unloaded
50,000 empty cases at one
cannery, and they told us
that was enough for one
and one-half days.*

—*Diary, August 25,
1923. From W. Leslie
Yaw,* Sixty Years in
Sitka *(Sheldon
Jackson College Press,
1985).*

Lona's Salmon Jerky

Friends and neighbors fortunate enough to have sampled it declare that Lona Schroeder of Dillingham makes the world's tastiest salmon jerky. Lona kindly mailed me some strips, and I have to agree it's top-notch: firm but not hard, chewy but not jaw-breaking, sweet but not cloying, and nearly translucent.

Fortunately for fish jerky aficionados, Lona was willing to share her recipe, the recipient of many blue ribbons. A favorite brand of soy or teriyaki sauce may be used instead of the Yoshida's Gourmet Sauce that she prefers.

*Fresh sockeye salmon
Yoshida's Gourmet Sauce*

Fillet the salmon and skin it. "You should have big slabs [sides]," Schroeder says. "Make real thin strips the length of the slabs, and bone them."

Marinate the strips for 24 hours, refrigerated, in Yoshida's Gourmet Sauce. To make the marinating easier, Schroeder uses gallon zipper-lock plastic bags. Swish the bags gently occasionally to make sure the strips marinate evenly.

After 24 hours, take the marinated strips to your smokehouse and lay them over wire racks. Smoke for 3 days over birch. "There's very little warmth in there, so it's pretty much a cold smoke," Schroeder says.

Turn the strips after the first 6 hours so they don't stick to the rack. The jerky is done when it looks almost transparent.

Cut the smoked fish into 5- or 6-inch lengths. Store them in plastic refrigerator containers or bags in the freezer.

TEN 5- TO 6-POUND SALMON WILL YIELD
8 QUART-SIZE FREEZER BAGS FULL OF JERKY.

RAVEN BARGAINS FOR SALMON

Having procured light, fresh water, and halibut for man, wily Raven set his nets wider. He determined to trick the powerful Taboo tribe into handing over the world's salmon supply.

When he rowed to the steep, rocky island where the Taboos lived, he heard strange music drifting from the windows of their stone house. The Taboos were inside, eating salmon, dancing, and playing games. Raven donned his lustrous black feather blanket and ran thrice around the house, calling, "Caw! Caw! Caw!" Soon he was invited to join the party. He began to play the stick game, using his blanket, beads, and medicine club as bargaining tools.

Grease-That-Is-Sticking-to-the-Stone wanted Raven's blanket. Dry-Boxes-in-Which-Fish-Are-Kept wanted his blue beads. Little-Chief-of-Canoes wanted his carved club. All wagered their shares of the world's salmon.

At first, the playing sticks favored Raven. But then Taboo magic turned against him, and he lost.

"Give me my club!" insisted Little-Chief-of-Canoes.

"Give him his club!" shouted all the Taboos.

"Take your club!" cried Raven, splitting the chief's skull like a length of dry kindling. "Now I am chief," Raven declared. "How shall I punish you for your lack of hospitality?"

The Taboos knelt at Raven's feet, begging for mercy. Raven finally agreed to let them live, on condition that once a year they would send to his people all the salmon they might need.

> —A legend told by Southeast Alaska Natives, adapted from The Box of Daylight by William Hurd Hillyer (Alfred A. Knopf, 1931). Collected in Alaska ca. 1909.

Salmon Omelet Pie

Chinook salmon

Hook-M-Up Tours in Aniak, on the banks of the Kuskokwim, is a small fishing lodge known to its clients as the "Kuskokwim Hilton." Fish, served every day, is seldom cooked the same way twice, says lodge owner Woody Wooderson. "We've been told that if the fishing ever gets bad, we can always start a restaurant."

One of Woody's favorite dishes is this frittata-like omelet. On the riverbank, Woody wields a 24-inch skillet to cook up 2 dozen eggs at a time—enough to serve 12. His recipe has been trimmed here for home cooks.

For a low-fat variation, boil the potatoes instead of frying, combine them with the other ingredients (using skim milk if you like), and bake instead of fry. Sprinkle low-fat cheese on top, let it melt, and serve.

2 tablespoons oil
5 potatoes, scrubbed and diced
1 small onion, chopped
⅓ pound mushrooms, sliced
8 eggs
½ cup milk
2 tablespoons flour
Salt and freshly ground black pepper to taste
Garlic powder to taste
1½ cups cooked and chunked salmon, bones removed
1½ cups grated Cheddar cheese

Heat the oil in a 12- or 14-inch skillet. Fry the diced potatoes until golden and almost fork-tender, about 5 minutes. Add onion and fry another 2 minutes. Add mushrooms; cover and cook for 1 more minute. Meanwhile, in a large bowl whip the eggs, milk, flour, salt, pepper, and garlic powder vigorously until thoroughly mixed.

Pour the egg mixture over the potato mixture in the skillet. Fold in the salmon. Cover the pan and cook over low heat until the eggs are set.

Remove from the heat. Sprinkle the cheese on top of the entire omelet, cover, and allow to rest. As soon as the cheese is melted, cut the omelet into wedges and serve.

MAKES 4 TO 5 SERVINGS.

Northwest Risotto

Risotto is a Northern Italian dish. Traditionally a side dish crammed with fresh vegetables such as baby artichokes, Swiss chard, and porcini mushrooms, it is a delectable choice for the health-conscious cook. Risotto is one of the dishes served at the occasional "Tuscan Tuesdays" of the Marx Brothers Cafe in Anchorage. Risotto also lends itself to this main dish featuring salmon.

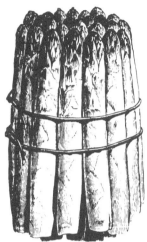

Asparagus

2 cups chicken stock, more if needed
1 tablespoon olive oil
1 large onion, coarsely chopped
1½ cups arborio rice (see Note)
¾ cup dry white wine
¼ teaspoon salt
½ pound fresh asparagus, cut into 1-inch pieces (2 cups)
1 pound salmon, poached and broken into chunks, or 1 can
  (15 ounces) sockeye salmon, drained and broken into chunks
1 teaspoon grated lemon zest
3 fresh porcini mushrooms, sliced (optional)
¼ cup heavy cream
1 green onion, cut into short julienne strips
Freshly ground black pepper to taste

Bring the chicken stock to a boil in a small saucepan, then reduce the heat and leave the stock at a low simmer.

Heat the oil in a 10-inch skillet and sauté the onion until tender, about 4 minutes. Add the rice; cook and stir 1 minute, or until the rice is well coated with oil. Add half of the warm stock and the wine to the skillet. Stir in the salt. Bring to a boil and cook, stirring for 10 minutes over medium heat, gradually adding about two-thirds of the remaining stock. Continue to stir until the rice is cooked and has absorbed all of the liquid. Do not let it dry out.

Stir in the asparagus, salmon, lemon zest, and mushrooms. Stir over low heat for 2 minutes. Remove from the heat. Cover and let stand until the asparagus is crisp-tender, about 5 minutes. Stir in the cream. Sprinkle with the green onions. Add freshly ground pepper at this point if you wish. Serve at once.

MAKES 4 TO 5 SERVINGS.

NOTE: Arborio rice, customary in risotto recipes, is a short-grain Italian variety. A pearl of starch in the center of each grain helps it retain its texture when cooked. (It should be slightly soupy but still hold its shape if mounded up.)

Copper River King Salmon Chili

The dining room at the Reluctant Fisherman Inn in Cordova is famed not only for its pressed copper ceiling—made from copper mined nearby at Kennecott—and its view of the busy small boat harbor, but also for its assertively seasoned king salmon chili. Inn owner (and Cordova's first woman mayor) Margy Johnson told me, "The secret, of course, is the great salmon from the Copper River." Cooks far from a river of kings can use any salmon. For a flavor boost, toast whole cumin seeds instead of using ground cumin. Simply heat the seeds in a dry skillet over low heat until fragrant, about 8 minutes, then grind with a mortar and pestle.

The Reluctant Fisherman dishes up its chili in crispy fried flour tortilla "bowls." Alternatively, warmed flour or corn tortillas may be served on the side. See Note.

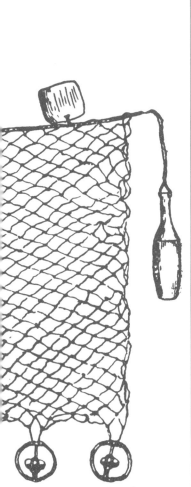

Nettle-fiber gillnet

> *1½ cups dried kidney beans*
> *8 cups water*
> *¼ cup olive oil*
> *½ teaspoon cayenne pepper*
> *1 teaspoon ground cumin*
> *1 teaspoon dried oregano*
> *2 tablespoons chopped garlic*
> *½ cup diced green pepper*
> *1 cup diced celery*
> *1 cup diced white onion*
> *4 cups canned, diced tomatoes packed in purée*
> *3 cups hot water*
> *2 tablespoons chili powder, or to taste*
> *2 pounds Copper River king salmon, skinned and boned*
> *3 quarts water*
> *2 cups grated Cheddar cheese*

Soak the dried beans overnight in the 8 cups water.

The next day, cook the beans slowly over medium heat until barely tender. Drain the beans and rinse with cold water.

Heat the olive oil in a skillet. Add the cayenne, cumin, oregano, garlic, green pepper, celery, and onion, and sauté lightly. Add the tomatoes.

Mix together the 3 cups hot water and the chili powder in a large pot. Add the sautéed tomato mixture and the drained beans. Simmer for 20 minutes.

Meanwhile, prepare the salmon. Cut the salmon into ½-inch cubes. Bring the 3 quarts of water to a boil. Place the fish cubes in the water and stir gently for 1 minute. Drain in a strainer and rinse gently with cold water.

Remove the chili mixture from the heat. Fold in the salmon. Garnish each serving with some of the grated cheese.

MAKES 8 TO 10 SERVINGS.

"Some royal good sport," king salmon, early 1900s

NOTE: Phyllis's Cafe in Anchorage serves up its salmon chowder in sourdough bread bowls.

Smoked Salmon and Pasta

Alaskans typically dole out their precious hoard of smoked fish as an hors d'oeuvre. Anchorage journalist Nancy Jordan, however, has an extra-large supply of smoked fish, because her writer husband, John Strohmeier, is an avid fisherman, so Nancy serves smoked salmon in an entrée.

Vinegar in the pasta water helps to keep the strands from clumping. In the interests of reducing cholesterol, Nancy occasionally substitutes evaporated skim milk for the light cream.

The brilliant green color and crisp texture of asparagus make it a perfect side dish for this rich pasta entrée.

6 tablespoons butter
6 tablespoons flour
2½ cups light cream or half-and-half
½ cup chicken stock
¼ cup sherry or Madeira, or 1½ tablespoons lemon juice
½ teaspoon salt
½ teaspoon white pepper
½ teaspoon nutmeg
8 ounces fettuccine
2 teaspoons vinegar
½ cup flaked smoked salmon, some in large chunks
Grated lemon zest, for garnish
Chopped fresh parsley, for garnish

Melt the butter in a medium saucepan. Add the flour, stirring constantly until blended. Remove from the heat and add the cream and stock. Return to the stove and bring to a boil while continuing to stir. Add the sherry, salt, pepper, and nutmeg, and stir until well blended. Keep the sauce warm in a double boiler.

Cook the fettuccine al dente, adding the vinegar to the water. Drain and rinse in hot water; drain well.

Arrange the cooked pasta on 4 warmed dinner plates. Add the smoked salmon to the sauce and reheat very briefly. Divide the sauce among the plates, ladling it over the pasta. Garnish with a sprinkle of lemon zest and/or chopped parsley.

MAKES 4 SERVINGS.

Haida canoe paddle design

Whole Baked Stuffed Salmon

Although she doesn't live in Bethel or Eek, Alaska Northwest Books managing editor Ellen Wheat of Seattle cooks as if to the seashore born. Her stuffed baked salmon reminds me of the stuffed cod my mother fed me back in Massachusetts. Yum! Comfort food!

Whole salmon, 4 pounds, head and tail off, cleaned, boned, and
  filleted but still connected along skin at top
1 cup dry white wine
Salt, pepper, dill, garlic powder to taste
1 medium onion, sliced
1 lemon, sliced

Stuffing:
  3 cups prepared seasoned bread stuffing cubes, dry
  2 stalks celery, diced
  ¼ medium onion, diced
  ¼ cup dry white wine
  Salt, pepper, garlic powder to taste

Prehead oven to 350°.

To prepare Stuffing, combine seasoned bread stuffing cubes, celery, onion, wine, and salt, pepper, and garlic powder. Toss to mix.

Place Stuffing between 2 halves of the prepared salmon and fold over to close up.

Place the stuffed fish on a large piece of heavy aluminum foil on a baking sheet. Fold the edges of the foil into a dish shape, then pour the wine over the fish. Sprinkle with salt, pepper, dill, and garlic powder to taste. Overlap onion and lemon slices on top. Seal foil.

Bake for 1 hour.

MAKES 6 SERVINGS.

Salmon

Daniel's Dreams

Every evening, chef Daniel Wendell of Anchorage's Sacks Cafe dreams up an entrée or two based on fresh, local fin fish. Wendell relies heavily on pecans and pine nuts, Asian reductions, and ginger. A recent creation, for example, was a fillet of wild Alaska salmon set on a peanut and ginger sauce, topped with a tasty lava flow of black bean salsa.

PIROG

A Primer of Pirog, Alaska's Fish Pie

The first Europeans to see Alaska were two Russians, Ivan Feodorov and Mikhail Gvozdev, in 1732. After Vitus Bering confirmed their sighting in 1741, the territory was colonized—chiefly along its deeply indented coastline—by Russian seamen, fur traders, and missionaries. Russia was interested in Alaska primarily as a source of luxurious furs like the "soft gold" of the sea otter, but colonists also dabbled in gold and coal mining, agriculture, ship building, and ice harvesting. The domain remained in Russian hands until 1867, when the vast territory was purchased by the United States.

Although there were never more than 580 Russians in the territory at any one time, Russian influence was far-reaching and pervasive. One of the most delicious reminders of that period of Alaska's history is a fish pie called *pirog* or *perok* (or, with an Aleut spelling twist, *perox*).

Pirog is traditionally served on various special occasions and holidays, particularly Russian Christmas, celebrated on the evening of January 6 by Alaska's Orthodox believers. For a menu suitable to this festive occasion, see Suggested Menus (page 262).

Pirog is a rustic country cousin to the classic French *coulibiac* and the Russian *kulebiaka*, a square pie resembling a plump pillow, filled with chopped hard-boiled eggs, mushrooms, rice or *kasha* (cooked buckwheat kernels), smoked haddock or fresh salmon, onion, sour cream, and dill. The recipe derives from the *kulebiaka,* but Alaska's Aleuts apparently borrowed the name from another pastry-wrapped import introduced by the Russians, the pirog (the Russian word for "pie" or "tart").

Food writer Robert J. Courtine believes that the roots of pirog can be traced to the German *kohlgeback,* or "cabbage pie." Courtine thinks that "this cabbage pie was brought to Russia by German exiles. However the Russians stuffed the original puff-pastry recipe with salmon, rice, and eggs."

The most important ingredient of the pirog, says Courtine, is *vesiga,* dried sturgeon bone marrow. Vesiga brings an added richness to an already rich winter dish.

Aleut cook Mary Bourdukofsky of Anchorage skips the sturgeon marrow when she prepares half a dozen huge fish pies for the annual Russian New Year Masquerade Ball. She also bakes fish pies for Emyanniny, or Name Day.

Mary grew up on Saint Paul in the remote Pribilof Islands, where

Emyanniny is an important festival. "Emyanniny is a [Russian Orthodox] religious day, celebrating the saint's day for whom you were named," she explains.

Mary's Name Day Pirog (see page 146) reflects her own style: she uses halibut rather than salmon; her mother, Marina Kozloff, always used halibut "bellies," the moistest part of the fish."

Flaky Pastry

2 cups all-purpose flour
1 teaspoon salt
6 tablespoons cold butter, lard, or shortening
2 tablespoons corn oil
2 teaspoons white vinegar
2 tablespoons ice water, or as needed

Combine flour and salt in a bowl. Cut in butter with a pastry blender, knives, or a grater.

Add oil gradually, working it in with your fingers. Then add ice water and vinegar until mixture forms a ball. Knead dough briefly on a floured board.

Roll out and use as pastry for a 2-crust, 9-inch pie.

MAKES PASTRY FOR A 2-CRUST, 9-INCH PIE.

Note: For Name Day Halibut Pirog, this recipe must be multiplied by 4; i.e., 8 cups flour, 4 teaspoons salt, 1 cup butter, 8 tablespoons corn oil, 2½ tablespoons vinegar, 8 tablespoons ice water.

Chinook salmon

A Very Singular Present

Devoted to preventing scurvy among his crew, Captain James Cook noted nutritional matters in his journals.

On his third and last voyage of exploration, Cook navigated the Inside Passage and then the body of water later named Cook Inlet. Finding the way blocked, he steered west. His ships came to the Aleutian island of Unalaska. Anchored in Samganoohda Harbor, Cook made the first written record of the pirog's Alaskan presence: "On the 8th [of October, 1778], I received by the hands of an Oonalashka man, named Derramoushka, a very singular present, considering the place. It was a rye loaf, or rather a pie made in the form of a loaf, for it enclosed some salmon highly seasoned with pepper."

The rye crust and the black pepper in this gift document the influences of Russian imports upon Native Alaskan cuisine.

In Russia, fillings 🖝

Oonalashka Pirog

This recipe aims to reproduce what Cook savored in 1778. You can use Court Bouillon (see page 38) in place of the poaching liquid, if you prefer.

Poaching Liquid:
> Cold water to cover salmon
> 2 teaspoons white vinegar per cup of water
> 1 bay leaf per cup of water
> Dash each salt and pepper per cup of water

Filling:
> 4 salmon steaks, 1 to 2 inches thick, about 1 pound each
> ⅓ cup butter
> ½ cup finely chopped shallots or wild onions
> 1 clove garlic, minced
> ¾ pound fresh wild mushrooms, such as shaggy manes, sliced
> 2 tablespoons snipped fresh dill
> 1 teaspoon salt
> ¼ teaspoon freshly ground black pepper, more to taste

Dough:
> 1 envelope active dry yeast
> ¼ cup lukewarm water
> ½ cup butter
> 1 cup milk
> 2 teaspoons sugar
> 1 teaspoon salt
> 1 cup rye flour
> 3 eggs, lightly beaten
> 3½ to 4 cups all-purpose flour

Assembly:
> 4 cups cooked white rice or buckwheat groats (kasha)
> 6 hard-boiled eggs, peeled and coarsely chopped
> Salt and freshly ground black pepper to taste
> 1 egg yolk, lightly beaten
> 2 tablespoons water

To prepare the Poaching Liquid, combine water, vinegar, bay leaf, and salt and pepper.

To prepare the Filling, put the salmon steaks into a pan and cover with Poaching Liquid. Simmer as gently as possible for 20 minutes, or 6 to 8 minutes per pound. Cover the pot, but check it often to make sure it is not boiling. Gently remove the steaks from the liquid. Skin and bone the salmon, and flake it into large pieces. Reserve ½ cup of the Poaching Liquid.

Melt the butter in a large, heavy saucepan and sauté the shallots and garlic until tender, about 4 minutes. Add the mushrooms and dill, and sauté for 3 to 5 minutes. Add the reserved ½ cup poaching liquid, salt, and pepper, and bring to a boil. Remove from the heat and mix with the flaked salmon. Cool to room temperature. The Filling may be completed the day before and refrigerated, covered, overnight.

To make the Dough, dissolve the yeast in the warm water in a large bowl. Melt the butter in the milk. Add the sugar and salt; cool to lukewarm (110°F). Add the milk mixture to the yeast mixture. Beat in the rye flour. Beat in the eggs, then gradually mix in enough of the white flour to make a soft dough.

Turn the dough out onto a lightly floured board and knead until smooth and elastic, 4 to 8 minutes. Place the dough in a lightly greased bowl, turning it once to grease the top. Cover with a damp cloth and leave in a warm place until the dough doubles in bulk, about 2 hours.

Preheat the oven to 400°F.

To assemble the pirog, roll the dough out on a surface lightly coated with rye flour to a rectangle about 18 inches by 14 inches. Spread 2 cups of the cooked rice in the middle of the rectangle, leaving 4 inches on each side clear. Spread half of the fish mixture on top of the rice. Cover with the chopped eggs. Sprinkle with salt and pepper. Pile the remaining fish and then the remaining rice on top, making a meat-loaf shape. Draw the long edges of the dough together over the filling and pinch to seal. Cut off a triangle from each corner, then fold the ends, like envelope flaps, up over the filling and seal. Place a lightly greased and floured baking sheet next to the pirog and roll the pirog gently onto the sheet so that the sealed side is down. Mix the egg yolk with the 2 tablespoons water, and brush the top of the pirog with this mixture. Cut 3 or more steam slits in the top of the dough and bake for 15 minutes, or until browned. Reduce the oven temperature to 350°F. Bake for 15 minutes longer, or until the bottom is cooked.

MAKES 12 SERVINGS.

vary: from semolina to diced, sautéed carrots bound with Bechamel sauce, from cream cheese to game hash mixed with cooked buckwheat, from rice cooked in meat stock to cooked whitefish and vegetables.

Shaggy mane mushrooms

Name Day Halibut Pirog

A 300-pound halibut, 1904

Among Alaska's Orthodox faithful, pirog is suitable for all festive occasions. "Where I come from, even if they are eating turkey for Thanksgiving," Mary Bourdukofsky notes, "there will always be a pirog on the table."

Flaky Pastry, enough for 4 2-crust pies (see page 143)
¼ cup butter
1 large head green cabbage (about 2 pounds), chopped
2 onions, chopped
1 pound mushrooms, sliced
5 cups steamed rice
6 hard-boiled eggs, peeled and sliced
2 pounds halibut, skinned, boned, and sliced thinly crosswise
3 tablespoons chopped parsley
¼ teaspoon lemon pepper or other seafood seasoning
½ teaspoon salt
¼ teaspoon freshly ground black pepper
1 egg
1 tablespoon milk

To make the Flaky Pastry, follow the recipe on page 143, quadrupling it. Divide the pastry in half and roll out one half large enough to fit into a 9-inch by 13-inch pan with low sides. An inch of dough should hang over the sides of the pan.

Heat the butter in a large sauté pan and sauté the cabbage, onions, and mushrooms for about 10 minutes.

Preheat oven to 375°F.

Spread half of the rice evenly over the pastry, then top with half of the sautéed vegetables. Distribute the eggs on top. Lay the thinly sliced halibut on top, then sprinkle with the parsley, lemon pepper, salt, and black pepper.

Top with the remainder of the rice and vegetables. Roll out the remaining pastry and cover the pie, sealing the edges. Brush the top with the egg beaten with the milk. Bake for 1 hour.

Recipe may be halved.

MAKES 24 SERVINGS.

Alaskan waters play host to many shark species, including the mako, brown cat, leopard, sevengill, dogfish (see page 61), soupfin, salmon, Pacific blue, thresher, and white. Cooks in the know favor the mako, leopard, and the gargantuan thresher.

Shark retailed in Alaska's markets is usually harvested as a by-catch—that is, caught accidentally when the ship was after another species altogether. It is also rare for the Alaska sportfisherman to target sharks on purpose. However, sharks that are inadvertently hooked should be taken home and enjoyed.

Sharks are so well suited to their environment that they have altered little in the last 200 million years. Their entire body is armored with oblique rows of tooth-like scales. The teeth studding their powerful jaws are arranged in rows four deep, so that each razor-sharp triangle has three backups. Thus, should a tooth rip loose in a tussle, a new one eases forward into the empty socket.

Shark meat is rich yet mildly flavored, lean, and firm like swordfish. The meat is white when cooked, with a tender, soft consistency. Shark is sometimes marketed under the name "grayfish." Shark meat is best grilled, batter-fried, marinated and broiled, smoked, or pan-fried. Teriyaki marinade is particularly well paired with shark. Shark's "bonus" is that the meat is boneless, because this is a cartilaginous fish. Thus it is perfectly suited to the finicky diner who hates "picking out bones."

Shark loses moisture quickly, so avoid overcooking. Use pieces of shark at least 1¼ inches thick to prevent drying out while cooking. Urea in the flesh of shark can become ammonia if poorly handled, but if the skin of the shark is removed immediately after catching, the problem can be avoided. If necessary, urea concentration can be reduced by soaking in milk or acidulated water for 1 hour (see page 62).

Haida dogfish (shark) design

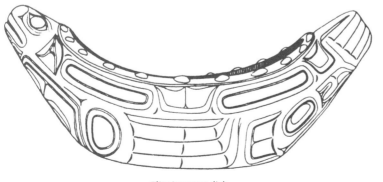

Tlingit grease dish

A Prehistoric Eskimo Kitchen

During the summer, the Eskimo kitchen was located in the open air. But during winter and periods of foul weather, the Inupiat Eskimos of Alaska's North Slope cooked inside.

According to excavations undertaken in 1982 of the mounds composing the 500-year-old village of Utqiagvik (today called Barrow), the kitchen was typically located in an ell off the entrance tunnel of the house. A round dome covered with sod, the house averaged twelve feet in diameter, and the kitchen was almost as large. The kitchen was a U-shaped room set to the right of the entrance tunnel. The one excavated was nine feet long and seven and a half feet wide, with the hearth located at the far end. A large skin could shut off the entrance.

This cramped space was warm but smoky. Two whale skulls supported the lip of the hearth, and wood chips from kindling production littered the floor. ☞

Shark and Chips

Fish and chips is a classic British fast food of batter-fried fish and french fries, seasoned with sprinkles of salt and malt vinegar. Pacific blue shark is delicious prepared this way, but you can substitute dogfish or other shark, orange roughy, or cod.

Serve with your favorite fries, salt, and malt or cider vinegar, or with Oscar's Tartar Sauce (see page 234), Thousand Island dressing, and baked potatoes. Or, for a Southern table, serve with hush puppies, beet greens or collards, and lemon wedges.

2 pounds shark fillets
Deep-fry Batter (see page 110)
Lard, vegetable oil, or shortening, for deep-frying

Dry the shark fillets with paper towels. Cut them crosswise into ½-inch by 2-inch strips.

Make the Deep-fry Batter (see page 110).

Heat 4 to 5 inches of lard, vegetable oil, or shortening to 375°F in a deep fryer.

Dip 2 or 3 portions of shark at a time into the batter. When they are well coated, carefully slide them into the hot oil. Fry for 3 to 5 minutes, or until golden and just cooked through, turning the fish strips occasionally during cooking so that they do not stick together. Serve hot.

MAKES 6 SERVINGS.

Haida dogfish design

Shark with Red Butter Sauce

Accountant and novelist Ted Leonard of Salcha (near Fairbanks) enjoys fishing and hunting when not standing watch at his computer. This is one of Ted's favorite fish recipes, also suitable for halibut, tuna, or marlin. Serve with rice, grits, or pasta to sop up the buttery sauce, which is colored an appetizing red by ripe tomatoes.

2 pounds shark fillets, of even thickness
¼ cup butter
2 medium zucchini, thinly sliced
2 ripe tomatoes, peeled and cut into eighths
Salt and freshly ground black pepper to taste
Garlic powder to taste

Cut the shark fillets into serving portions.

Melt the butter in a skillet large enough to hold the shark pieces in 1 layer. Add the fish, zucchini, and tomatoes, with salt, pepper, and garlic powder to taste. Simmer gently until the fish is cooked through, about 10 minutes. The tomatoes will liquefy, resulting in a rich red sauce.

Serve the zucchini over the fillets, topped with the sauce.

MAKES 4 TO 6 SERVINGS.

Tomatoes

Women cooked food at the wood-burning hearth and also over oil lamps, coating the inside of the kitchen—and the lungs of the cooks—with soot. The kitchen had areas for blubber stacking, blubber pounding, dumping ashes, and serving. (Blubber was pounded next to a pit, to encourage it to release oil which would flow into the pit. This was a temporary catch basin, because oil was stored in sealskin pokes.) Food was not eaten in the kitchen, but taken to the qargi (men's house, and communal meeting place) in bowls and on wooden platters. Butchering was carried out elsewhere, so preparation in the kitchen was confined to final trimming. Food was stored outside in the unheated tunnel, or in the open air on racks.

—A. A. Dekin, Jr., editor, Additional Reports of the 1982 Investigation by the Utqiagvik Archaeology Project, Barrow, Alaska (The North Slope Borough Commission on Inupiat History, Language and Culture, no date)

SKATE

Haida argillite platter design

Skate was once deemed "lobster bait," but this underappreicated fish is appearing more and more frequently on restaurant menus and fast becoming accepted in its own right.

Shaped like a diamond with a whip-like tail at one corner, the skate is also known as "ray." It has a wide, flat body that comes in a variety of colors: blue-purple with black dots, mottled brown, or gray, with a paler underside. The meat is cut from the "wings," with each wing yielding two fillets.

Skate fillets have a unique, fan-like outline. They are usually marketed with the skin off. The meat is deeply striated and rosy pink to gray, turning white quickly when heat is applied. Because of the skate's diet of mollusks and crustaceans—which it chomps down shell and all—its flesh is sweet, often compared to scallops. The best quality skate is harvested in winter.

Skates in Alaska waters include the longnose skate, the big skate, the Alaska skate, and the Aleutian skate. The Alaska and the Aleutian skates are the most common of the four. Skate wings began to surface in Alaska's supermarkets in January 1995, signaling growing interest in this fish family.

Serve skate poached, accompanied by Hollandaise sauce, or sautéed. An easy preparation consists of marinating it in a vinaigrette for 15 minutes before baking. It can also be deep-fried in Beer Batter (see page 31) or poached and used as an extender in crab salad.

Skate Piquant

This peppery-hot entrée is the creation of Clay Donohoe and Robin Alessi, the talented young pair of chefs who founded Anchorage's Atlasta Deli in August 1989. "Add your favorite pepper—Scotch bonnet, habanero, jalapeño, etc.—to taste," Robin advises. The chefs serve Skate Piquant with arborio rice and garlic bread. Dry sherry may be substituted for the pepper sherry.

½ ounce dried chanterelle mushrooms
1 cup white wine
1½ tablespoons pepper sherry
2 pounds skate, skinned
½ cup butter
3 scallions, chopped
2 cloves garlic, chopped
2 medium tomatoes, peeled and chopped
1 medium red bell pepper, cored, seeded, and thinly sliced
Chile peppers to taste
2 tablespoons chopped fresh basil
Salt and freshly ground black pepper to taste

Chanterelle mushrooms

Soak the chanterelles in the wine and pepper sherry for 30 minutes. Drain, reserving the liquid.

Cut the skate into 2-inch squares or disks. Slice each piece in half if it is thicker than 1 inch.

Heat ¼ cup of the butter in a heavy sauté pan. Sauté the skate squares, scallions, garlic, tomatoes, bell pepper, chile peppers, and drained chanterelles until the skate is barely opaque, about 4 minutes.

Add the remaining ¼ cup butter, basil, and reserved soaking liquid (the wine-sherry mixture). Add salt and pepper to taste. Simmer for 2 minutes to meld the flavors.

MAKES 4 SERVINGS.

SURIMI

Hair crab

Don't look for surimi at the city aquarium. Surimi is a man-made or "analog" seafood product, conjured up from a mixture of steamed pollock, shellfish flavorings, starch or gelatin, and seasonings. Tender, white, and boneless, surimi may masquerade as "scallops," but it is often shaded with red and shaped into faux crab legs, lobster claws, or shrimp. Japan has produced a gelatinous "fish cake" *(kamaboko)* for centuries, but the first U.S. surimi plant did not open until 1981, in Southern California. Now there are plants in the Aleutians.

When large trawlers make landfall at Dutch Harbor with holds awash in pollock, giant vacuum tubes suck the slippery fish into the holding tanks of a roaring processing plant. After passing through a maze of gleaming, stainless steel equipment, the fish end up as part of a 20-kilogram box of surimi, frozen solid and stacked in a warehouse freezer. Cargo ships flying Japanese flags await these boxes.

American consumption of surimi was slow to catch on, but surimi is now steadily growing as an inexpensive and versatile alternative to shellfish.

The least expensive surimi form is bite-sized slices or flakes, which over the past 15 years has made inroads in the take-out and fast food business, particularly in seafood enchiladas, casseroles, chowders, stir-fries, "Neptune Salad," and "krab" dip. Recently surimi has been surfacing in the shape of smoked salmon and whitefish.

The latest development in surimi is herring surimi, a silver gray paste first created in the U.S. in May 1994, at Unalaska, by Westward Seafoods. Pollock surimi is typically odorless, but the herring version still smells like herring. Exported to Japan, the product is reprocessed into a special fish cake.

Versatile surimi, delicate and ready to eat, should be added to stir-fries, pasta dishes, or chowders at the last moment—to heat rather than cook. When cooking with surimi, you may not need to add salt: sodium levels are quite high in most surimi.

Surimi in Rice Paper with Lemon Sauce

Thai dishes such as these rice-paper-wrapped rolls are popular with Alaska's burgeoning Asian populations, including Koreans, Chinese, and Japanese; they're also popular with world travelers.

Pan-fried or deep-fried, these delicate rolls and their tart Lemon Sauce make a memorable appetizer or luncheon dish. A pinch of sugar can be added to the water the rice paper is soaked in, to produce an even brown color during frying. Serve with kimchi, steamed rice, and snow peas. Crab may be substituted for the surimi.

2 egg whites, lightly beaten
8 ounces surimi, finely chopped
⅔ to 1 cup crabmeat
2 dried tree ear mushrooms, soaked and chopped (optional)
½ teaspoon lemon pepper
4 green onions, finely chopped
15 sheets (6½ inches across) Thai rice paper (see Note)

Lemon Sauce:
1 cup water
1 chicken bouillon cube
1 teaspoon sugar or honey
1 teaspoon vinegar
2 teaspoons cornstarch
1 tablespoon cold water
1 tablespoon soy sauce, or to taste
1 teaspoon grated lemon zest
¼ cup lemon juice
2 teaspoons chopped fresh chives

Combine the egg whites, surimi, crabmeat, mushrooms, pepper, and onions in a small bowl.

Soak the rice paper sheets in water for a few seconds, or until soft; drain. The brittle rice paper will become soft and pliable.

Cut the rice paper sheets in half. Place them on a clean dish towel. Top each half sheet with 2 level teaspoons of the seafood mixture. Fold in the long sides, then roll up from the narrow ends.

The rolls can be prepared to this point up to 3 hours before serving. Refrigerate if not using immediately.

Lemon

NOTE: Ubiquitous in Thai cooking, rice paper is a translucent, edible wrapper available in Asian groceries and some supermarkets.

Just before serving, prepare the Lemon Sauce: Combine the water, bouillon cube, sugar, and vinegar in a small saucepan. Stir over medium heat until the mixture boils. In a small bowl, mix the cornstarch with the cold water. Stir into the hot liquid. Boil and stir for 1 minute, or until the sauce thickens. Add the soy sauce, lemon zest, and lemon juice. Add the chives just before serving. Serve hot.

Place the rolls in a steamer in a single layer. Steam, covered, over simmering water for about 10 minutes, or until heated through. Serve at once with hot Lemon Sauce.

MAKES ABOUT 30.

Harvesting tanner crab in the Bering Sea, 1981

T he wolf fish (or wolffish) is an ugly character combining an eel-like body, a formidable turtle-like head with large eyes, and a set of prominent razor-sharp canines; its ferocious aspect earned the wolf fish its forbidding name. The dark brown Bering wolf fish can attain a length of 44 inches, and prowls depths of 200 to 500 feet.

The wolf fish is closely related to the little-known wolf-eel, harvested as a subsistence catch in small seaside communities like Whittier and Tununak.

Like skate, wolf fish fattens itself on clams, mussels, and other mollusks, producing firm, white flesh of superior quality. It's unfortunate this fish has been saddled with such daunting names as "wolf" and "ocean catfish," because its flesh is comparable to scallops and lobster. In Alaska, the wolf fish is primarily a by-catch—meaning fishermen accidentally catch it when out for other species—so it isn't regularly available in markets. Norwegians farm the Atlantic wolf fish as "loup de mer" and "steinbit"; it should soon be available in U.S. fish markets.

According to personable Eskimo painter, writer, and sculptor Edna Wilder of Fairbanks, indigenous peoples near Nome caught the wolf fish during a very short spring season, off the rocks, using roots as bait. After skinning, the fish were cut into chunks and boiled, then dipped in seal oil and eaten with fresh sprouted tundra greens such as roseroot.

Wolf fish is quite adaptable and may be substituted in recipes calling for cod, haddock, halibut, grouper, or other firm, white fish.

WOLF FISH

Skin Sewing

The sturdy, dark skin of wolf fish was used by Eskimos and Aleuts as a trim on kamleikas *(rain parkas) and water mukluks, and in any skin sewing application where a piece of very thin skin was needed. Salmon's tough skin was applied in similar ways.*

Haida design

Sautéed Wolf Fish with Alaskan Cabbage and Lemon-Herb Sauce

Executive chef Michael Flynn of the Alyeska Prince Hotel in Girdwood prepares wolf fish in an inventive combination with cabbage, two types of mushrooms, and Lemon-Herb Sauce. When he's not working over a hot stove or marinating venison with juniper berries, Michael, a former professional alpine ski instructor at Lake Tahoe, enjoys the slopes of Alyeska Resort.

4 wolf fish fillets, 6 ounces each
Salt and freshly ground black pepper to taste
2 tablespoons flour, more if needed
¼ cup olive oil
1 pound fresh shiitake mushrooms, stemmed
1 pound small fresh oyster mushrooms, sliced
1 head green cabbage, finely shredded, as for coleslaw
2 to 3 medium russet potatoes, peeled and thinly sliced
¼ cup white wine
¼ cup fish stock or chicken stock
2 cups heavy cream
2 tablespoons chopped fresh herbs (such as cilantro, tarragon, chives, or parsley)
Diced tomato and/or fresh herb sprigs, for garnish

Lemon-Herb Sauce:
1 teaspoon corn oil
4 shallots, peeled and coarsely chopped
¼ cup white wine
2 tablespoons lemon juice
1 cup fish stock or chicken stock
1 cup heavy cream
2 teaspoons butter
Pinch of saffron powder
1 tablespoon chopped fresh thyme
1 teaspoon grated lemon zest
Salt and freshly ground black pepper to taste

Wild chives

To make the Lemon-Herb Sauce, heat the oil in a medium saucepan, add the shallots, and cook until tender. Add the wine and lemon juice, and boil until reduced by half. Add the stock and boil until reduced by one-third. Add the cream and boil until reduced by one-third. Liquefy the sauce in a blender. Melt the butter in a small frying pan, stir in the saffron, and use this mixture to color the sauce a light yellow. Pour the sauce into a clean double boiler and keep warm until ready to serve.

Season the wolf fish fillets lightly with salt and pepper. Coat with the flour and pat off excess. Heat 2 tablespoons of the olive oil in a large, heavy saucepan, and sauté the fillets until both sides are golden and they are nearly done, 6 to 8 minutes. Remove from the pan and keep warm.

Add the remaining 2 tablespoons olive oil to the hot pan. Sauté the shiitake and oyster mushrooms for about 4 minutes, or until just soft. Add the cabbage and potato slices, and sauté for 6 to 7 minutes. Remove from the pan and keep warm.

Deglaze the pan with the wine. Add the fish stock and boil until reduced by half. Add the cream and boil again until the pan is almost dry. Stir well until very thick. Adjust the seasonings and add the herbs.

Just before serving, add the thyme and lemon zest to the sauce and season with salt and pepper to taste. Coat each warmed dinner plate with ¼ to ⅓ cup of the Lemon-Herb Sauce. Mound some of the mushroom-potato-cabbage mixture in the center. Place a fillet on top. Garnish with diced tomato and/or a fresh herb sprig.

MAKES 4 SERVINGS.

Tlingit design

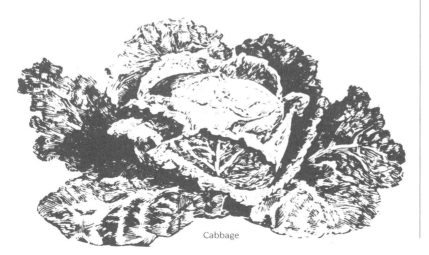

Cabbage

SHELLFISH

Eskimo girl, Frances, holding a king crab, ca. 1938

ABALONE

Abalone is commercially harvested in Auke Bay, Sitka, and Ketchikan. It is an important subsistence catch in Haida and Tlingit communities in Southeast Alaska, including Metlakatla, Wrangell, Craig, and Petersburg. Fiction writer Tara Neilson of Meyers Chuck near Ketchikan declares, "Everybody here eats abalone. . . . Most people put it into chowder."

The meaty abalone, a member of the snail family, is a univalve shellfish found just off the Asian and American shores of the Pacific Ocean. The coiled spiral shell typical of the snail has, in this cousin, been flattened into an ear shape, leaving the entire bottom open. The shell bears an arc of breathing holes, the number varying with the species.

The abalone is slow to mature, which is an important factor in the price of this delectable shellfish. The female is 6 years old before she can spawn. Typically, an abalone is 8 years old before it reaches the minimum Alaska legal harvest size of 4 inches.

Abalone's typical habitat is the intertidal zone and adjacent shallows. Early Native Americans easily gathered these oval delicacies at low tide, but, generations later, abalone have been gathered at such a rate by snorkelers and scuba divers that it is now necessary to dive or snorkel farther from shore to find ones large enough to meet harvest requirements.

The interior of the abalone's shell is lined with iridescent mother-of-pearl highly prized by craftsmen for buttons, jewelry, and reflective inlays. The Tlingit inlaid bits of abalone shell to dazzling effect in intricate masks, house screens, and totems.

Like the limpet, the abalone uses its abrasive tongue to scrape its diet of algae off rocks. The abalone creeps along with the powerful muscles of its large "foot," which is what we slice into delicious steaks.

Seven abalone species thrive along the shores of the Pacific. The red and pink species are the most important commercially. The pink of Alaska and British Columbia measures about 4½ inches in diameter at maturity, and its tender flesh needs scant pounding.

Abalone is available fresh during the summer months. You can also find it canned, frozen whole in the shell, or vacuum-packed (meat only). The lean, firm, mild, ivory, clam-like meat of the abalone toughens quickly when cooked; take care not to overcook it. Unlike the majority of seafood, fresh abalone is improved by aging in the refrigerator for a day or two before it is prepared: the meat becomes more tender. A favorite preparation of abalone is simple: cut across the grain into ½-inch steaks, dip in beaten egg, bread, and pan-fry for about 30 seconds in hot oil.

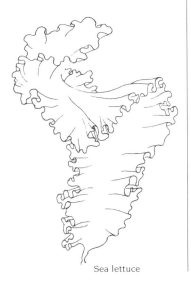

Sea lettuce

Abalone Seviche

Abalone Seviche, in which citrus juice "cooks" the abalone protein, is popular with beachcombers along the Inside Passage. Scallops may replace half the abalone. Canned abalone may be substituted for fresh. Rockweed and sea lettuce are tasty varieties of seaweed, the first ruddy brown and the second like green cellophane.

1 pound abalone meat
½ cup fresh lime juice
1 tablespoon corn oil
½ teaspoon salt
1 small clove garlic, finely chopped
½ teaspoon white pepper
⅛ teaspoon cayenne pepper
1 tablespoon finely chopped onion
Fresh rockweed or sea lettuce
Lime slices, for garnish

Pound the abalone between sheets of plastic wrap until it is paper-thin, being careful not to shred it. Cut the abalone into bite-sized pieces and place it in a glass or glazed crockery bowl.

In a small bowl, combine the lime juice, corn oil, salt, garlic, white and cayenne pepper, and onion. Pour over the abalone and toss to coat. Refrigerate, covered, for 24 hours.

Serve on fresh rockweed or sea lettuce, garnished with lime slices.

MAKES 6 APPETIZER SERVINGS.

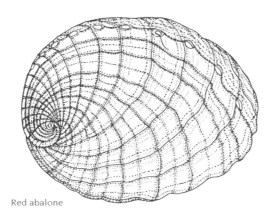

Red abalone

Harvesting Abalone

Wading or scuba diving, probe on the underside of rock ledges. Slip a long steel bar ("ab iron") under the shell and quickly pry it off before the abalone can tighten its grip. Do not attempt to pry off abalone with your hands, because a large abalone can grip your fingers and hold you under long enough to endanger you.

Preparing Abalone

To remove meat from shell, insert a flexible knife between the shell and the body and sever the attachment at the top of the shell. The large foot is the edible portion. Cut away the dark, soft viscera, including the inedible green gut. The remainder will resemble a large scallop. Slice this foot against the grain or "across" into steaks about 1 inch thick. Pound thoroughly with a rolling pin or meat-tenderizing mallet.

CLAMS

Tlingit Traditions

Black seaweed is sometimes used in Tlingit boiled seafood dishes such as red rockfish, clams in chowder, and smoked black cod boiled with potatoes. "But you never use it if a close relative of the same tribe has died within a year or before the payoff party [funeral potlatch]," explains Jane Lindsey-Mills of Hoonah in Southeast Alaska. "People still follow that practice today. You never serve seaweed or clams at a payoff party, because they are slippery and they might encourage the living to slip into the grave."

A favorite meal for walrus, clams are common in cold northern waters. Over two dozen species of clams call Alaska home: razor clams, butter clams, geoducks, littlenecks, horse clams or "gapers," soft shells, pink necks, surf clams, and many others. (The cockle, another variety of clam, is discussed on page 168.)

Although there is a handful of freshwater species, most Alaskan clams inhabit salt water along the state's wildly irregular 33,904-mile coast. The majority of these species are not harvested commercially— although many are prized by subsistence gatherers and individuals out to fill the evening's dinner pot.

During summer weekends of extreme low tides, Alaskans cause traffic jams as they head to Clam Gulch and other popular clamming spots on the Kenai Peninsula. Armed with the low-tech tools of the trade—rubber boots, shovels, and thermoses of hot coffee—entire families dig in, hoping for big harvests of razor clams. Many drive down in travel trailers and eat their catch at the site, their appetites honed by the briny breeze and the wet, gritty exertions of the hunt.

The littleneck is found from Alaska to California. Its ivory meat and brownish siphon are suitable for chowder.

The Pacific razor clam conceals its briny, excellent meat in an olive brown shell with a varnish-like gloss. The long, narrow shell may grow to 6 inches long, with a shape resembling the handle of an old-fashioned straight razor. The shell's interior is white or purplish.

The butter clam bears fine concentric ridges on a hefty, egg-shaped, white, gray, or black shell. Measuring to 5½ inches, the butter clam is found in intertidal and shallow water—easy prey. In a 5,000-year-old Alutiiq midden (refuse heap) on an island in Prince William Sound, I saw butter clam shells that were identical—except for the coloring they'd absorbed from minerals in the soil—to fresh shells on the beach nearby.

The horse clam or gaper (up to 10 inches in length) is distinguished by a muscular sumo wrestler's neck wreathed in tough, black skin. It is second in size only to the meaty geoduck (pronounced GOO-ee-duck), the king of clams. Weighing from 1 to 3 pounds, with lean pinkish gold to ivory flesh, the geoduck can live for 100 years. Its size, the strength of its closing mechanism, and its enviable longevity make the geoduck a fit subject for Tlingit legend.

Certain cautions must be observed when gathering any species of clam. See details on pages 278–79 and 282–83.

Freshly dug clams, especially small steamers, are apt to be gritty or sandy. To clean them, first scrub the shells well with a vegetable brush and cold water. Then put them on a rack in a bucket or lobster steamer and cover with clean, cold salt water or freshwater mixed with ¼ cup cornmeal. Soak for a minimum of 4 hours, or up to 48 hours.

The clams tend to spit out any grit, and take in the cornmeal.

If soaking for a long period, change the water every 8 hours, adding 2 tablespoons of fresh cornmeal each time.

The most universally popular clam dish is undeniably chowder, a thick soup whose name apparently derives from a big, French copper cauldron or *chaudière*. Tradition has it that Basque fishermen in Newfoundland invented chowder: when the fishing fleet returned to home port, each crew tossed part of its catch into a common cauldron, and the entire village celebrated the men's safe return over hot bowls of the resulting "kettle of fish."

Despite this catchy tale, Algonquian tribes of the Atlantic Coast have since prehistoric times simmered many a kettle of fish (or fish and beans), a basic hot pot to which European settlers introduced milk and cream.

Clam lovers will insist that the best way to eat clams is simply steamed, perhaps with embellishment from a splash of white wine, drizzle of olive oil, or sprinkle of fresh herbs. The tasty nectar left at the bottom of the bowl is a bonus, great for sipping or dunking crusty bread.

But clams have life beyond steaming and chowders. They're great in pasta dishes, stir-fries, and even on pizza. Generally, clams are steamed open first and the meat removed before using it in a recipe. Try geoduck uncooked as sashimi, and also steamed or sautéed.

If fresh clams seem tough—as is often the case with larger varieties—dice or coarsely grind before using.

Clam Yields

Eight quarts of clams in the shell will yield about 1 quart of shucked meat.

Clam

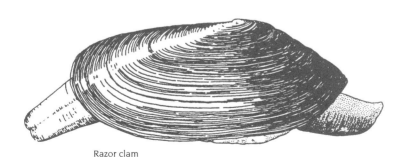

Razor clam

NOTE: Certain seafoods, such as clams or mussels, can harbor parasites or harmful bacteria. Before preparing clams, please read Seafood Safety, page 282.

Exploring Alaska

Together we explored the many wild bays of Kodiak and Afognak islands where the giant brown bear left tracks in the black sand—climbed mountains to the clear lakes hidden beyond the green shoulders—gorged ourselves on fat butter clams steamed over campfires that flickered before shelters of driftwood and saplings of spruce.

—Sam Keith, preface to One Man's Wilderness *(Alaska Northwest Books, 1973)*

Clams Steamed in Their Own Juices

Steaming is one of the most basic ways to cook clams and is the method that least disguises their intrinsic flavors. Clams can be steamed in a pot on the beach.

3 pounds small butter clams, scrubbed
½ pound Clarified Butter, for dipping (optional; see page 232)

Scrub the clams. Soak and clean, then drain (see pages 162–63).

Place the clams in a large, heavy pot. Do not add water. Cover and cook over high heat until the clams open, about 10 minutes. Using a slotted spoon, transfer the clams to a bowl. Discard any clams that did not open.

Serve the clams immediately with a dip of Clarified Butter, or remove the meat from the shells and use it in a recipe.

The pan juices may be used in other recipes. Strain them first through a sieve lined with moistened cheesecloth to remove any sand.

MAKES 3 OR 4 APPETIZER SERVINGS.

Tsimshian plaited cedar bark storage basket

Butter Clams Steamed with Aromatics

Butter clams steamed with herbs and olive oil is simple, speedy, and sure to please a medley of demanding gourmets. It's slightly more complex than Clams Steamed in Their Own Juices (see preceding page), but still serves to showcase the clams' briny flavor. Serve with crusty bread to sop up the juices.

2 tablespoons olive oil
4 cloves garlic, chopped
Grated zest of ½ lemon
¼ cup minced onion, or 2 teaspoons dried onion flakes
1 tablespoon chopped fresh rosemary
Juice of 1 lemon
1 cup dry white wine
4 pounds small butter clams, scrubbed

Garlic

Heat a large, heavy pot on medium heat without added water. Add the olive oil, garlic, lemon zest, onion, rosemary, lemon juice, and wine.

When the mixture boils, add the clams. Cover and cook over high heat for 7 minutes, or until the clams open, shaking the pot every 2 minutes to redistribute the clams. If the pot goes dry, add ¼ cup water. Discard any clams that do not open. Strain the pan juices through a strainer or colander lined with moistened cheesecloth to remove any sand.

Serve the clams with the cooking juices in soup bowls.

MAKES 4 APPETIZER SERVINGS.

Butter clam

Spanish Clam Stew

Cathy Fisher of Eagle River and her family regularly spend Fourth of July weekends at Clam Gulch on the Kenai Peninsula. They bring home enough clams for several meals. "I do clam fritters and New England clam chowder. This Spanish clam stew is kind of like chili," Cathy says. Other clams may be substituted for the razors. Serve with cheese rolls or garlic bread and a green salad.

4 cups salted water
6 fresh razor clams, shucked and cut into bite-sized pieces
  (or about 2 cups clam meat)
3 slices bacon, diced
1 small onion, diced
2 stalks celery, diced
½ green, red, or yellow bell pepper, cored, seeded, and sliced
3 tablespoons flour
Salt and black pepper to taste
Chili powder to taste
Dash of Worcestershire sauce
Dash of Tabasco sauce
1 teaspoon ground cumin
½ teaspoon minced garlic or garlic salt
1 large can (28 ounces) Italian-style stewed tomatoes
1 can (8 ounces) tomato sauce

Heat the salted water to a low simmer. Add the clams and simmer gently for 10 minutes; don't boil, or they will turn leathery. Drain.

In a large frying pan or heavy saucepan, sauté the bacon, onion, and celery until tender. Add the bell pepper, then the flour, and stir. Add salt, pepper, and chili powder to taste.

Then add the Worcestershire and Tabasco sauce, cumin, garlic, tomatoes, and tomato sauce, and simmer until blended. Add drained clams. Heat and serve.

MAKES 6 SERVINGS.

Clovisse en Pasta

This tasty low-calorie, low-fat clam and pasta entrée, perfect for late summer, is the creation of Chris Cikan of Statewide Services' ARCO Cafeteria. Chris notes, "Timing is the most important ingredient in this colorful dish."

If you prefer a thicker clam juice-vegetable sauce, after it is cooked you can thicken it by adding a mixture of 2 tablespoons butter and 1 or 2 tablespoons flour and cooking briefly until it thickens. You can also thicken it with 2 teaspoons of arrowroot or cornstarch dissolved in a little water. Other vegetables can be substituted, such as asparagus or yellow peppers.

3 cloves garlic, minced
2 cups bottled clam juice
1 cup sliced carrots (see Note)
1½ cups sliced celery (see Note)
1 cup sliced zucchini (see Note)
½ cup sliced green and/or red bell pepper (see Note)
1 teaspoon fresh thyme leaves, or ¼ teaspoon dried thyme
⅛ teaspoon fennel seed
Cracked black pepper to taste
48 butter clams or littlenecks (or 1½ cups canned clams,
*   minced or diced)*
8 ounces angel hair pasta

In a medium saucepan, combine the garlic with the clam juice. Note: Slice all vegetables to a uniform shape on the diagonal.

Steam or simmer the carrots, celery, zucchini, and bell pepper in the clam juice until they are crisp-tender, adding the zucchini and bell pepper last (as they require the least cooking time). Stir in the thyme and fennel. Add black pepper to taste. Turn off the heat if you are not ready to serve.

If using fresh clams, follow cleaning method on pages 162–63. Place cleaned clams in a steamer basket over boiling water, covered, for 7 minutes. Discard any unopened clams. Shuck, reserving meats.

Cook the pasta al dente. Drain well. Combine the vegetables and clams. Serve over the hot pasta.

MAKES 6 SERVINGS.

Clovisse *is the French term for "cockle" or "winkle," but Chris Cikan uses the term here to mean its relative, the clam.*

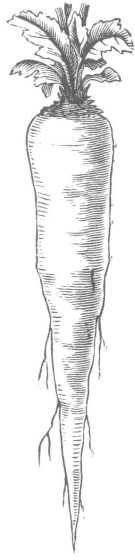

Carrot

COCKLES

Cockle Salad

Sasha Smith of the village of Ouzinkie on Spruce Island near Kodiak makes a Cockle Salad using the proportions of 3 cups of steamed cockles to 1 diced hard-boiled egg and 2 tablespoons diced onion. Grind the cockles. Mix with egg and onion; add mayonnaise to taste. Serve on lettuce.

The cockle is a variety of clam, distinguished by deeply ridged markings running from the pointed hinge end to the broad lip of the shell (as compared to most other clams, whose striped ridges travel side-to-side). Some cockle look-alikes may have similar distinctive ridges—as few as 6 or as many as 45—but the cockle has 35 such ridges.

There are over 250 species of cockle distributed worldwide; they are sometimes known as the "heart clam" due to the shape when viewed from the side. Several varieties of cockles are common or abundant in Alaska's waters: the Northern cockle, Nuttall's cockle (which grows to 5 inches, named for the naturalist who discovered it), the Greenland cockle, and the Iceland cockle. Young shells have prominent color patterns; older shells are gray or yellow-brown.

Alive, alive oh, cockles may be found lying on pebbly beaches, but they are usually buried just below the surface in the sand or fine gravel of the intertidal or shallow subtidal zone.

Cockles, along with clams and chitons, were important backup foods for the Tlingit and Haida during "starving times"—those lean winter months when fresh foods were unavailable and supplies of dried fish and dried clams had been exhausted. Cockles are also a favorite food of shorebirds and starfish.

The average marketable cockle is 1 inch long and 2 or 3 years old. Cockle meat is ivory, chewy, and lean. It is sometimes eaten raw or preserved in salt and vinegar. Prepare cockles as you would clams, though, keeping in mind that they yield less meat than clams. Cockles are more perishable than other clams and should be cooked right away.

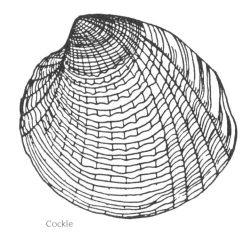

Cockle

Cockle-Corn Fritters

Crispy, silver-dollar-sized fried cakes called "corn oysters" are a favorite dish of the Midwest—best made with leftover corn on the cob, grated from the cob to produce a creamed corn. The Alaska version of these is made with ground cockle meat. These fritters are delicious for a hearty breakfast when preparing for a strenuous morning of winter outdoor activity. Tenderized, aged, diced abalone may be substituted for the cockles.

3 cups grated fresh corn
3 eggs, well beaten
1 cup finely diced or ground cockle meat
½ teaspoon salt
1½ teaspoons baking powder
¼ teaspoon freshly ground black pepper
3 tablespoons light cream or half-and-half
⅓ cup flour

In a medium bowl, combine the corn, eggs, cockle meat, salt, baking powder, pepper, light cream, and flour, and beat until smooth and well blended. Drop by tablespoons onto a hot, buttered griddle or into a heavy, greased skillet, and fry over medium-high heat until golden brown on both sides. Serve at once as a cocktail tidbit or main dish. For breakfast or brunch, serve with birch syrup.

MAKES 6 TO 8 SERVINGS.

Corn

CRAB

Crab Trivia

In 1901, comedian Rex Beach appeared on stage in Nome with an act in the vaudeville tradition— relying heavily on the gradual sagging of his baggy pants to his knees and finally to the floor. Beach's costume also included an oversized jacket with oyster cracker buttons and a necklace of spider crabs, which he munched on during his monologue.

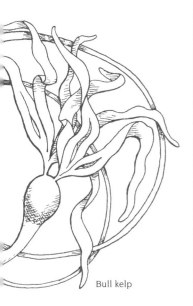

Bull kelp

To the everlasting glee of Alaska's cooks, Alaska produces a high percentage of the world's crab—from the large king crab to the smaller snow crab (bairdi and opilio, also known as tanner crab), hair crab, and Dungeness crab.

The Dungeness is, commercially, the most important crab of the Pacific Coast. The main body of the marketable male is 7 to 9 inches wide and 4 to 5 inches long, generally weighing close to 2 pounds. It has a reddish brown upper surface; its legs and underbody are yellowish. The shell of a live Dungeness—named for Dungeness Spit on the coast of northwest Washington state, where the crabs are abundant—is a purplish brown, turning a bright orange when cooked.

The knobby-shelled red king is one of the largest members of the crab family. Major historical fishing grounds have been near the Pribilof Islands and St. Matthew and Hall islands in the Bering Sea. The record king weighed nearly 25 pounds and measured an impressive 6 feet from tip to tip of its spider-like legs. Commercially caught males average 7 pounds and are 8 to 9 years old—about 3 feet wide with legs extended. (The males are larger than the females; when crab pots are hauled aboard, the smaller females are thrown back into the sea to produce more crabs.) King crab meat is easily recognized: porcelain white, edged in brilliant red—inspiration for the common colorations of surimi (imitation crabmeat).

Other king crabs, including the "golden" and the "blue," are also commercially fished in Alaska. Goldens are the latest Alaska "gold rush." These 4- to 9-pound kings are being caught in increasing numbers for domestic consumption. The 1988–1989 season in Alaska yielded 11.5 million pounds of golden king crabs worth about $37 million to fishermen.

Alaska's crab fishery changes species and waxes and wanes with supplies available. So, the consumer may find that a crab abundantly available at a good price one year may be in short supply—and at higher prices—the next, and vice versa. It's still hunting on a wild frontier when it comes to crabbing in Alaska, so there are few guarantees.

King and snow crabs are large and unwieldy to maintain alive, so these crabs are cooked by processors as soon as they get to shore, then quickly frozen to preserve the quality of the meat. They reach the market in leg sections or "clusters," split leg pieces, and canned. Dungeness crab is often sold whole—live or freshly cooked—but is also available in bulk flaked meat, claw pieces, or canned. You may find "krab" at the seafood counter: it is a fish paste shaped to resemble meaty claws, legs, and other shellfish parts (see Surimi, page 152).

Crab ingratiates with its sweet, delicate flavor and tender, boneless flesh. Succulent king crab deserves to be served simply steamed, with Clarified Butter (see page 232) or Homemade Mayonnaise (see page 233) alongside. But king, and other crab, can be used in a myriad of recipes, including salads, omelets, chowders, quiches, soups, sautés, and pasta dishes. Master chef and Northwest native James Beard called Dungeness "sheer, unadulterated crab heaven!"

Crab

When choosing whole crabs, larger ones are a better buy, yielding a better ratio of meat to shell. Whether small or large, crabs should seem heavy for their size.

For live crab, all you need to do to prepare them is bring a large pot of water to a rolling boil, add the crab in one fell swoop, bring back to a boil, and simmer for about 8 minutes per pound. Immerse the cooked crab in cold water for a moment to stop the cooking process. Let it cool, then dig in!

To shell crabs, devotees wield claw hammers, nutpicks, and nutcrackers. With large crabs like the king, if you loosen one joint from another, the joint of one piece often draws out the meat of the next for you. I use kitchen shears to open the large claws and leg sections to remove the meat. It is easier to cut along the edge of the claw or leg than to smash it with a hammer: the meat gets less damage and you don't have to deal with shell slivers in the meat.

Harvesting tanner crab in the Bering Sea, 1981

Hair crab

Curried Crab Casserole

Kathy Hunter, a humorist and writing instructor, who formerly lived in Fairbanks and before that hailed from king crab country—Kodiak Island—passed along this entrée. Kathy has built her home-style dish around fresh broccoli harvested from her bountiful garden on Lazy Mountain outside Palmer. Serve with steamed jasmine rice, along with mango chutney, slices of peeled kiwifruit, or fresh pineapple spears on the side.

> *1½ pounds broccoli*
> *1 cup grated sharp Cheddar cheese*
> *¼ cup butter or margarine*
> *2 tablespoons chopped onion*
> *2 tablespoons flour*
> *¼ teaspoon curry powder or more to taste, up to 1 tablespoon*
> *½ teaspoon salt*
> *1 cup milk*
> *1 tablespoon lemon juice*
> *2 cups crabmeat*
> *⅓ cup dry bread crumbs*

Cut the broccoli florets from the stalks. Peel the stalks and slice 1 inch thick. Steam the florets and stalks on a rack over simmering water for 3 or 4 minutes, or until just tender but not limp.

Arrange the broccoli in the bottom of a buttered casserole dish. Sprinkle the grated cheese over the broccoli.

Preheat the oven to 350°F.

In a frying pan, melt the butter and sauté the onion for 3 to 4 minutes. Stir in the flour, curry powder, and salt. Cook and stir for 2 minutes to eliminate any floury taste. Gradually stir in the milk. Cook and stir until thick. Add the lemon juice and crabmeat.

Pour the crab mixture over the broccoli and sprinkle with the bread crumbs. Bake for 30 minutes.

MAKES 6 SERVINGS.

Mrs. Gruening's Crab Bisque

Trained in Luxembourg, Marguerite Doucette ruled the kitchen at the Governor's House in Juneau for 14 years (1939 to 1953), during Ernest Gruening's term as territorial governor.

Marguerite Doucette met Ernest and Dorothy Gruening in Washington, D.C., when she was cooking for a member of the diplomatic corps. "The Gruenings liked all kinds of fish and crab, oysters, and clams," says Marguerite, now 86.

The Gruenings' formal dinners for 12 often began with a sherried crab bisque. Marguerite's creamy first course is based on a recipe from first First Lady Martha Washington, who used 8 hard-shelled crabs. True to Colonial methods, Martha boiled her crabs for half an hour before considering them done.

2 king crab legs, or ½ pound crabmeat
2 hard-boiled eggs
1 tablespoon butter, softened
1 tablespoon flour
Grated zest of 1 lemon
Freshly ground black pepper to taste
4 cups milk
½ cup cream
¾ cup dry sherry
1 teaspoon Worcestershire sauce
Salt to taste

Crack the crab legs and remove the meat. Cut into bite-sized portions. Pick through the crabmeat, discarding any bits of shell or cartilage, and set aside.

In a large, heavy saucepan, mash the hard-boiled eggs to a paste with a fork. Add the butter, flour, lemon zest, and a little pepper.

In a medium saucepan, bring the milk to a boil, and pour it gently into the egg mixture, whisking constantly. Place over low heat; add the crabmeat and allow to simmer for 5 minutes. Add the cream and bring just to the boiling point, but do not boil. Add the sherry, Worcestershire sauce, and salt. Heat but do not boil. Serve at once in warm bowls.

MAKES 6 SERVINGS.

Cooking on the Beach

Kodiak Island residents prefer to cook their king crab in nature's own cooking liquid—seawater. Simply bring a large pot or washtub of salt water to a boil. Place a whole Dungeness or sections of snow or king crab in the water. Boil rapidly for precisely 12 minutes. This method is recommended by high school teacher and baidarka (kayak) builder Dave Kubiak of Kodiak. A lifelong resident, Dave says 12 minutes is perfect for kings. Having eaten king crab cooked by Dave on the beach there, I must agree. If beginning with freshwater, add ¼ cup of salt per gallon.

Lemon

Eskimo girl holding a king crab

Tofu with Crab Sauce

Bernie Souphanavong founded Northland Soy Products more than a decade ago, giving Anchorage its first taste of locally produced tofu and bean sprouts. Bernie uses protein-rich tofu in everything from a creamy pumpkin pie to crab entrées like this one, in which a small amount of crab goes a long way. Serve with noodles or steamed rice.

12 to 16 ounces tofu, drained
½ cup chicken stock
2 cups water
1 teaspoon salt
3 tablespoons vegetable oil
4½ teaspoons grated or finely minced fresh ginger
1 cup crabmeat
1 teaspoon mirin *(rice wine) or dry sherry*
2 tablespoons cornstarch
¼ cup cold water
1 egg white, beaten until frothy
2 teaspoons chopped green onion
1 teaspoon dark sesame oil, or to taste

Cut the tofu into ¾-inch cubes. Combine the chicken stock, the 2 cups water, and salt in a small bowl. Mix well and set aside.

Heat the vegetable oil in a wok over medium heat for 1 minute. Add the ginger and crabmeat, and stir-fry for 15 seconds. Add the *mirin* and the water–chicken stock mixture. Mix well. Stir in the tofu cubes. Reduce the heat to low and cook for 3 to 4 minutes.

Dissolve the cornstarch in the ¼ cup cold water. Slowly add the cornstarch mixture to the crab in the wok. Stir gently until the sauce thickens slightly. Slowly stir in the egg white, stirring in one direction. Cook just until the egg white is opaque. Remove from the heat and sprinkle with the green onion and sesame oil. Serve at once.

MAKES 4 TO 6 SERVINGS.

The mussel is a bivalve mollusk with blue-black exterior and pearly interior. Myriad mussel shells in prehistoric middens (refuse heaps) along the shores of Prince William Sound show that early Alaskans found them tempting fare.

Mussels are easily gathered from rocks where the adults have formed dense colonies. But check with local environmental authorities first to be sure water in the area is not polluted or experiencing "red tide" (see page 283). Also, a permit or license might be required.

The blue mussel gets its name from the color of its shell, which is blue or blue-black. The horse mussel, the black mussel, the discord mussel, and the California mussel are all common in Alaska as well, but the blue mussel is considered the tastiest of the five.

Most mussels cluster on rocks, wharf pilings, and the hulls of wrecked vessels near the low-tide mark. Like some scallops and all pearl oysters, mussels anchor themselves with tough, brownish strands called byssal threads, often referred to as the "beard."

Mussel aquaculture has ancient roots. They were grown on stakes interwoven with brushwood as early as the 13th century in Europe. The same method is still used on France's Bay of Biscay. Today mussels are grown in Alaska locations such as Halibut Cove Lagoon. Brenda Hays of Bay Blue Mussel Farm in Halibut Cove, for example, is raising excellent crops—but visiting sea otters sometimes dine on them before humans get a chance.

Mussel flesh is mild and buttery, plump, and delectably tender, generally in a Halloween combination of bright orange fringed with black. For mussel lovers, all that's needed to enjoy them is to steam the mussels until they open, then eat them straightaway (see Mussels Steamed in Their Own Juices, page 176). For use in recipes, mussels are generally opened first, then added to a dish. They can be steamed open on the stovetop or in the microwave, or plunged into a large pot of boiling water just until they open. (Mussels that do not open should be discarded.) They can then be marinated, broiled, sautéed, fried, or used in casseroles, soups, salads, or stews.

Mussels and clams can often be used interchangeably in recipes, or you might choose to use half mussels and half clams. Mussels have thinner shells than most clams, so they cook more quickly. Try mussels in your favorite clam spaghetti recipe.

MUSSELS

A Birthday Feast

During British navigator George Vancouver's voyage to survey and map the Northwest Coast, good food for the crew became a priority. Each ship carried enough wheat flour and beef extract to provide the crew with two hot meals a day. To provide additional supplies, the men would fish and hunt. On the eve of King George III's birthday, June 3, 1793, one crew was so successful on shore that they were able to feast on "Bear Steaks, stewd Eagle, and roasted Muscles, with as much glee as a City Alderman attacks his Venison," Vancouver noted in his journal.

NOTE: Certain seafoods, such as mussels and clams, can harbor parasites or harmful bacteria. Before preparing mussels, please read Seafood Safety, page 282.

Mussel Yields

Six pounds of mussels in the shell equals about 4½ quarts, yielding close to 3 cups of meat. Prepared in a dish like paella or pasta, this is enough to serve four to six people. When planning to serve the mussels solo, however, purchase about 1 pound per person for each appetizer, or about 2 pounds for a main course.

Mussels Steamed in Their Own Juices

Bliss is the perfume rising from steaming mussels. For an easy Italian variation, add 2 cups chopped fresh tomatoes or two drained canned tomatoes while the mussels are steaming.

2 pounds mussels, scrubbed and debearded (see Note)

Put the mussels in a large, heavy pot. Do not add water. Cover and cook over high heat until the mussels open, about 6 minutes. Transfer the mussels to a bowl. Discard any that have not opened.

The pan juices may be used in a recipe, or they may be served with the mussels, to be sopped up with crusty bread. (When straining shellfish juices, use a fine-mesh sieve lined with moistened cheesecloth to make sure all of the grit is removed.)

MAKES 2 SERVINGS.

NOTE: Do not debeard mussels until just before you plan to cook them, because they will die and spoil. The dark beard fibers are not harmful to eat but are generally removed before cooking. Use your fingers, shears, or a small knife.

THE MOST BEAUTIFUL PLACES IN THE WORLD

Barbara Svarny Carlson is an Aleut storyteller who performs in a replica of a traditional long dress decorated with beads, shells, and feathers, with her face "tattooed" in traditional Aleut designs (using eyeliner). Carlson has taken an Aleut name, Waygix (wayee gujek) or "Blue Mussel."

"I chose it because I think the tide pools are the most beautiful places in the world, and if I had a choice, I would stay there—forever."

—*The* Dutch Harbor Fisherman, *April 23, 1993*

Marinated Mussels with Lovage

Seeking a distinctive mussel recipe, I asked Janice Schofield of Fritz Creek, author of the encyclopedic *Discovering Wild Plants* (Alaska Northwest Books, 1989) and an enthusiastic and creative herb gardener. Janice sent a favorite mussel recipe via letter from a winter vacation, with an apologia: "Dining in New Zealand on Marinated Mussels—I remembered your request." Schofield grows her own lovage, an herb with an earthy perfume similar to celery; celery leaves may be substituted. Serve these mussels on beds of greens on salad plates, accompanied by crackers.

1 cup white wine or ½ cup herbal vinegar
2 tablespoons brown sugar
2 tablespoons chopped fresh parsley
3 tablespoons diced onion
2 tablespoons diced lovage
2 cups steamed, shucked mussels (see Note)

Follow the recipe for Mussels Steamed in Their Own Juices (see preceding page) as the first step of this recipe.

Combine the wine, brown sugar, parsley, onion, and lovage to make a marinade. Marinate the steamed mussels in this mixture for 24 to 48 hours, covered, in the refrigerator.

Note: The flavors in this recipe meld best if the mussels have just been steamed and are still warm when combined with the marinade.

MAKES 4 APPETIZER SERVINGS.

Mussel

Lovage

OCTOPUS

Tenderizing Octopus

If you catch your own octopus, Jim Tsacrios of Ouzinkie recommends a tenderizing method reminiscent of streamside laundry drubbing: After gutting, beat the carcass hard on rocks at the water's edge, giving it 75 to 80 whacks. After each set of 10 blows, scrub the carcass on a rock until it foams, then rinse in seawater. Repeat until the octopus ceases to foam.

Cleaning Octopus

To clean the head of an octopus, turn it upside down, sever the muscles that hold the viscera, ☞

The lively, leggy, and highly evolved octopus is kin to both clams and oysters, and—despite its unprepossessing appearance—not unlike them in flesh quality. Octopus is a mollusk and defined as a "shellfish," although it's not enclosed in a shell.

The reclusive octopus has just one bone in its body—the sharp, black beak, named for its resemblance to a parrot's beak. It uses this tool to break open crab shells and tear food into bites. The rough tongue inside the beak can efficiently rout crabmeat from its shell.

Expert at embraces and the source of many a salty tall tale, the wrinkly common or giant Pacific octopus is the world's largest; its body can grow to 40 inches, with arms averaging three to five times the length of its body. The overall length, then, could stretch a diver-daunting 16 feet. It can weigh 100 pounds or more.

The giant Pacific octopus uses its multitalented arms to pile up rocks and shells, feel in holes for crab and shy shellfish, and even sniff out prey. It dines on fish, mollusks, and crabs, and is preyed upon in turn by halibut and sea lions. Intrepid Alaskans seek out these creatures by poking around in seaside cliff holes at low tide or turning over stones on outer flats during extremely low tides; it's not unusual for them to catch octopus weighing 35 to 40 pounds. Fishermen who don't care to eat octopus often use it as halibut bait. Artists like Diana Tillion of Halibut Cove near Homer use octopus ink for drawing. It may also be used to color homemade pasta.

Alaska's Aleut and Tlingit peoples relied on foods like octopus when game, fish, or large marine mammals were scarce. Octopus commonly wound up simmering in traditional chowders. Today at Old Harbor on Kodiak Island, Alutiiq villagers boil the meat until tender (30 to 40 minutes) and then fry slices in butter or oil. Octopus meat can also be ground and used as you would minced clams.

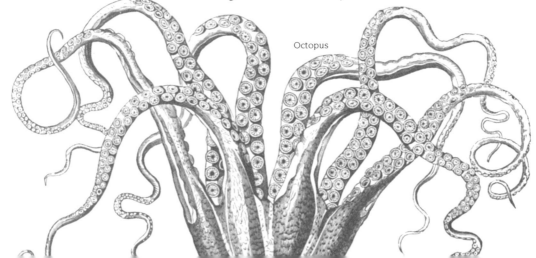
Octopus

Pickled Octopus

Libbie Graham serves Pickled Octopus at the Powder House, a tavern overlooking Cordova's Eyak Lake. (The Powder House derives its name from the fact that it stands near the spot where blasting powder was stored for the construction of the Copper River Railroad.)

"We've been serving Pickled Octopus for years," Graham says. " It's served whenever I can get fresh octopus. I add it to the salad bar. It's great on a green salad." You can also serve it with crackers.

2 pounds cleaned octopus (see Note)
2 teaspoons salt
6 cloves garlic, coarsely chopped
¼ cup chopped fresh parsley
2 teaspoons chopped fresh basil
Freshly ground black pepper to taste
1 stalk celery, chopped
4 green onions, chopped
½ cup olive oil
2 cups red wine vinegar

Rub the octopus with the salt. Rinse. Put it in a large pot over low heat, covered. Don't add water; the octopus will produce its own broth. Cook over low heat until you can pierce it with a fork and the skin has turned a fairly dark purple, about 30 minutes. Don't overcook the octopus or the suckers will come off.

Plunge the octopus at once into cold water to stop the cooking. Then peel off the purple skin. Dice the mantle and suckers into ½-inch pieces. In a medium bowl, combine the garlic, parsley, basil, pepper, celery, green onions, oil, and vinegar, and stir the diced octopus into this mixture.

Allow the octopus to marinate for 1 hour at room temperature before serving, or preferably overnight in the refrigerator.

MAKES 8 TO 10 SERVINGS.

and turn the head inside out. Remove the viscera and any dark ink sacs inside. Be especially careful to clean the moss and slime out of the suckers.

Parsley

NOTE: If you do not wish to catch your own octopus, substitute octopus tentacles from a fish market.

OYSTERS

Festival Fare

During the 1993 Anchorage Oyster Festival, Simon & Seafort's Bar and Grill offered oysters on the half shell, pan-fried oysters, Cajun oyster stew, and oysters baked with cracker crumbs, butter, cream, caramelized onions, and bacon.

NOTE: Certain seafoods, such as oysters and halibut, can harbor parasites or harmful bacteria. Before preparing oysters, please read Seafood Safety, page 282.

Found around the globe, the oyster is a bivalve relative of clams and mussels. A curious creature, the oyster begins life as a male and becomes female in middle age.

Two varieties of oyster are common along America's Pacific Coast: the Pacific oyster (introduced experimentally from Japan in 1875) and the Olympia oyster (the only oyster native to the Northwest, small and prized). Both are commercially important, but the larger Pacific carries much more weight in the industry.

During the gold rush, when successful prospectors wished to gobble up the rewards of their rich claims, they were served shucked oysters brought north from Seattle. Around the turn of the century, fishermen hailing from the port of Seattle, anxious to expand the oyster population, cast live oysters upon Alaska's beaches. These experiments never took, because Alaska's waters are generally too cold for oysters to reproduce.

Today, Alaska has its own supply of oysters grown on dozens of "farms" spread over a bountiful ocean arc curving from Yakutat to Prince William Sound. Since the oysters here generally don't reproduce on their own, tiny "spat" (young oysters) are brought in from Outside and suspended in the water in tiered baskets with room to grow crisp, plump, and flavorful.

Oysters feed on minute organic particles, which they harvest by filtering seawater through their feeding siphons at a great rate—2 to 3 gallons of water an hour. The water in which an oyster grows will have considerable impact on its quality, in terms of both flavor and of undesirable chemicals borne by pollution. As discriminating palates can identify wine from a particular vineyard, so some oyster lovers claim that they can distinguish oysters of a particular habitat.

Some Alaskan oysters are marketed under specific names, like Sea Otter Sweets (Prince of Wales Island) and Pristines (Prince William Sound).

During summer months outside Alaska, oysters spawn as the waters become warmer, which leaves them flabby and soft—less ideal for the table. But in Alaska, where waters are always cold and oysters seldom spawn, firm oysters are never lacking.

In addition to in the shell, oysters are also available shucked by the pint, often in glass jars. Shucked oysters should always be stored submerged in their liquor—or natural juices—to maintain the quality of texture and flavor.

Tried-and-true oyster fans are loyal to eating these creatures raw, but oysters offer numerous options cooked, too. Oysters are tender, easy to eat, and quickly prepared. Somewhat gelatinous raw, the off-white flesh grows firmer when cooked. Oyster stew—little more than cream, butter, oysters, and a grinding of black pepper—can be sublime, as are oysters lightly breaded and pan-fried. Oysters broiled or baked in their shell, with a topping of sauce, minced vegetables, or cheese, are also delicious. Smoked oysters are a real treat.

Oyster Trivia

During the Klondike gold rush (1896–1898), milk was $30 a gallon, eggs $4.50 a dozen during the winter, and imported delicacies like oysters were $25 for a 1-pound tin. So many oysters were sent north that natural beds around Seattle were seriously depleted.

Tlingit girls, Juneau, ca. 1890s

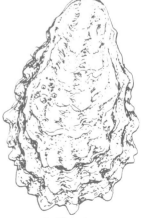

Pacific oyster

Opening Oysters

Observe an oyster in profile and you will see that one shell is rounded or humped, while the other is somewhat flat. Place the oyster on a firm surface, flat side up, and nip off some of the shell edge until you create an opening large enough to insert a knife blade. Slip a thin but sturdy kitchen knife or oyster knife into the opening and slide it back against the flat side of the shell until you sever the adductor muscle. Pull the flat side of the shell off. To remove the oyster from the shell still cradling it, slide your knife under the oyster to sever its moorings.

Chef Ray Estes of Sea Galley in Anchorage sometimes runs through four 10-dozen bags of fresh oysters a day. Shucking tips, Ray? "Just be sure you don't mutilate the oyster," Estes says, using a protective glove with rubber grippers on the palm on his left hand and wielding an oyster knife in his right. "Open it very carefully so you retain the original ☞

Grizz's Grilled Oysters

Since 1980, Don "Grizz" Nicholson and family have operated the Canoe Lagoon Oyster Company on Coffman Cove, 95 miles north of Ketchikan. The Nicholsons call their product the "Alaska Sterling," describing it as sweet, lightly salty, and succulent. "The Sterling is only from this lagoon," Don said, "and we feel there are significant flavor differences." Don considers grilling one of the best ways to showcase his harvest.

6 pounds fresh, raw oysters in the shell
Cocktail sauce or hot pepper sauce

Prepare coals for grilling. When the coals are hot, put the oysters, in their shells, in a single layer on the grill. Cook just until they open. "They will be perfect," Don says.

Serve with cocktail sauce or hot pepper sauce.

MAKES 6 SERVINGS.

Sterling Microwaved Oysters

Don Nicholson recommends microwaving oysters as a form of steaming; it dries out the meat less, he says.

4 pounds fresh, raw oysters in the shell
Cocktail sauce

Place the oysters on a paper plate or other microwavable plate. They will need to be cooked in batches, each batch placed in a circle in a single layer.

Cook on medium high just until the shells pop open, 3 to 5 minutes. Serve hot with the cocktail sauce of your choice.

MAKES 4 TO 6 APPETIZER SERVINGS.

Beverly's Oyster Wontons

Wasilla real estate agent Beverly Schiemann owns Blue Water Seafoods, an oyster farm on Sea Otter Sound, on the west coast of Prince of Wales Island. At any one time, Beverly has from 100,000 to 300,000 oysters growing. Four caretakers live at the farm year-round, while Beverly visits three or four times every summer. "We're not going to get rich, but I love the lifestyle," she says.

Clever Beverly invented this appetizer to showcase her Sea Otter Sweets, which won best of show in a taste testing of 10 Alaska-raised oysters during Anchorage's 1993 Oyster Festival.

⅓ cup butter
4 cloves garlic, minced
3 green onions, finely chopped
1 can (6 ounces) water chestnuts, finely chopped
1 bunch spinach, washed, drained, and coarsely chopped
Dash of black pepper
Dash of lemon juice
24 wonton wrappers
24 oysters, shucked and drained
Oil for deep-frying
Hot mustard or other dipping sauce

Melt the butter in a large sauté pan. Sauté the garlic, green onions, water chestnuts, spinach, pepper, and lemon juice over medium heat for 3 to 5 minutes.

Place about 1 teaspoon of the vegetable mixture in the center of a wonton wrapper, and top with 1 oyster. (If the oysters are large, cut them in half.) Bring the lower left corner of the wrapper to the center, followed by the lower right corner and the upper left corner. Finally, fold the upper right corner on top and seal with a little water. Continue with the remaining wrappers, oysters, and vegetable mixture.

Place enough oil to just cover the wontons in a large frying pan, and heat it to 375°F to 400°F. Deep-fry the filled wontons for about 2 minutes, or until golden brown. Serve immediately with hot mustard or the dipping sauce of your choice.

MAKES 8 TO 12 APPETIZER SERVINGS.

content. We try to loosen the muscle—not to nick them, scar them, or leave any shell bits."

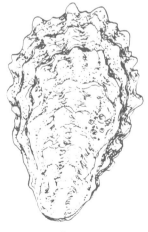

Pacific oyster

NOTE: Chef Flynn blanches his basil in boiling water for 5 seconds, then plunges it into an ice-water bath and squeezes out the excess water. Blanching locks the chlorophyll into the basil, retaining its fresh green color.

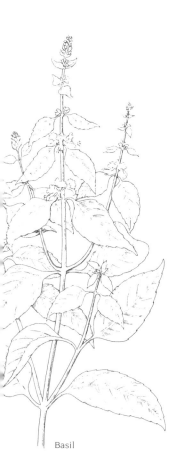

Basil

Pesto Roasted Oysters

Michael Flynn, executive chef with the Alyeska Prince Hotel, worked as an alpine ski instructor before attending California Culinary Academy. "I wanted to be a chef, not only for the creative career possibilities but because I genuinely love great food," Flynn says.

This dish is one of the unique recipes Michael developed for the elegant new Seven Glaciers Restaurant at Alyeska. Located on a mountainside at an elevation of 2,300 feet, the restaurant is reached by an aerial tram. The oysters are presented on a bed of greens topped with Vinaigrette. Leftover Pesto can be served over pasta. Leftover Vinaigrette doubles as a dressing for mixed greens.

> *16 medium or large Pacific oysters in the shell*
> *2 ripe tomatoes, quartered and seeded*
> *2 ounces mixed baby greens (mesclun)*

Pesto:
> *Leaves from 2 bunches fresh basil, picked from the stems (about 2 to 3 cups loosely packed) and blanched (see Note)*
> *2 tablespoons finely chopped garlic*
> *2 tablespoons grated Parmesan cheese*
> *2 tablespoons toasted pine nuts*
> *½ cup olive oil, or more to achieve desired consistency*
> *Salt and freshly ground black pepper to taste*

Vinaigrette:
> *1 tablespoon Dijon-style mustard*
> *¼ cup good-quality red or balsamic vinegar*
> *½ cup olive oil*
> *1 tablespoon chopped fresh mixed herbs*

To make the Pesto, place the blanched basil and garlic in a food processor. Pulse until the basil is coarsely chopped. Add the cheese and pine nuts. With the motor running, add the oil slowly in a steady stream until the mixture is emulsified and reaches a soft paste consistency. Add salt and pepper to taste.

To make the Vinaigrette, place the mustard, vinegar, oil, and herbs in a jar and shake vigorously until mixed. The vinaigrette may be prepared the day before and stored in the refrigerator.

Preheat the broiler.

Wash the oysters well under cold water to remove any dirt or grit. Open them with a shucking knife and loosen the meat from the shell (see page 182). Cut the tomato quarters into halves diagonally. Place a piece of tomato in the bottom of each shell, with an oyster on top. Top each oyster with 1 teaspoon of the Pesto. Place under the broiler and broil until the oysters are plump and hot, 6 to 10 minutes.

Divide the baby greens among 4 salad plates. Drizzle some of the Vinaigrette over and around the greens. Place 4 oysters, evenly spaced, atop the greens on each plate. Serve immediately.

MAKES 4 SERVINGS.

Oyster Yields

Shucked Pacific oysters, by grade:
Large: Less than 8 meats per pint
Medium: 9 to 12 meats per pint
Small: 13 to 18 per pint
Extra-small: 19 or more per pint

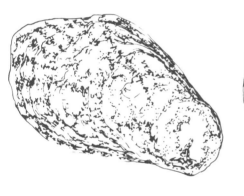

Olympia oyster

SEX AND OYSTERS

Oysters rarely spawn naturally in Alaska because they require a sustained water temperature of 68°F to 72°F for approximately 1 month in order to reproduce. Alaska's supply of oysters doesn't rely on oysters reproducing, but instead hinges on "spat" or baby oysters being brought in from Outside and planted.

SCALLOPS

How Turnagain Arm Got Its Name

When Captain James Cook sailed north to Alaska in 1798, he was seeking that elusive Northwest Passage—a water connection between the Pacific and the Atlantic. During his quest, he explored the southern arm of Cook Inlet. But there was no passage here; Cook's crew was forced to "turn again" as the snowcapped mountains loomed closer on both sides and the water grew shallower.

Like oysters, clams, and mussels, the scallop is a mollusk with two curved shells, a bivalve. The deeply grooved shells are hinged, with wing-like projections on either side of the hinges.

Scallop shells range in size from 1 inch to 7 inches across. They range in color from red to purple, orange, yellow, pink, and white. Since prehistoric times these attractive shells have been recycled as bowls and tools.

The family of scallops includes more than 400 species distributed worldwide. The Alaska species of scallops are the larger weathervane and the smaller Pacific pink, Hinds', and arctic pink. The weathervane is locally abundant south of the Alaska Peninsula and is the major food scallop of the northeastern Pacific. A weathervane shell can grow to 12 inches across.

The cube-shaped scallop meat sold in supermarkets is the large adductor muscle cut from the shell (the adductor muscle in other bivalves is tiny in comparison). The muscle grows to great size because it has been spasmodically used by the scallop to open and close its shells—with such force that water jets out and propels the animal forward or upward. Some scallops are immobile, attached to a stationary object for life; others are adventurers who flit from place to place like pastel saucers.

Singing scallops are grown commercially in British Columbia and northern Washington and imported to Alaska. These small pink-shelled scallops are eaten whole, unlike other scallops in which only the adductor muscle is harvested.

Scallops have a sweet, inimitable taste. They are delicious poached, breaded and fried, used in fondue instead of beef, or combined in sauced dishes with other shellfish such as shrimp and crab. Like halibut cheeks, scallops are tender, boneless seafood, universally relished when they're cooked correctly—which means briefly.

Scallop

Turnagain House Mushrooms

Turnagain House, a Continental restaurant located in the village of Indian, a 25-minute scenic drive south of Anchorage, boasts an unbeatable vista across Turnagain Arm to the peaks of the Kenai Range.

Turnagain House prides itself on flying in fresh seafood year-round. When scallops and shrimp are available, this signature appetizer graces the menu.

18 large mushrooms suitable for stuffing
6 tablespoons dry white wine
2 tablespoons brandy
Juice of ½ lemon
1 cup chopped scallops
1 cup chopped shrimp
4 green onions, chopped
1 tablespoon chopped fresh tarragon, or 1 teaspoon dried
   tarragon, crumbled
12 ounces cream cheese, softened
Salt, black pepper, and cayenne pepper to taste
2 tablespoons butter
½ cup grated Parmesan cheese
½ cup buttered bread crumbs

Remove the stems from the mushrooms and chop them. Set the whole caps aside. Combine the white wine, brandy, and lemon juice in a medium saucepan. Add the scallops, shrimp, mushroom stems, green onions, and tarragon, bring to a simmer, and poach until the seafood is just cooked through, about 3 minutes. Drain and chill. This step may be done the day before.

Combine the chilled seafood mixture with the cream cheese. Add salt, black pepper, and cayenne to taste.

Preheat the oven to 375°F. In a large frying pan, heat the butter over medium heat and lightly sauté the mushroom caps for 2 to 3 minutes, adding salt and pepper to taste. Stuff the caps with the seafood mixture and set on a baking sheet. Top with the grated Parmesan and buttered bread crumbs. Bake for 20 minutes. Serve at once.

MAKES 6 APPETIZER SERVINGS.

Bore Tide

An added attraction at the Turnagain House Restaurant is the occurrence of a bore tide—a wall of water moving across the Arm— one of only two such tides in North America. Diners sometimes make their reservations to coincide with the tide.

Chanterelle mushrooms

Scallop

Scallops with Raspberry-Tomato Chutney

Serving scallops with a fruit and red onion chutney is the notion of Anchorage chef Scott Evers, a talented ice carver who left the restaurant business to found his own catering firm, Glacial Reflections. Evers's recipe is designed to meet the calorie and fat requirements of the Providence Heart Diet. He prefers weathervane scallops in this dish.

Although cultures are not quick to mix in terms of who's coming to dinner, recipes are quick to meld together in the kitchen's pots. In Alaska's fusion cuisine, Tex-Mex blends with East Indian quicker than you can say "cross-cultural."

Serve these scallops with Thai jasmine rice.

1 pound sea scallops (1½ to 2 inches in diameter)
1½ teaspoons olive oil
1½ teaspoons tequila
1 tablespoon Rose's lime juice
½ teaspoon finely chopped fresh lemon thyme or common thyme

Raspberry-Tomato Chutney:
1 tablespoon honey
1 teaspoon molasses
¼ teaspoon brown sugar
1 teaspoon balsamic vinegar
½ cup seeded, diced ripe papaya (½-inch dice)
½ cup peeled, diced pineapple (½-inch dice)
2 tablespoons finely diced red onion
½ cup chopped ripe tomato
¼ cup chopped fresh mint
2 tablespoons chopped cilantro
6 large strawberries, hulled and halved
1 cup raspberries

To make the Raspberry-Tomato Chutney, combine the honey, molasses, brown sugar, vinegar, papaya, pineapple, onion, tomato, mint, and cilantro in a saucepan and simmer, stirring, for 15 minutes. Add the strawberries and raspberries, and simmer for another 15 minutes. The chutney will keep, refrigerated, for 1 week. Makes 2 cups.

Carefully pat the scallops dry. In a heavy skillet, heat the olive oil.

Sear (brown the outside) of the scallops quickly, about 1 minute per side. Remove the scallops to a warm oven.

Add the tequila to the skillet, and stir to dissolve all the brown bits. Add the lime juice and lemon thyme, and stir. Pour this mixture over the scallops and serve at once on warmed dinner plates with the Raspberry-Tomato Chutney.

MAKES 6 SERVINGS.

Wild raspberries

Alaskan Seafood Chowder

Floating a wealth of fish, shellfish, and smoked fish in a rich stock, Alaskan Seafood Chowder is a specialty of Roberto Alfaro, chef de cuisine of the Crow's Nest Restaurant in the Hotel Captain Cook in Anchorage. Any leftover fish stock can be frozen to use at another time.

Celery

¼ cup plus 1 tablespoon Clarified Butter (see page 232)
½ cup flour
1 tablespoon chopped garlic
1 small white onion, diced
1 teaspoon chopped shallot
¼ cup diced celery
¼ cup white wine
2 tablespoons Pernod (anise liqueur, optional)
2 cups diced red potatoes
2 bay leaves
4 cups nonfat milk
1 cup heavy cream
2 ounces halibut, cut in cubes (½ cup)
2 ounces scallops, cut in half (½ cup)
2 ounces peeled, deveined spot shrimp (½ cup)
4 ounces king crabmeat (1½ cups)
2 ounces smoked salmon, cut in ½-inch cubes (½ cup)
1 teaspoon minced fresh thyme
1 teaspoon minced fresh basil
Dash of cayenne pepper
Salt and freshly ground black pepper to taste

Alfaro's Fish Stock:
1 tablespoon olive oil
1 small clove garlic, chopped
1 teaspoon diced white onion
¼ cup sliced celery
¼ cup sliced carrots
¼ cup sliced leeks
1 bay leaf
1½ pounds halibut bones
1 cup shrimp shells

¾ cup white wine
4 cups water

Croutons:

24 slices (¼ inch thick) French baguette, about 2 inches in diameter
1 tablespoon extra-virgin olive oil
2 tablespoons grated Parmesan cheese

To make Alfaro's Fish Stock, heat the oil in a medium saucepan over medium-high heat. Add the garlic, onion, celery, carrots, and leeks. Sauté lightly. Add the bay leaf, halibut bones, shrimp shells, white wine, and water, and bring to a boil. Strain.

To make the Croutons, preheat the oven to 350°F. Brush the bread rounds with the olive oil. Sprinkle with the cheese. Place on a baking sheet and bake until the cheese is melted, about 5 minutes. Keep warm while making the chowder.

Heat ¼ cup of the Clarified Butter in a small, heavy saucepan. Whisk in the flour. Whisk over medium heat until thickened, 3 to 5 minutes; do not allow to brown. Set this roux aside.

Heat the remaining 1 tablespoon Clarified Butter in a large stockpot over medium-high heat. Add the garlic and sauté for 1 minute. Add the onion, shallot, and celery, and sauté until the onion is translucent. Add the white wine and Pernod. Light with a match and flame until the alcohol is completely gone. Add the red potato and bay leaves. Sauté for 2 minutes. Add 4 cups of the Fish Stock with the milk and heavy cream. Bring almost to a boil and add the roux. Stir lightly over low heat. Make sure the chowder does not burn to the bottom of the pan.

Add the halibut, scallops, and spot shrimp, and simmer for 10 minutes longer. Add the crabmeat and smoked salmon, and cook until just heated through. Stir in the thyme, basil, and cayenne pepper with salt and black pepper to taste. Remove the bay leaves. Ladle the chowder into heated bowls and pass the Croutons separately, or float 3 on each serving of chowder.

MAKES 8 SERVINGS.

Onions

Terrine of Leeks, Scallops, and Sole with Fresh Tomato Sauce

This feather-light terrine was developed by chef Craig McCloud of the Rose Room Deli at Providence Alaska Medical Center in Anchorage. It's a dieter's dream: only 122 calories per serving.

2 envelopes (2 tablespoons) unflavored gelatin
½ cup water
6 medium leeks, roots and green ends trimmed, washed, and
    blanched
1 pound sole fillets
½ pound scallops
2 egg whites, at room temperature
1 teaspoon salt
1 teaspoon white pepper
½ teaspoon nutmeg
1½ cups very cold evaporated skim milk
4 ounces morel mushrooms, washed and cut into rings
1 red bell pepper, diced and blanched

Fresh Tomato Sauce:
8 large tomatoes
2 tablespoons corn oil
⅓ cup minced chives
1 tablespoon tomato paste

Preheat the oven to 325°F.

Sprinkle the gelatin over the water in a small saucepan and let sit until softened, about 5 minutes.

Line a lightly oiled terrine mold or 9-inch by 5-inch loaf pan with plastic wrap. Chill the terrine for 5 minutes. Halve the leeks lengthwise and separate them into layers. (Remove any grit between layers.)

Gently heat the gelatin mixture until it is dissolved and smooth. Dip a leek strip in the gelatin and let excess drip off. Lay the strip in the chilled terrine across the width, pressing well into the bottom, with either end hanging over the edge. (The cold terrine solidifies the gelatin so the leeks stay in place.) Repeat with the remaining leeks to line the whole terrine mold.

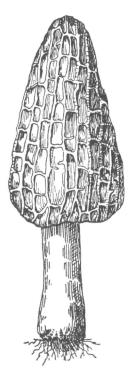

Morel mushroom

Prepare a mousse by whirling the sole, scallops, egg whites, salt, pepper, nutmeg, and evaporated milk in a food processor until fluffy. Fold in the morels and bell pepper.

Spoon the mousse into a piping bag with a large tip. Pipe the mousse into the terrine mold carefully. Trim excess leek ends to within ½ inch of the filling. Cover the top with parchment paper or the terrine cover. Place the terrine in a pan of hot water and bake in the oven for about 1 hour, or until it reaches an internal temperature of 135°F. (Test with an instant-read food thermometer.) Cool slightly, then chill in a refrigerator.

Make the Fresh Tomato Sauce while the terrine is chilling. Blanch, peel, and seed the tomatoes, then dice them. Heat the oil in a large frying pan; add the tomatoes, chives, and tomato paste, and sauté, stirring, until the sauce is the desired consistency.

To serve, slice the chilled terrine and serve it with the hot sauce.

MAKES 6 SERVINGS.

Leek

Eskimo woman emerging from an "ice cellar," King Island, ca. 1938

Smoked Scallops in Angel Hair Pasta

Chris K. Olson of Valdez and her teenage daughter, Spring Alaska Olson, live a challenging bush lifestyle—one many Alaskans favor. "We live on a houseboat out in the woods," Chris says. "No electricity and no phone." Chris studied business, food, and restaurant management at Washburn University in Kansas. In Valdez, she works as a caterer and part-time cook. During the summer, she manages a campground of 101 sites. "I help make the tourists happy—and negotiate with the bears," she says with a laugh.

Smoked scallops are available seasonally in many markets; other smoked seafood—or fresh scallops—may be substituted. You may also use 1 cup of either Romano or Parmesan cheese, rather than both.

12 ounces angel hair pasta
2 tablespoons Clarified Butter (see page 232)
4 large cloves garlic, minced
1 pound smoked scallops, quartered
2 cups heavy cream
¼ teaspoon salt
¼ teaspoon cracked black pepper
½ cup finely grated Romano cheese
½ cup finely grated Parmesan cheese
6 green onions, minced
Additional grated Romano or Parmesan cheese (optional)

Cook the pasta al dente and drain well.

In a large skillet or wok, heat the Clarified Butter. Add the garlic and smoked scallops, and cook over medium-high heat for about 90 seconds to sear them slightly.

Add the cream, salt, and pepper, and cook for 2 minutes more.

Add the drained pasta and both cheeses, and toss the mixture over medium heat until it is thoroughly heated and the cheese is melted. Serve topped with the green onions and additional cheese, if desired.

Makes 6 servings.

Scallop

Tequila Lime Scallops

This eclectic recipe was invented by chef Peter Ostrinsky for the Raven's Nest restaurant in Fairbanks. "We've gotten lots of compliments on it," says Ostrinsky, now a resident of Anchorage. Ostrinsky first became acquainted with a restaurant kitchen when he worked as a dishwasher in Scribners, a four-star seafood house in his hometown, Milford, Connecticut. Just 15 then, he was sufficiently intrigued to set his sights on graduating from the Culinary Institute of America. He later worked at another four-star establishment, the Occidental, in Washington, D.C. After three years of electrical construction in Fairbanks, he dived back into cooking, rising to the level of sous-chef at the Raven's Nest.

Serve these scallops with wild rice pilaf and the fresh vegetable of your choice.

½ cup Clarified Butter (see page 232) or extra-virgin olive oil
2 pounds sea scallops
2 tablespoons chopped fresh herbs (a mixture of basil, oregano, thyme, chives, and mint)
2 tablespoons finely chopped garlic
2 teaspoons salt, or to taste
1 teaspoon freshly ground white pepper, or to taste
1½ cups gold tequila, preferably José Cuervo
1½ cups Rose's lime juice or fresh lime juice

Heat a large sauté pan until medium hot. Add the butter, followed by the scallops. When slightly browned, turn the scallops and add the herbs, garlic, salt, pepper, and tequila. Be careful when adding the tequila; it will flame up in the pan. This burns off the alcohol.

While the sauté is flaming, shake the pan to deglaze it, or loosen the flavorful food solids from the bottom of the pan.

When the flames subside, pour in the lime juice and allow the mixture to simmer for 2 to 3 minutes. When the scallops are semi-firm, remove them from the pan and keep warm. Continue to simmer the sauce until it reaches a syrupy consistency. Arrange the scallops on 4 warmed plates. Pour the sauce over the scallops and serve.

MAKES 4 SERVINGS.

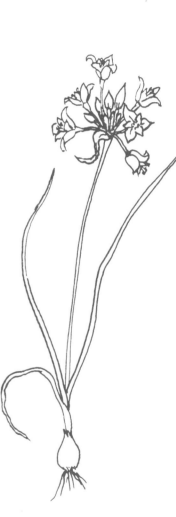

Wild onion

Scallop

Littleneck clam

Scallops and Clams with Ginger Sauce

Larry Pi is cook and manager of the only Chinese restaurant in Valdez, Fu Kung's on Kobuk Street. Larry serves a school of seafood specialties, including this scallop and clam dish that reflects his Korean roots. Serve over steamed rice.

¼ cup Clarified Butter (see page 232)
1 large onion, sliced
2 cloves garlic, sliced
1 tablespoon tomato paste
1 teaspoon salt
1 pound frozen whole-leaf spinach (see Note)
1 pound scallops or peeled and deveined shrimp
2 cups cooked, diced clams

Ginger Sauce:
4 dried black mushrooms, soaked in warm water for ½ hour, drained, and minced
2 tablespoons minced green onions
2 teaspoons minced red chile peppers
1 tablespoon light soy sauce
¾ cup minced sweet pickled ginger (the shell-pink Japanese sushi condiment beni shoga)
½ cup white vinegar
½ cup sugar
¾ cup water
1 tablespoon cornstarch
1 tablespoon cold water

To make the Ginger Sauce, place the mushrooms, green onions, chiles, soy sauce, pickled ginger, vinegar, sugar, and water in a small saucepan, bring to a boil, and simmer for 3 minutes.

Mix the cornstarch with the cold water, and stir it into ginger mixture over low heat until the sauce is thickened; keep warm. If making the sauce ahead, refrigerate and use within 2 days.

Melt the Clarified Butter in a large, heavy saucepan. Add the onion and garlic, and sauté gently until soft. Stir in the tomato paste and the salt, and cook, stirring, for 1 minute. Add the frozen spinach and cook until the spinach has thawed, breaking it up with a wooden spoon.

NOTE: Equivalent fresh spinach may be substituted.

Add the scallops and clams, and cook on medium heat for another
5 minutes, turning the seafood gently to coat it with the spinach. Serve
immediately with the warm Ginger Sauce.

MAKES 6 SERVINGS.

Koodlahlook jigging for tom cod through the ice, Bering Strait, 1916

SEA URCHINS

Eskimo Pancakes

With the Western introduction of flour and pancakes, Eskimos made this dish using sea gull or murre eggs, or sometimes sea urchin roe. Roe from six urchins was used as the equivalent of three hen's eggs. The pancakes were fried in whatever oil was available, including whale oil.

A porcupine of the sea, the sea urchin is a spiny invertebrate, kin to the starfish and sand dollar. Most sea urchins are oblate (pumpkin-shaped) and armored all over with long, movable spines. Sea urchins commonly attach themselves to bottom-growing seaweed and then feed upon it, sometimes clear-cutting whole kelp forests. Their special feeding apparatus—"Aristotle's lantern"—consists of five sharp, constantly growing teeth.

There are 500 species of sea urchin worldwide—all edible. The sea urchin has no flesh per se, but it does house edible gonads or "roe," as delicate in flavor and texture as the finest caviar. The roe ranges in color from nearly white (male) to bright orange (female); the brighter the color, the better the taste.

Sea urchins gather in depressions, rocky crevices, and tide pools at low-water line. The most prized of the Pacific Coast urchins is the giant or "red" urchin, with a shell (or "test") reaching nearly 7 inches in diameter. It has two color phases, red-brown and dark purple, and ranges from Kodiak Island to Mexico. The green urchin is circumpolar. A less desirable cousin is the Pacific purple urchin.

These delectable shellfish are more available in restaurants—often as *uni* at sushi bars—than they are in supermarkets for the home cook. But Alaskans are often seen out gathering their own. The best months to gather sea urchins are July through December. It's important to collect from only very clean waters (check with local authorities), and to wear heavy leather gloves as protection from sharp spines. Native Alaskans do away with the spines by roasting whole urchins in the fire until the spines are burned away.

Sea urchin roe is generally eaten raw. An easy appetizer is fresh roe served on sourdough bread slices with a dribble of lemon juice over it. But sea urchin roe can also be poached in egg cups or custard cups, setting the cups in hot water and simmering 3 to 5 minutes. Sea urchin roe is rich in iodine, delicate, and nutty when raw, like hen's eggs when fried in butter.

Sea Urchin Sauce

This sauce was recommended by Lynn Abernathy of Ocean Fresh Seafood. It is a unique complement to any white-fleshed fish, including whitefish, lingcod, and rockfish.

½ cup heavy cream
2 tablespoons gewürztraminer wine
½ cup chopped sea urchin roe (from 3 or 4 medium urchins)

In a small saucepan, bring the cream and wine to a low boil. Cook for 2 to 3 minutes to reduce it. The sauce is properly reduced when it coats the back of a spoon. Add the roe and stir well. Serve hot over poached, broiled, or baked unseasoned or lightly seasoned fish.

MAKES 4 SERVINGS.

Tlingit spruce-root basket

A Trial Harvest

In January 1995, Ocean Fresh Seafood Products of Fort Bragg, California, was awarded a contract to conduct a trial commercial harvest of red sea urchins off Ketchikan. The company projects bringing up 2.7 million pounds of urchins, the roe of which will be marketed to Japan.

Extracting Roe

Turn the urchin upside down so the five-toothed mouth is exposed. Crack the shell all around with sharp blows from a hammer or cut a circle out of the bottom of the shell. The viscera will come away with this circle, revealing the five tongues of roe clinging to the top of the shell. Loosen the tongues with your fingertips, removing them whole like a clutch of tangerine sections.

SHRIMP

At Tempura Kitchen in Anchorage, raw shrimp are offered on a bowl of vinegared rice, accompanied by a small bowl of deep-fried shrimp heads. Squeeze lemon on a raw shrimp, top with a fried head, and crunch down, antennae and all.

FRESHNESS: "Spot shrimp are very perishable because they have a low water content," says Anchorage supermarket owner Paul Reid. "Fishermen may store them on ice and hold them on board four or five days. You can tell how old they are by the shells; fresh shells are slippery, almost as if they've been coated with silicone; old shells feel rough because they have oxidized. To me they're old and stinky! I think shrimp frozen at sea are superior; they take their heads off and flash freeze them right there."

The Alaska shrimp harvest is comprised of four main cold-water or northern species, the pink, spot, side-stripe, and coon-stripe. Pink shrimp account for about 85 percent of the total harvest.

In Alaska and the western Unites States, large shrimp are marketed as "prawns." The Food and Agricultural Organization, however, calls freshwater species "prawns" and saltwater species "shrimp."

Meaty, firm, boneless, and mild in flavor, shrimp are eagerly devoured by diners who "don't like fish." Not only are shrimp one of the most popular seafoods, they are also among the most versatile. They can be poached, baked, steamed, pan-fried, deep-fried, stir-fried, grilled, you name it. Spot shrimp, hailed for their succulent flavor, are often simply steamed and served with cocktail sauce or drawn butter for dipping. For extra color and gastronomic panache, add any eggs found on the shrimp's belly to shrimp dishes at the last moment of cooking.

Tsimshian design

Sophie Station Fettuccine

Timothy Frank, executive chef of Sophie Station Hotel in Fairbanks, offers a pasta and shrimp duet, one of his most popular entrées. "This dish takes its inspiration from the incomparable Gulf of Alaska shrimp," says Frank, "so sweet and delicate they require only the lightest of touches to showcase."

1 pound fettuccine
½ cup butter
4 green onions, finely chopped
¼ cup dry white wine
2 tablespoons white wine vinegar
¼ cup sherry
1 tablespoon A-1 steak sauce
1 teaspoon dried tarragon
¼ teaspoon Tabasco sauce
½ teaspoon dry mustard
2 cups light cream or half-and-half
1 pound shrimp, peeled and deveined
¼ cup freshly grated Parmesan cheese

Cook the fettuccine al dente and drain well.

In a saucepan, heat 2 tablespoons of the butter and add the green onions. Sauté for 1 minute. Add the wine and vinegar, and boil until reduced by half. Add the sherry, A-1 sauce, tarragon, Tabasco sauce, and dry mustard. Boil again until reduced by half. Add the cream and bring to a boil. Reduce slightly.

Add the shrimp. Simmer and stir until the shrimp are opaque through, 3 to 5 minutes; the shrimp will be evenly pink and partly curled. Stir in the remaining 6 tablespoons butter and the Parmesan cheese. Toss the sauce with the drained pasta. Serve at once on warmed plates.

MAKES 4 SERVINGS.

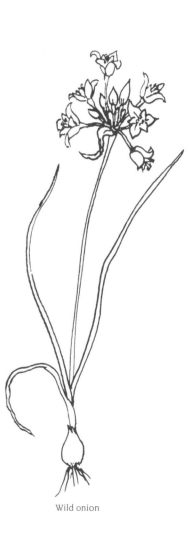

Wild onion

Celery

Shrimp Étouffée

Brett Connor is a massage therapist in Kotzebue whose clientele includes members of the Maniilaq Medical Center staff as well as mushers competing in the Kobuk 440, an annual sled dog race. In his "former life," Brett spent 18 years in restaurant kitchens. He cooked at Land's End in Homer for five years, in Hawaii for a winter, at the popular Double Musky Inn in Girdwood, and at the Nul-luk-vig Hotel in Kotzebue. At both the Musky and the Nul-luk-vig, diners applauded his spicy Shrimp Étouffée, a bold Cajun favorite. It uses Brown Sauce, a Louisiana-style roux of browned butter and flour, usually made in large batches and kept in the refrigerator.

As the ingredients of this recipe are increased to serve more people, you may need a little less than ¼ cup of the Brown Sauce per person. Accompany the étouffée with steamed rice and crisply steamed okra. Consider Double Musky Pie (see page 256) for dessert.

2 tablespoons butter, softened
1 tablespoon plus 1 teaspoon minced garlic
¼ cup chopped celery
¼ cup chopped green onions
Dash of white wine
½ cup Shrimp Stock (see page 93) or water
2 canned tomatoes
¼ cup tomato liquid from can
1 bay leaf
½ teaspoon Tabasco sauce
1 teaspoon dried thyme leaves
Salt and black pepper to taste
6 to 8 ounces medium shrimp, peeled and deveined

Brown Sauce:
1 cup butter
1 cup flour

To make the Brown Sauce, melt the butter in a heavy saucepan. Stir in the flour and cook over medium heat, stirring and watching carefully, until the mixture is a rich brown. Set aside. Makes 2 cups.

In a heavy pot, cream the butter with 1 teaspoon of the garlic. Heat the garlic butter, and sauté the celery and green onions until slightly

browned and transparent, about 4 minutes. Add the white wine and
Shrimp Stock. Crush the tomatoes and add to the onion mixture along
with the ¼ cup tomato liquid. Add the bay leaf, Tabasco sauce, thyme,
the remaining 1 tablespoon garlic, and salt and pepper to taste.

Cook this mixture down for about 10 minutes, stirring
occasionally, until it is as thick as a chunky soup.

When ready to serve, remove the bay leaf. Add ¼ cup of the Brown
Sauce. Shake, stir, and incorporate well. Do not allow the mixture to
stick and burn. Add the shrimp and study the density of the dish. It
should be neither runny nor pasty. If it's too thick, add a little more
shrimp stock or water.

Watch carefully as the shrimp cook. When they are opaque
through, evenly pink, and partly curled, serve immediately over rice.

MAKES 1 SERVING

Basic Boiled Shrimp

*Use seawater or add
¼ cup of salt to each
quart of freshwater. Bring
enough water to cover the
whole shrimp to a boil.
Add the shrimp. When
the water resumes boiling,
allow the shrimp to cook
for another 3 to 8 minutes,
depending on their size.
Do not overcook, or the
shrimp will lose their
desirable firmness.*

*Cool. Pinch off head and
tail, then peel away the
shell. To remove the dark
entrail tract from the
back, use a sharp paring
knife to score, and rinse
away entrails with cold
water. Serve with tomato
cocktail sauce or
Homemade Mayonnaise
(see page 233), or atop
salads.*

Billy Nicoli and other Ahtna Indians at a fish camp, early 1900s

Prawns Bhuna Masala

Tourists who stereotype Alaska as the "north woods" are often surprised to learn that Anchorage boasts two East Indian and three Thai eateries. This spicy, bright red and green shrimp dish originates with Maharaja's, Anchorage's oldest East Indian restaurant, owned by Raj and Brijinder Basi.

Hailing from the fish-rich Punjab, the north of India, Raj Basi has a varied background for a restaurant owner. Brijinder explains: "Raj has a Ph.D. in business management. He was one of the economists to the government of Saudi Arabia for several years. Then he taught at Kent State. After four students were killed in riots there, Raj served as head of the Center for Peaceful Change, but when his friend Glenn Olds was hired away to head Alaska Pacific University, Olds in turn hired Raj as provost.

"People always enjoyed our Punjabi food, and I always said I should have my own restaurant," Brijinder says. "My nephew, trained in the restaurant field, helped me to open in 1989."

I love this dish served over steamed basmati rice flavored with chicken stock and a dash of golden turmeric. Raita (see page 237) is an ideal side dish.

Peppers

1 pound large shrimp, peeled and deveined
2 tablespoons oil
1 large onion, diced
3 cloves garlic, finely chopped
1 teaspoon finely chopped fresh ginger
½ teaspoon ground cumin (see Note)
2 medium tomatoes, chopped
¾ teaspoon salt
½ teaspoon freshly ground black pepper
½ teaspoon ground coriander (see Note)
¼ teaspoon crushed red pepper flakes
¼ teaspoon ground cloves
¼ teaspoon ground cinnamon
¼ teaspoon ground cardamom
1 large green bell pepper, cored, seeded, and sliced
¾ cup water
1 tablespoon cornstarch

Rinse the shrimp in cold water and pat dry with paper towels.

In a large frying pan, heat the oil and sauté the onion, garlic, and ginger. When browned, add the cumin and tomatoes. When the mixture becomes a paste, add the salt, black pepper, coriander, red pepper flakes, cloves, cinnamon, and cardamom. Let simmer for 5 minutes, stirring and watching carefully so it does not burn.

Add the shrimp. When they are somewhat opaque (about 3 minutes), add the bell pepper and the water mixed with the cornstarch. Let simmer for 3 or 4 minutes more.

Note: The flavor is heightened if you use whole cumin and coriander, grinding them with a mortar and pestle before adding them to the dish.

MAKES 4 SERVINGS.

"E-Z Peel" Shrimp

A recent development is the "E-Z Peel" shrimp. Each shrimp has been mechanically slit along two-thirds of its spine, cutting deep enough to remove the dark line of digestive tract ("vein"). This process makes removing the shell a simpler matter.

Tsimshian plaited cedar bark storage basket

Toni's Shrimp Pizza with Roasted Garlic

Toni Bocci manages the Cordova terminal of the Alaska Marine Highway. "That means I tie up the ship, sell tickets, and make reservations," she explained. "I'm the only one here, so I'm jack of all trades when the ferry comes in." Toni's specialty is a delicious white pizza—a shrimp pizza made without tomato sauce.

1 pizza crust (14 inches), unbaked, or prebaked crust
1 head garlic
2 tablespoons plus 1 teaspoon olive oil
1 tablespoon dried basil
1 teaspoon dried oregano
8 ounces mozzarella cheese, or more to taste, grated

Toppings:
1 cup peeled and deveined shrimp
½ cup sliced Greek olives
4 ounces feta cheese, cut into small cubes
½ cup sliced mushrooms
½ cup grated Parmesan cheese
½ cup sun-dried tomatoes or sliced Roma tomatoes

Preheat the oven to 375°F.

Roast the head of garlic as follows: Remove the loose outer skins, place the garlic head in an ovenproof dish, and drizzle with 1 teaspoon of the olive oil. Bake for 20 to 30 minutes, or until the individual cloves are tender.

Peel the garlic cloves, mash them, and spread on the prepared crust. Sprinkle with the remaining 2 tablespoons olive oil. Then sprinkle with basil and oregano. Sprinkle all but ½ cup of the mozzarella onto the crust.

Increase the oven temperature to 425°F.

Top the pizza with the shrimp, olives, feta, and mushrooms, distributing them evenly. Over the toppings, sprinkle the remaining ½ cup of mozzarella and then the Parmesan. Top with the tomatoes. Bake for 15 minutes, or until the cheese is melted and the crust is baked.

MAKES 6 TO 8 WEDGES.

Oregano

Sweet and Sour Shrimp McKinley

Freeze-dried foods are required by mountain climbers who need to minimize the weight in their backpacks. This recipe was developed by Rachel Holzwarth, founder of Alaska Women of the Wilderness, for climbers on North America's highest peak, Mount McKinley (Denali). Her *Menu Planning Guide for the Backcountry* (1989) gives menus and recipes for nine people for an expedition of 21 days. For expeditions, climbers usually package meal-size portions of ingredients in zipper-top bags.

Pineapple

4 cups brown rice
9 cups water
1 package (1 ounce) soy sauce
2 packages (5 ounces each) spaghetti sauce mix
3 packages (2.75 ounces each) sweet-and-sour mix
1 cup raisins
6 ounces tomato paste
2 packages (6 ounces each) dried shrimp
1 cup dried green pepper
1 cup dried onions
1 cup dried pineapple
2 ounces margarine
1 can (1 pound) chow mein noodles

Cook brown rice with water and soy sauce in one big camp pot over backpacking stove. Watch to see that mixture doesn't run dry and burn; add a bit more water if needed. Cooking time will vary with altitude.

When rice is nearly done (about 40 minutes), mix spaghetti sauce mix, sweet-and-sour mix, raisins, and tomato paste in a second pot over a second stove, adding water as necessary to reconstitute. Add shrimp, green pepper, onions, and pineapple, and heat. Mix in margarine at the end. Serve sauce over rice. Sprinkle chow mein noodles over each serving.

MAKES 9 SERVINGS.

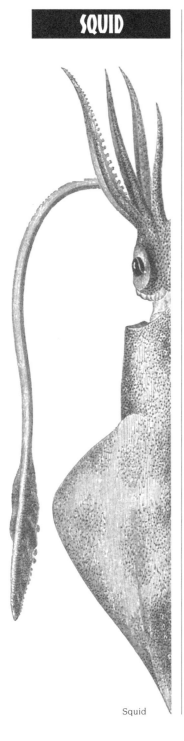

SQUID

The squid is a small relative of the octopus, but with 10 arms rather than 8, 2 much longer than the others. Its soft body has a hard axis, a flat bone called the "quill." The native squids of Alaska are the Pacific bobtailed squid and the majestic, both subsistence catches. The bobtailed grows to only about 4 inches, and is common north and south of the Alaska Peninsula. The majestic, which has a red, cylindrical body, occupies the same habitat, but can reach 18 inches long. The California or Monterey squid, which inhabits the Lower 48's West Coast, is the species most often available in Alaska's supermarkets. Squid, like octopus, are mollusks and are considered shellfish although they lack shells.

From Alaska down to California, squid (also known by their Italian name, "calamari") congregate in gregarious schools, zipping hither and yon as if jet propelled. Fishermen catch them in traps or snag them with specialized jigs.

Squid are commonly available whole, needing to be cleaned at home before cooking. Some stores do sell pre-cleaned squid pouches and tentacles, though. The meat from large squid is marketed as "steaks," tenderized pieces of the oversized pouch; these are ready to be cooked as is, often pan-fried or cut in strips for stir-frying.

Squid rings (neat little white circles of cleaned squid body) are available both fresh and frozen. Rings may be poached and added to salads, or coated and deep-fried, emerging nearly as tender as onion rings.

Squid flesh is milky white when raw, bright white when cooked. The flavor is slightly sweet, the meat firm and tender. If necessary, tenderize steaks with a mallet, pounding paper-thin before pan-frying. Squid rings, tubes, or strips may be thawed and refrozen without affecting quality. Squid cooks in a flash; take care not to overcook or the meat becomes quite tough.

Squid

Squid Sagaya

This is another recipe from the New Sagaya supermarket, which specializes in seafood, with live tanks for crab and one of the largest selections of fresh fish and shellfish in Anchorage. This main dish is intended to be one among many in an Asian-style menu, so the servings are smaller than usual. If this will be the sole entrée on the menu, increase the amounts of the ingredients accordingly.

Served over rice or noodles, with almond cookies and juicy tangerines for dessert, Squid Sagaya makes a complete meal.

½ pound cleaned squid
2 tablespoons oil
1 small onion, sliced
¼ pound edible pea pods (snow peas)
1 cup sliced zucchini
1 5-ounce can sliced bamboo shoots, drained
1 8-ounce can sliced water chestnuts, drained
2 tablespoons chicken stock or water
1 to 2 tablespoons mirin *(rice wine)*
1 tablespoon black bean sauce (see Note)
Salt to taste
1 tablespoon cornstarch mixed with 2 tablespoons water (optional)

Cut the cleaned squid bodies (tubes) into 1-inch squares. Chop the tentacles into 1-inch lengths, or leave intact. Allow it to drain, or dry with paper towels.

Heat 1 tablespoon of the oil in a wok or heavy skillet. Add the squid and stir-fry for 1 minute, or until squares curl up at the edges and tentacle clusters form "chrysanthemums." Remove and set aside.

Wipe out the pan with paper towels. Add the remaining 1 tablespoon oil. Add the onion, pea pods, zucchini, bamboo shoots, and water chestnuts, and stir-fry for 2 to 4 minutes, or until onion is brown. Add the stock, *mirin,* black bean sauce, and salt. Return the squid to the wok and continue cooking until most of the sauce has evaporated, or thicken the sauce with the cornstarch, if desired.

MAKES 4 SERVINGS.

Future Food

High in protein and low in fat, squid is potentially the largest single source of animal protein in the sea, according to experts at the Division of Agricultural Sciences at the University of California, Davis. The current annual world catch exceeds a half million tons, and could increase to 100 million tons. Squid is the food of the future.

NOTE: Black bean sauce is available in Asian markets or in the Asian cuisine section of most supermarkets.

Grand Aleutian Stuffed Calamari

James White is one of the talented chefs introducing sumptuous cuisine to the Aleutians. White graduated from the Western Culinary Institute in Portland, Oregon, in 1987. He opened the kitchen of the new Grand Aleutian Hotel in Unalaska in May 1993.

Tourists visit Unalaska chiefly in May through October. Part of the adventure is the distinct possibility of getting "socked in" for an extra week by the notoriously unpredictable Aleutian weather. Such an unplanned stay might allow one to taste a wide array of White's delectable dishes, including this squid entrée. Serve with steamed rice and sautéed leeks or another green vegetable of your choice.

¼ pound finely chopped sea scallops
¼ pound crabmeat
1 small red onion, diced
½ red bell pepper, cored, seeded, and diced
½ green bell pepper, cored, seeded, and diced
2 tablespoons finely chopped fresh cilantro
1 cup fine dry bread crumbs
1 egg
½ cup heavy cream
Salt and white pepper to taste
8 whole squid (calamari) tubes, cleaned (see Note)
2 teaspoons prepared Cajun seasoning (see page 35)
⅓ cup flour
¼ cup olive oil

Citrus Glaze:
Juice of 4 oranges
Juice of 1 lemon
Juice of 1 lime
¼ cup white wine
¾ cup unsalted butter, softened
1 tablespoon honey, if needed

To make the Citrus Glaze, pour the orange, lemon, and lime juice into a saucepan and place over medium heat. Add the white wine. Bring to a simmer and boil until thickened. (This may be done an hour or so ahead and reheated at serving time.)

NOTE: Squid vary greatly in size. The average squid tube found in markets is 5 to 8 inches long. Restaurants can sometimes request tubes that are all of a certain size.

This recipe takes 8 tubes if they are 8 by 3 inches, 16 if they are 4 by 1¾ inches. Avoid tubes with openings of less than 1½ inches, because they will be difficult to stuff. Run your finger around the inside of each tube before stuffing, because sections of the transparent quill sometimes remain.

Remove from the heat and stir in the butter. Taste the glaze. If it is too sharp, add about a tablespoon of honey. Makes 12 ½ cups.

Combine the scallops, crab, red onion, red and green bell peppers, cilantro, and bread crumbs in a bowl. Whisk the egg with the cream, and stir into the seafood mixture. Add salt and pepper.

Stuff each squid tube with an equal amount of stuffing. Fold the wide end of the tube and hold it closed with a toothpick, running the toothpick in and out as if basting a hem.

Combine the Cajun seasoning and flour, and dredge the squid in this mixture.

Preheat the oven to 350°F.

In a sauté pan, heat the olive oil. Add the squid and pan-fry until golden. This should be done in batches, so that the squid are not crowded. Immediately put the squid in a lightly greased, ovenproof baking dish, in 1 layer. Bake for 8 to 10 minutes. Remove the toothpicks.

Divide the warm Citrus Glaze among 4 warmed plates, and place 2 calamari tubes on top of the sauce on each plate. Serve at once.

MAKES 4 SERVINGS.

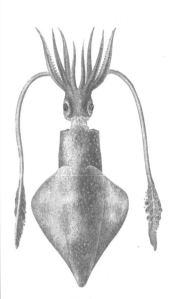

Squid

Peppers

Kachemak Calamari Salad

This recipe comes from brewmaster Wade Hampton Miller of Anchorage, who created it for a large gathering, using 8 pounds of squid tubes. (I've modified it here to serve 8.) Wade recommends garlic bread on the side.

2 cups water
1 cup pilsner beer
¼ cup vinegar
1 bay leaf
Salt and pepper to taste
2 pounds squid tubes, cleaned
Juice of 2 to 3 lemons
3 large, ripe tomatoes, diced
½ cup sliced black olives
¼ cup chopped parsley
¼ cup minced marinated pimientos
2 tablespoons chopped chives
1 tablespoon drained capers
⅛ teaspoon dried basil
⅛ teaspoon dried thyme
⅛ teaspoon dried oregano
¼ cup balsamic vinegar
3 cloves garlic, minced
1 teaspoon dried tarragon
½ cup extra-virgin olive oil
Red lettuce leaves, washed and dried
1 pint alfalfa sprouts, for garnish

In a large saucepan, combine the water, beer, vinegar, bay leaf, salt, and pepper. Bring to a boil. Add the squid tubes. Return to a boil, and simmer for no more than 60 seconds, until the squid are firm but not overcooked. Drain. Place the squid in a bowl of ice water and stir to firm the flesh. Drain and set aside.

Slice the squid into ½-inch rings, combine with the lemon juice, and season with salt and pepper to taste. Add the tomatoes, olives, parsley, pimientos, chives, and capers. Toss well. Add the basil, thyme, and oregano, and toss again to distribute the herbs.

In a food processor, blend the vinegar, garlic, and tarragon. Add the

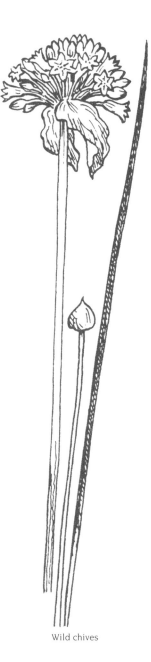

Wild chives

olive oil in a steady stream until blended. Taste, and adjust the seasoning if necessary. Pour over the squid and toss lightly. Cover and marinate, refrigerated, for 1 to 2 hours before serving.

Serve on a bed of lettuce leaves garnished with alfalfa sprouts.

MAKES 8 SERVINGS.

Child, dog, and giant squid, Dutch Harbor, 1982

RECIPES TO ROUND OUT THE MEAL

Siberian Yup'ik fishermen with cod, Saint Lawrence Island, 1897

SIDE DISHES

Cooks appreciate knowing of regional dishes that perfectly comple-ment Alaska's seafood. In this section, I've included recipes for dishes to round out your meal—side dishes, sauces, leftovers, and desserts—many with authentic Alaskan flavor.

Alaskan cooking is a fusion cuisine that incorporates many influ-ences, from Filipino to Tex-Mex to Continental. It also incorporates such local greenery as kelp, fiddlehead ferns, and goosetongue. Alaskans are accustomed to borrowing sauces from India, seasonings from Spain, and pasta from Italy. And all this borrowing and appropriating adds up to intriguing, delicious menus.

What goes best alongside your fish? It's often a matter of personal preference, but below I've included a few ideas to fuel your inspiration. From honest biscuits to mellow mushroom and blue-cheese custards, these recipes offer good companions for Alaska's seafood, with flavors from near and far.

Salmon troller near Noyes Island, west of Ketchikan, 1970s

Bannock with Baking Powder

Prospectors, stampeders, and early lawmen in Alaska craved the comfort of fresh bread. But dry yeast must be kept cool, and is thus unreliable for folks on the move. Portable sourdough came into vogue during the gold rush, when many prospectors earned the nickname "sourdough" for the form of leaven they favored. But sourdough, too, is a baker's ball and chain, a tender infant requiring constant care. So many early Alaskan bakers shunned it for simpler breads like bannock.

It is part and parcel of the Alaskan lifestyle to spend considerable amounts of time camping, hunting, hiking, boating, and fishing and, therefore, cooking outdoors. Cookie Whaley of Barrow developed this bannock recipe for campfire cooking, but it can also be cooked at home. It is delicious with trout, char, or chili.

1½ cups unsifted flour
2 teaspoons baking powder
2 teaspoons sugar
1 teaspoon salt
2 tablespoons powdered milk
1 tablespoon corn oil or melted shortening
¾ cup water
Butter or bacon fat

At home, measure the flour, baking powder, sugar, salt, and powdered milk into a mixing bowl. Mix well. Add the oil and work with a fork or pastry blender until the mixture is fine and crumbly. Form a well, pour in the water, and work into a stiff dough that holds its shape. Store in a zipper-top plastic bag. (It should keep for at least 2 days.)

In camp, on a floured surface, working with lightly floured hands, pat the dough into a flat cake the size of the griddle or pan. Grease the pan lightly with butter or bacon fat. Heat the pan, and set the bread on it. Cook for 10 minutes on one side. Flip the bread with a spatula and cook for 10 minutes on the other side. Cut into wedges and serve.

Bannock may also be cooked at home on the stovetop in a lightly greased, heavy cast-iron skillet.

MAKES 4 TO 6 SERVINGS.

A Sourdough Menu

At the Yukon Sourdough Rendezvous held every February in Whitehorse, Yukon Territory, the menu includes sourdough pancakes, meaty moose stew, and flaky bannock.

Grilled Polenta with Prosciutto di Parma and Shiitake Mushrooms

For a change of pace from bannock's simplicity, turn to a more complex side dish, grilled polenta as served by Jens Nannestad, executive chef of O'Malley's on the Green in Anchorage. Under Jens's leadership, the Crow's Nest restaurant of the Hotel Captain Cook was featured in *Bon Appetit*. His polenta appetizer is broiled and served with a colorful garnish of vegetables and salty, cured Italian ham.

Polenta:
> *6 cups water*
> *⅔ cup Clarified Butter (see page 232)*
> *2 teaspoons chopped fresh oregano*
> *2 cups cornmeal*
> *Salt and black pepper to taste*

Garnish:
> *2 red bell peppers*
> *2 green bell peppers*
> *2 tablespoons olive oil*
> *2 cloves garlic, finely chopped*
> *3 shallots, finely chopped*
> *2 tablespoons demi-glace or chicken stock*
> *4 ounces fresh shiitake mushrooms, julienned*
> *4 ounces prosciutto di Parma, julienned*
> *3 tablespoons chopped Italian parsley*
> *Salt and pepper to taste*

To make the Polenta, place the water, Clarified Butter, and oregano in a saucepan and bring to a boil. Add the cornmeal. Simmer until the mixture is thick and smooth, 5 to 10 minutes, stirring frequently. Add salt and pepper to taste.

Spread the Polenta on a greased baking sheet, and chill. The Polenta may be prepared the day before and refrigerated, covered.

To prepare the Garnish, char the red and green peppers over a gas flame or in a broiler until they are blackened on all sides. Place them in a paper bag, fold the top closed, and let stand for 10 minutes to loosen the skin. Peel and seed the peppers, then julienne them.

Heat the olive oil in a sauté pan. Sauté the garlic and shallots for 3 minutes, or until transparent. Add the demi-glace or chicken stock, and stir to deglaze the pan. Add the peppers and mushrooms. Sauté for 1 minute, or until warmed. Sprinkle the prosciutto and parsley over the top. Add salt and pepper to taste and keep warm.

Preheat a stovetop or gas grill, or light the barbecue coals. Cut the Polenta into 2-inch triangles and grill to heat it through and to create attractive grill marks.

Spoon the bell pepper mixture onto warmed plates, with the Polenta triangles alongside.

MAKES 8 SERVINGS.

Eskimo women cooking walrus meat on the beach, Nome, 1905

"Let's Give Texas Back to Mexico" Beer Biscuits

When Alaskans begin cogitating about the size of their state, they sometimes wax poetic, as did musician/songwriter Wade Hampton Miller when he wrote a tune called *Let's Give Texas Back to Mexico.* He even invented a biscuit with that name. Miller adds that, because of the stout, "these biscuits come out like hockey pucks—dark and malignant looking—but they're amazingly tasty." Serve with his Slammin' Salmon-Halibut Salad (see page 242).

3 cups sifted flour
4½ teaspoons baking powder
1½ teaspoons chili powder, regular or hot
½ teaspoon dried cilantro
½ teaspoon dried dill
¾ teaspoon salt
½ cup butter
½ cup buttermilk or sweet milk
½ cup stout or dark ale

Preheat the oven to 450°F.

Sift together the flour, baking powder, chili powder, cilantro, dill, and salt. Cut in the butter until the mixture is like coarse crumbs. Make a well, and pour in the buttermilk and stout together. Stir with a fork just until the dough follows the fork around the bowl.

On a floured surface, knead dough very gently 10 to 12 times. Pat or roll out to a thickness of ½ inch. Cut with a 2½-inch biscuit cutter or the open end of a clean, empty, 1-pound can. Bake on an ungreased baking sheet for 12 minutes.

MAKES 16 BISCUITS.

Ferguson's Fireweed Salad

"Anything that's green, if you live in Alaska, you value it much more," says Judy Ferguson, who lived on the Tanana River near Fairbanks for 15 summers, on a parcel accessible only by water. After struggling to create appetizing meals so far from sources of fresh produce, Judy says, "I watch my sister in Oklahoma put the tops of onions down the disposal and just cringe!"

Fireweed *(Epilobium angustifolium)* or willow herb is most recognizable in August, when it produces spikes of magenta flowers. In spring, harvest the green and red shoots for a salad rich in vitamin A.

To guarantee mellow taste and maximum crispness, gather the greens early in the season (before the plants bloom) and shortly before you plan to serve them. Fireweed is best when it is 3 to 5 inches tall; it wilts quickly after picking.

2 cups fireweed shoots
2 cups lamb's-quarter
1 cup dandelion greens
1 cup willow leaves

Mustard Vinaigrette:
1 cup light olive oil
⅓ cup red wine vinegar or balsamic vinegar
2 tablespoons finely chopped fresh parsley
1 teaspoon salt
½ teaspoon Dijon mustard
¼ teaspoon freshly ground pepper

To make the Mustard Vinaigrette, combine the olive oil, vinegar, parsley, salt, mustard, and pepper in a pint jar. Cover tightly and shake well. The vinaigrette will keep for a week in the refrigerator.

To prepare the greens, trim off any tough stems. Wash well and dry. Tear all the greens into bite-sized pieces, and toss in a serving bowl. Add just enough of the Mustard Vinaigrette to coat the greens, and toss gently. Serve at once.

MAKES 6 SERVINGS.

Fireweed

Two-Color Chilled Borscht

A 1984 graduate of Anchorage's East High, chef Tanya Newall of Seven Glaciers Restaurant in Girdwood trained at both the University of Alaska and the Culinary Institute of America in New York. Tanya then polished her credentials at a "little chocolate place" in Belgium and aboard a Hawaiian cruise ship. She likes to kick off a meal with the classic Russian beet soup, borscht. But as an elegant twist, she uses both yellow and red beets, puréed separately. The contrasting purées are spooned into opposite sides of a tureen and swirled with sour cream. For added panache, Tanya garnishes the cold soup with salsify strips, deep-fried after marinating overnight in purple beet juice.

Beet

4 medium red beets, sliced
3 medium yellow beets, sliced
½ cup beef stock, or as needed
½ cup chicken stock, or as needed
Salt and pepper to taste
¼ teaspoon cayenne pepper
2 tablespoons sour cream

In a pan with a steaming rack, cook the red beets and the yellow beets separately until tender. Drain, cool, and purée the beets separately. Add enough beef stock to the red beets to achieve the desired consistency, and add enough chicken stock to the yellow beets to achieve the desired consistency. The purées should not be too liquid or they won't remain separate when dished. Season with salt and pepper to taste. Chill for 2 hours or overnight.

Stir the cayenne into the sour cream. Let sit for 1 hour. Stir again. For a chef's touch, put the sour cream into a squeeze dispensing bottle to make the decorating process easier.

Place the puréed beets in a serving bowl or tureen, red on one side, yellow on the other. Stripe with the sour cream. Serve cold.

MAKES 4 SERVINGS.

Fiddleheads with Chardonnay and Bacon

Fiddlehead ferns—the tightly coiled spring shoots of shield, ostrich, or lady ferns—are a valued wild spring green in Alaska. Like artichokes, fiddleheads have a taste all their own, which might be compared to raw string beans or okra.

At the red-roofed Grand Aleutian Hotel in Dutch Harbor, UniSea executive chef Dave Wood serves fiddleheads with entrées such as Steak Calamari. "We pick fiddleheads in the spring when they are a few inches high," Dave says. Before cooking, rub off the bitter brown chaff on the stalks of shield fern *(Dryopteris dilatata)*, and rinse thoroughly.

Young dandelion leaves, lamb's-quarter, and sourdock are other greens that may be mixed with the fiddleheads to taste. Asparagus may be substituted for the fiddleheads. Pancetta (smoked Italian bacon) can stand in for the American bacon.

1 tablespoon butter
1 cup washed and cleaned fiddleheads (see Note)
¼ cup chardonnay wine
Salt and pepper to taste
2 strips bacon, cooked until crisp and crumbled

In a heavy sauté pan over moderate heat, melt the butter and sauté the fiddleheads, stirring with a wooden spoon, for 2 to 3 minutes, until almost tender but not brown. Pour the chardonnay into the pan and cover immediately, allowing the fiddleheads to steam until slightly wilted. Season with salt and pepper to taste. Garnish with cooked bacon bits, and serve.

MAKES 2 SERVINGS.

Fern fronds and fiddleheads, from left: shield, ostrich, lady

Shield fern fiddlehead

NOTE: Avoid serving fiddleheads raw; they contain a vitamin B-depleting enzyme destroyed by heat. Gather fiddleheads from shield, ostrich, or lady ferns only. The bracken fern, formerly considered edible, is now suspected of causing stomach cancer.

Spanish Artichokes

Valdez helicopter pilot Chet Simmons serves Spanish Artichokes with his Halibut Olympia Simmons (see page 81). The artichoke recipe comes from his grandmother. "I was raised by my Spanish grandmother, a mail-order bride 'acquired' at age 19 and set to cooking at a mine in Nevada for 300 people. She was an excellent chef—and a bootlegger," Simmons explains. "So consequently I enjoy a little wine with my dinner—and artichokes with my fish."

6 large artichokes
1 teaspoon salt
2 tablespoons olive oil
2 tablespoons red wine vinegar
6 large cloves garlic, chopped
Melted butter or mayonnaise, for dipping

Remove the spiny points from the artichoke leaves with scissors and slice off the top 1½ inches of each artichoke. Leave about an inch of stem. Set the artichokes upright in a large, deep pan. Sprinkle with the salt, olive oil, and red wine vinegar. Then place them upside down in a large saucepan with 1½ inches of water. Add the garlic to the pan.

Cover the pan and steam the artichokes for about an hour. (If necessary, add water during cooking so that the pan doesn't go dry.) Serve with melted butter or with mayonnaise as a dip. The boiling motion of the water will have forced the garlic bits up among the leaves.

MAKES 6 SERVINGS.

Aleut twined fish basket

Artichoke

Fried Goosetongue Salad

Residents of Alaska's seaside areas traditionally harvest the wild plants typical of coastal habitats. Native gatherers could recognize more than 100 edible or medicinal plants. One such plant is goosetongue or ribwort, favored for salad by Diane Triplet, manager of Haida Way Lodge at Craig on Prince of Wales Island in Southeast.

Named for its long, narrow leaves, goosetongue *(Plantago maritima)* favors beaches and salt marshes from southeastern Alaska to the Aleutians, sinking its roots a bit above the high tide line. One of the most popular seaside greens, both raw and cooked, it is prime from spring to early summer.

Triplet picks and cleans goosetongue greens, then blanches them for 20 seconds. She next cans them in plain water for winter use. If your larder lacks canned goosetongue, use freshly gathered, blanched goosetongue or buttery beet greens.

6 slices bacon or salt pork, diced
1 medium onion, diced
1 pint canned, drained goosetongue
1 cucumber, peeled and coarsely diced
Vinegar to taste (optional)

In a frying pan, fry the bacon and onion together until the onion is translucent and the bacon is crisp. Remove from the drippings. Add the goosetongue to the drippings in the pan and stir over medium heat until warmed through. Combine the bacon-onion mixture, goose-tongue, and cucumber, and add vinegar to taste, if desired. Serve hot.

MAKES 3 SERVINGS.

Goosetongue

Morel mushroom

Warm Mushroom and Blue Cheese Custard with Red Pepper Sauce

Featured on the Anchorage television show *Alaska Home and Garden* and a specialty of executive chef Michael Flynn, this appetizer is one I'm always tempted to order when dining at the Seven Glaciers Restaurant. Combining two of my favorite tastes—blue cheese and sultry roasted red peppers—it's light as a cloud and tasty as a foodie's dreams.

Alaska's edible wild mushrooms include the hedgehog, the king bolete, the easily recognized shaggy mane, and the black morel.

> 1 tablespoon butter
> 6 ounces wild mushrooms, cleaned and sliced
> 1 cup crumbled blue cheese
> 1 cup heavy cream
> 3 eggs, beaten
> ½ teaspoon Dijon mustard
> Salt and pepper to taste
> 1 ounce mixed greens (about 1 cup)

Red Pepper Sauce:
> 2 red bell peppers
> 8 ounces cream cheese, softened
> ¼ cup sour cream, more if needed
> 1 teaspoon chili powder
> 1 teaspoon paprika
> Salt to taste

To make the Red Pepper Sauce, char the peppers over a gas flame or in a broiler until they are blackened on all sides. Put the peppers in a paper bag or bowl and let stand, covered, until cool enough to handle. Peel the peppers and rinse them. Then quarter the peppers lengthwise, discarding the seeds, stems, and ribs. Slice roughly.

Place the peppers and cream cheese in a blender and purée. Add enough sour cream to make a pourable sauce. Add the chili powder, paprika, and salt. Pour the sauce into a mustard-type squeeze dispenser for drizzling, if you like.

Heat the butter in a frying pan and sauté the mushrooms in the

Peppers

butter. Set aside one-third of the sautéed mushrooms for the garnish. Set aside half of the blue cheese for the garnish.

Preheat the oven to 300°F.

Combine the cream, eggs, mustard, salt, and pepper in a bowl. Divide the remaining mushrooms and blue cheese equally among four 4- to 6-ounce custard cups or molds. Fill the cups with the egg mixture. Set the custards in a pan with 1 inch of water (a water bath) and bake for 1 hour and 15 minutes, or until the custard is set. Remove from the oven.

To loosen the custards from the cups, run a narrow-bladed knife twice around the edge of each cup. Turn the custards upside down and unmold them in the centers of 4 plates. Arrange a tuft of greens next to each custard. Sprinkle the reserved mushrooms and crumbled blue cheese around the plate. Drizzle lightly with Red Pepper Sauce (extra sauce can be refrigerated for another use). Serve at once.

MAKES 4 SERVINGS.

Salmon gill netter in Clarence Straits, 1972

Pasta Cousteau

This spinach-laced side dish, named in honor of the famous French marine conservationist, originates with Shan Johnson of Northwoods Lodge near Skwentna. It could be dished up with baked pike, barbecued salmon, or Shan's Gravad Lax (see page 126). For additional panache, garnish it with the edible petals of a tuberous begonia, rose, nasturtium, or marigold.

1 cup heavy cream
3 ounces Gorgonzola or other blue cheese, crumbled
⅓ cup ricotta cheese
3 tablespoons butter
Freshly ground black pepper to taste
2 tablespoons vodka
1 teaspoon Grand Marnier (optional)
1 package (10 ounces) frozen chopped spinach, thawed and
*   well drained*
1 pound linguine or fettuccine
½ cup freshly grated Parmesan cheese
Edible flower petals, for garnish (optional)

In a small saucepan, heat the cream over medium heat. Add the Gorgonzola, ricotta, and butter, stirring until blended. Add the pepper, vodka, Grand Marnier, and spinach. Heat through. Keep warm in a double boiler until ready to serve.

Cook the pasta al dente. Drain and toss with the warm sauce. Serve immediately with Parmesan cheese sprinkled over the top. Garnish with edible flowers, if you like.

MAKES 4 TO 6 SERVINGS.

Wild rose

Pecan Wild Rice

Pecan Wild Rice is a savory side dish unique to Simon & Seafort's Bar and Grill in Anchorage, where it is dished up with fish entrées such as Cod Baked with Sun-Dried Tomato-Thyme Butter (see page 60) and Rockfish with African Peanut Sauce (see page 106). This is my own version, enhanced with tangerine rind.

3 cups water
½ cup raw wild rice, rinsed and drained
2 cups rich beef stock
1½ cups raw long-grain white rice
½ cup fresh orange juice
1 tablespoon finely chopped dried tangerine rind (see Note)
1 tablespoon olive oil
1 tablespoon butter
1 medium onion, coarsely chopped
1 clove garlic, finely minced
½ cup coarsely chopped pecans
Salt and freshly ground black pepper, to taste

In a heavy saucepan, bring the 3 cups of water to a boil. Add the wild rice, reduce heat slightly, and cook at a gentle simmer, uncovered, for 40 to 45 minutes, or until the rice is just tender. Drain. Keep warm.

In another heavy saucepan, bring the beef stock to a boil. Add the white rice, reduce the heat slightly, cover, and simmer for 15 minutes. Add the orange juice and stir. Cover and simmer for another 5 minutes, or until the rice is tender and the liquid has been absorbed. Stir in the tangerine rind.

Heat the oil and butter in a frying pan over medium heat. Add the onion and sauté, stirring, for 5 to 7 minutes, or until wilted. Add the garlic for the final 2 minutes. Add the pecans and cook for 2 more minutes, stirring. Remove from the heat.

Combine the rices and the onion mixture. Season to taste with salt and pepper, fluffing the rice with a fork. Serve hot.

Note: For the subtle Chinese fillip of tangerine rind, simply eat a tangerine 3 or 4 days ahead, saving the rind. Dry the rind at room temperature. Break the dried rind into little bits and fold it into the rice.

Makes 6 servings.

Kelp Pickles

Seaweeds and seaside vegetables are an important food source for many Alaskans. One of the most easily recognized marine wildings is giant kelp (also known as bull kelp or bull whip kelp, *Nereocystis luetkeana*), distinguished by a spherical bulb attached to a long stem. The plant's roots attach themselves to a rock in a shallow bay or channel, while the leaves and stem wave in the currents above this anchor like the uppermost story of a sea forest. At the top of each hollow stipe (stem) is the gas-filled float (bulb), which supports the bronze leaves and lifts them toward the light. Kelp can grow up to 45 feet in a single season, but the plants are often uprooted by fall storms.

Gather kelp from June to August. Gather only rooted (live) stems and bulbs, not the stuff that has washed up at the high tide line. Wash and peel. Use the kelp within 24 hours of gathering.

Firm green rings, Kelp Pickles provide a topic of conversation as well as a delicious relish at fish barbecues. They are a typical side dish on any buffet during Petersburg's Little Norway Festival.

> *4 pounds giant kelp, washed and peeled*
> *1 cup salt*
> *2 gallons plus 2 quarts water*
> *½ teaspoon alum*
> *3½ cups sugar*
> *2 cups white vinegar*
> *½ teaspoon oil of cloves*
> *½ teaspoon oil of cinnamon*
> *Green food coloring (optional)*

Cut the kelp stems in 12-inch lengths. Split the bulbs and pare off the dark surface. Dissolve the salt in the 2 gallons of water, and soak the kelp for 2 hours in this brine. Be sure to keep all of the kelp under the surface of the brine.

Remove the kelp from the brine and rinse with cold water. Dice the kelp into 1-inch cubes, or slice it in rings about ¼ inch thick. Dissolve the alum in the 2 quarts cold water, and soak the kelp in this mixture for 15 minutes. Drain and rinse in cold water. Drain again.

Place the prepared kelp in a nonreactive pot and add boiling water to cover. Simmer just until the kelp can be pierced with a fork, about 15 minutes. Drain.

NOTE: These pickles keep well for 4 or 5 months; then the texture begins to deteriorate.

Combine the sugar, vinegar, and oil of cloves and cinnamon; boil for 2 minutes. Pour this mixture over the cooked kelp. Let stand, covered, overnight in a nonreactive bowl or crock.

In the morning, drain the syrup into a saucepan and bring it to a boil. Pour the hot syrup back over the kelp and allow it to stand for 24 hours.

On the third morning, heat both the kelp and the syrup to boiling. A dash of green food coloring may be added to give a brighter hue. Pack the kelp in sterilized jars and seal according to the manufacturer's directions. Process the sealed jars for 10 minutes in boiling water to cover. See Note at left.

MAKES 3 PINTS.

Bull kelp

SAUCES

auces are not an indigenous tradition; a Continental influence arrived in Alaska during the gold rush, and has made sauces a fixed aspect of haute cuisine. The addition of a tasty sauce means an extra-special dish to most Alaskans—something a little beyond the call of duty. Here are a number of sauce recipes that add a particularly delicious touch to seafood.

Clarified Butter

Many chefs are trained to use clarified butter when cooking because it has a higher scorching point than whole butter. Clarified butter is the clear yellow liquid that separates from the milk solids when melted butter cools. Known to Yankee cooks as drawn butter, it is also served as a dipping sauce for steamed shellfish.

1 cup unsalted butter

In a heavy saucepan, melt the butter over medium-high heat. Skim off any foam that rises to the surface of the butter. Remove from the heat and allow the butter to cool.

When cool, drain off the clear liquid at the top; this is the clarified butter. Discard the milk solids at the bottom of the pan. Keep the clarified butter in a covered glass jar in the refrigerator. It can be prepared several weeks in advance.

MAKES ABOUT ⅔ CUP.

Haida dogfish design

Homemade Mayonnaise

A cold sauce with the sensuous mouth-feel of premium ice cream, mayonnaise takes advantage of the emulsifying qualities of egg yolks. A good mayonnaise is the crowning touch to many fish dishes (see Grayling en Gelée, page 36). I prefer extra-virgin olive oil in mayonnaise, but corn oil and sunflower seed oil have their fans, too. Special seasonings for mayonnaise are legion (see Note at end of recipe).

2 egg yolks (see Cautionary Note)
1½ tablespoons cider vinegar
1 cup extra-virgin olive oil
2 tablespoons fresh lemon juice
½ teaspoon salt
Freshly ground black pepper to taste

In an electric blender container, process egg yolks until thick—about 3 minutes. Add vinegar and blend 1 minute longer. Gradually drizzle in oil, then lemon juice, salt, and pepper. Process until smooth and thick.

Recipe may be doubled.

This mayonnaise keeps well in the refrigerator in a covered container for up to 2 weeks, but may separate a bit upon standing.

Note: Chopped parsley, chives, chervil, basil, tomato paste, horseradish, Dijon mustard, sorrel, or dried onion bits may be added to taste.

MAKES 1⅛ CUPS.

CAUTIONARY NOTE: Acid—vinegar or lemon juice—is believed to kill *salmonella* bacteria. But because we don't know the extent of the *salmonella* problem with raw eggs, we all eat raw eggs at our own risk. Many cooks now use poached egg yolks in mayonnaise.

Oscar's Tartar Sauce

After cooking for oil field and pipeline workers for 14 years at Prudhoe Bay, Al Sharpnack used his grubstake to open his own restaurant, Oscar's, in Valdez, Alaska's scenic "Little Switzerland." Because Oscar's is located on the harbor, chef Al buys his seafood right off the boat. With every seafood item on his international menu, Al serves his Tartar Sauce.

Classic Tartar Sauce surprises with little bursts of cornichons and capers. Al Sharpnack takes another tack.

2¼ cups Homemade Mayonnaise (see page 233)
⅛ cup sweet pickle relish
⅓ cup chopped dill relish
¼ cup finely minced onion
2 teaspoons lemon juice
½ teaspoon Worcestershire sauce
Garlic powder or minced garlic to taste
Salt and white pepper to taste

Mix Homemade Mayonnaise, pickle relish, dill relish, onion, lemon juice, and Worcestershire sauce. Sample. Then season to taste with garlic, salt, and pepper.

Sauce will keep in the refrigerator, covered, up to 2 weeks.

MAKES ABOUT 2½ CUPS.

Aleuts in their baidarkas, Iliamna Bay, ca. 1906

Apricot Kiwi Salsa

This speedy salsa is delectable with grilled salmon. It suavely combines fruits and vegetables with hot peppers for a palate-tingling side dish—the modern equivalent of the Colonial "relish." The recipe originated with the Providence Nutrition Center, Anchorage.

4 apricots, cleaned, seeded, and diced
2 kiwifruit, peeled and sliced
6 cherry tomatoes, seeded and julienned
½ bunch green onions, finely sliced
2 pepperoncini peppers, seeded and finely sliced (see Note)
6 fresh basil leaves, julienned
2 teaspoons sugar
Juice of ½ lime
¼ cup red wine vinegar

Prepare apricots, kiwifruit, tomatoes, green onions, peppers, and basil leaves. Dissolve sugar in lime juice and vinegar. Toss all ingredients together in a nonreactive container. Serve at once.

MAKES ABOUT 2 CUPS.

NOTE: Wear gloves or oil hands well when preparing the pepperoncini peppers, and avoid touching your eyes. Discard seeds.

Mexican Mayonnaise

Piquant salsa becomes more subtle when mixed with mayonnaise. Serve this quick and easy combo as a sauce for grilled, poached, or broiled fish. It adds zip and allure. Use the same day it is made.

1 large ripe tomato, peeled, seeded, and coarsely chopped
2 cups prepared mayonnaise
1 cup prepared salsa
1 tablespoon lime juice

Combine tomato, mayonnaise, salsa, and lime juice in a small serving dish. Chill until ready to serve.

MAKES 3½ CUPS.

Aleut twined fish basket

Saffron-Dill Sauce

Creative Karen Crabb has been cooking in Alaska's wilderness lodges and hotels since her youth. She currently works as a chef in the Top of the World restaurant at the Anchorage Hilton. Crabb recommends this subtle golden sauce with hot fish mousse or broiled fish.

1½ tablespoons butter
1½ tablespoons flour
1 cup milk
Pinch of saffron threads
Juice of 1 lemon
1 teaspoon minced fresh dill
Salt and white pepper to taste

In a small, heavy saucepan, melt the butter. Whisk in the flour to form a thick paste. Slowly add the milk, continuing to whisk. Bring the mixture to a boil over medium-low heat, whisking constantly. Add the saffron, lemon juice, and dill. Cook, stirring, for about 5 minutes, or until the sauce reaches the desired consistency. Season with salt and white pepper to taste. Serve hot.

Note: For a plain dill sauce, omit saffron.

MAKES 1 CUP.

Dill

Canoes by Yindastuki, Tlingit village on the Chilkat River, 1895

Raita

A proper East Indian meal includes a chutney, a pickle, and a raita—the latter being a chopped vegetable mixed with yogurt, to cool the mouth after an onslaught of spicy curry. Cool, creamy, chunky, refreshing raita marries well with poached fish, steamed shrimp, deep-fried fish, or seafood curry, as well as lentils or raw vegetables. The most popular raita is made with cucumbers, but it is also delicious with radishes. Once you taste it, you may start serving it with burgers. I serve cucumber raita with Prawns Bhuna Masala (see page 204).

1 cup plain nonfat yogurt
1 teaspoon sugar
2 medium cucumbers, peeled, seeded, and chopped
2 tablespoons minced fresh cilantro or 1 teaspoon ground cumin
Salt to taste

Combine the yogurt and sugar in a bowl. Stir in the cucumbers and cilantro. Season to taste with salt. Raita may be prepared 2 hours ahead. Cover and refrigerate until served.

MAKES 3 CUPS.

Eldon's Sauce for Poached Halibut

This unctuous sauce was invented by rockhound and inn proprietor Eldon Glein of Cordova. The petal-pink shrimp and fresh green herbs add appetizing color to the ivory halibut.

½ cup sour cream
½ cup mayonnaise
½ cup cooked, peeled, and chopped shrimp
Fresh herbs, for garnish

Mix the sour cream, mayonnaise, and shrimp. Serve over cold or hot poached halibut. Garnish with the fresh herbs of your choice.

MAKES 1½ CUPS, OR 6 SERVINGS.

VARIATIONS: For a Greek version of raita called *tzatziki,* omit the sugar and cilantro, and add 1 tablespoon minced fresh mint and 2 cloves minced garlic, plus pepper to taste.

For an American variation of this sauce, combine 2 cups sour cream, 1 diced cucumber, ¼ cup diced onion, 2 pressed garlic cloves, ½ teaspoon salt, and 1 teaspoon dill. Chill for 2 hours. Both of these sauces are delicious with barbecued or grilled salmon.

The Nan-Sea Sandwich

A mainstay on the menu of the Cafe Cups in Homer is the Nan-Sea Sandwich, a succulent layering of broiled halibut, Brie, fresh spinach, tomato slices, the cream sauce from Oysters Rockefeller, and freshly made aïoli.

Wild chives

Aïoli

A lusty variant on prepared mayonnaise, aïoli hails from southern France, where it is sometimes called "the butter of Provence." Traditionally, it is served with cold, poached salt cod and boiled potatoes or spread on the toast floated atop steaming bowls of bouillabaisse.

Aïoli can also be spread on fish steaks that are about to be broiled and is appropriate laved on any cold, cooked fish. Try it as a dip for cooked spot shrimp, too.

For a low-fat aïoli, replace most of the oil with cottage cheese—or with mashed potatoes. Two other variants include *rouille* (with the addition of minced red chile pepper) and *aïoli au basilic* (with chopped fresh basil leaves).

> *3 or 4 cloves garlic, crushed*
> *2 egg yolks*
> *½ teaspoon salt*
> *¼ teaspoon freshly ground black pepper*
> *1¼ cups olive oil, preferably extra-virgin*
> *Juice of 1 lemon*

In a bowl, combine the garlic, egg yolks, salt, and pepper. Whisk well. Gradually add the olive oil, a drop at a time, until you have added about half of it and the mixture looks thick and shiny. Add the lemon juice, then incorporate more oil quickly.

Alternatively, aïoli can be prepared in the food processor or blender.

When all of the oil is incorporated, taste the mixture and adjust the seasonings, if necessary.

MAKES 1¾ CUPS, OR 6 SERVINGS.

Garlic Oil

Simple and pungent, this recipe will make a splash at your next outdoor grilling party.

20 peeled garlic cloves
1 pint olive oil

Soak the garlic cloves in the olive oil for 1 week, covered and refrigerated. Remove cloves and discard. Use oil in seafood salads, as a rub and baste for grilled vegetables like Japanese eggplant as well as seafood such as salmon and shrimp, and as a sauce over grilled or poached seafood.

Garlic can carry botulism spores found in soil. According to the Food and Drug Administration, a way to make flavored oils safe is to simmer them in a 300°F oven for 1 hour.

Garlic Oil keeps, covered and refrigerated, 1 month.

MAKES 1 PINT.

Garlic

Chive Sauce

Chives grow wild in Alaska, and the Koyukon Athabascans ate them raw or mixed them with cooked fish. Serve chive sauce with broiled, poached, or sautéed fish. The pale violet flowers of chives may also be used as a perky edible garnish.

3 hard-boiled egg yolks
3 tablespoons corn oil
1 tablespoon vinegar
2 teaspoons chopped fresh chives
1 teaspoon dried onion flakes (optional)
Salt and pepper to taste

Press the egg yolks through a fine strainer or use a ricer. Gradually whisk in the oil, drop by drop. Then beat in the vinegar, chives, and onion flakes. Season to taste with salt and pepper.

MAKES ½ CUP, OR 2 TO 4 SERVINGS.

DILL SAUCE: Omit the chives, and add 1 tablespoon chopped fresh dill. Serve with Bistro 401 Salmon (see page 129).

Gooseberry Sauce

Gooseberries grow wild in Southeast Alaska and have been introduced farther north. Like applesauce with roast pork, a piquant gooseberry sauce complements oily fish such as mackerel and herring. This sauce goes especially well with Broiled Split Mackerel (see page 97). Alaskans who cultivate the tart, green fruit also relish this sauce with hooligan.

A few drops of ginger juice squeezed through a garlic press may be added, at the cook's whim.

If gooseberries are not available, red currants may be substituted.

1½ cups water
1 cup fresh gooseberries, washed and picked over
2 tablespoons sugar
3 tablespoons butter
1 tablespoon flour
Salt and pepper to taste

Bring ¾ cup of the water to a boil in a small saucepan. Add the gooseberries and simmer for 20 minutes, or until the berries are soft.

Remove from the heat and strain into a bowl, discarding the seeds. Add the sugar and stir.

Melt 1 tablespoon of the butter in a small saucepan. Add the flour and cook, stirring, for 2 minutes. Gradually stir in the remaining ¾ cup of water and bring to a boil, stirring well. Reduce the heat and stir in the gooseberry purée. Gradually add the remaining 2 tablespoons of butter to the pan in small pieces. Add salt and pepper to taste.

MAKES 2½ CUPS, OR 4 SERVINGS.

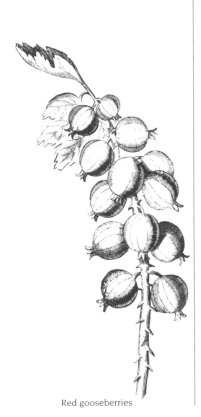

Red gooseberries

Tomorrow and Tomorrow and Tomorrow

Confronted with bowls of leftover salmon or cod, cooks may automatically reach for the mayonnaise and whip up sandwiches. This is an undeniably tasty solution, but there are many other ways to warm up a cold fish.

Indeed, leftover seafood is as versatile as leftover beef or lamb. Rather than a pain in the pantry, leftovers should be considered manna from the sea—they can be turned into so many wonderful things. You may actually want to consider "planning over" fish—that is, cooking more than you need for one meal with a plan to re-use it in a specific manner.

Salmon Salad with Cashews

This memorable luncheon salad contrasts creamy and crunchy with salty and fruity elements. The invention of Fort Richardson speech therapist Tanya Munro, it can be prepared in just a few minutes with leftover poached, grilled, or canned salmon. Serve with sourdough rolls.

2 cups cooked salmon
1 zucchini, diced
½ cup salted cashews
¼ cup diced green onion
½ cup sour cream
¼ cup mango chutney, chopped
1 ripe honeydew melon, cut in quarters and seeded
Clusters of red grapes, washed

Flake the salmon into large chunks, discarding any skin and bone. Combine the salmon, zucchini, cashews, and green onion, tossing gently.

Stir together the sour cream and chutney. Arrange the melon and grape clusters on 4 plates. Mound the salmon mixture over the melon quarters. Top with the sour cream–chutney mixture.

MAKES 4 SERVINGS.

Grapes

Slammin' Salmon-Halibut Salad

For a completely different approach to fish salad, consider this recipe created by freelance writer and composer Wade Hampton Miller of Anchorage. "This recipe has been road-tested many times," says Wade. "I invented it when I had a gig working at the Anchorage Salmon Bake as a strolling musician. At the end of each evening, they would give me leftover grilled salmon and halibut." Wade serves this beer-laced salad with his "Let's Give Texas Back to Mexico" Beer Biscuits (see page 220). Try it as a filling for tuna melt sandwiches.

1 cup leftover grilled salmon, boned and flaked
1 cup leftover grilled halibut, boned and flaked
1 teaspoon liquid smoke (optional)
½ cup light lager or pale ale (see Note)
¼ cup finely chopped celery
2 tablespoons finely chopped onion
3 cups coarsely grated red cabbage (as for coleslaw)
1 cup mayonnaise
1 tablespoon Dijon mustard
1½ teaspoons chopped fresh dill or ½ teaspoon dried dill, or to taste
½ teaspoon chili powder, or to taste
Salt and pepper to taste

Put the flaked salmon and halibut into a large bowl. Drizzle with the liquid smoke, if using. Add the lager, celery, onion, and cabbage. Mix in the mayonnaise, mustard, dill, chili powder, and salt and pepper to taste. See Note on page 249.

MAKES 5 SERVINGS.

NOTE: For those unaccustomed to the bitter, almost peppery taste of beer brewed with a hefty dose of hops, Miller recommends trying a lightly hopped beer the first time you make this salad.

Tlingit wood salmon sculpture, Juneau, ca. 1890s

Linguine with Garlic and Cod

Any leftover grilled fish such as cod, salmon, or halibut works well in this simple and speedy pasta entrée from wildlife photographer Alice Shields of Douglas. The sun-dried tomatoes add a subtle depth of taste, plus welcome color. Serve with peas or a mixed green salad.

8 sun-dried tomatoes
1 pound linguine
⅓ cup olive oil
3 cloves garlic, finely chopped
1 small onion, finely chopped
2 cups leftover grilled cod, flaked or cut into bite-sized pieces
¾ cup chicken stock
¼ cup chopped parsley
½ teaspoon dried red pepper flakes

Put the tomatoes in a small, heatproof bowl or measuring cup, and cover with boiling water. Let stand for 30 minutes, until plump. Drain and quarter.

Meanwhile, cook the linguine al dente. Drain and keep warm.

Heat the olive oil in a saucepan over medium-low heat. Add the garlic and onion, and cook for 3 minutes, or until the vegetables become translucent. Stir in the cod, chicken stock, parsley, and pepper flakes. Increase the heat slightly. Cook, stirring, until the sauce is heated through. Add the tomatoes and toss.

Place the pasta on a warmed serving platter. Top with the sauce. Serve at once.

MAKES 6 SERVINGS.

Garlic

Rockfish Cakes

Fish cakes are a simple and appetizing way to recycle leftover hake, cod, Irish lord, sheefish, pike, or salmon may be substituted for rockfish. A similar recipe was popular with Juneau homemakers in the 1960s. As a first course, serve a nettle soup.

2 cups cooked, boned, and flaked rockfish
4 medium potatoes, boiled and mashed
1 tablespoon chopped chives
1 tablespoon chopped parsley
½ teaspoon garlic powder or granulated garlic (optional)
1 teaspoon salt
½ teaspoon pepper
2 eggs, beaten
⅓ cup flour
1 teaspoon paprika
¼ teaspoon salt
Freshly ground black pepper, to taste
½ cup dry bread crumbs
2 tablespoons butter
2 tablespoons corn oil

In a mixing bowl, combine the rockfish, potatoes, chives, parsley, garlic powder, salt, and pepper. Stir in half of the beaten eggs. Form into cakes about 1 inch thick. Roll the cakes in the flour seasoned with paprika, salt, and pepper. Dip in the remaining beaten egg, then in the bread crumbs.

Heat the butter and corn oil in a heavy skillet and fry the cakes on both sides until golden. Serve hot.

MAKES 4 SERVINGS.

Nettles

Mae's Salmon Omelet

Born in 1908, poet Mae Martin relishes cooking in the sunny kitchen of her Anchorage log home. Mae attributes her sharp wit, good health, and ability to demonstrate waist-high karate kicks to cooking delicious dishes from scratch, like this savory salmon omelet.

Mae serves her crisp Zucchini Pickles on the side.

4 eggs
1 teaspoon water
Salt and pepper to taste
2 teaspoons oil
1 cup leftover steamed or poached salmon
1 green bell pepper, chopped
4 green onions, sliced
4 canned tomatoes, drained and coarsely chopped (optional)
Liquid smoke to taste (optional)

Salmon

Whisk the eggs in a bowl with the water. Add salt and pepper to taste. Heat the oil in a skillet, and add the egg mixture. When the eggs are almost set, combine the salmon, bell pepper, green onions, tomatoes (if used), and liquid smoke (if used). Fill the omelet with the salmon mixture, folding it over. Cook for another minute, then serve on warmed plates.

MAKES 2 SERVINGS.

Brailing a fish trap, Kachemak Bay, 1917

Fish and Rice-Stuffed Tomatoes

When truly ripe tomatoes are plentiful and the refrigerator holds leftover smoked sablefish or poached salmon, try this recipe. You could also use smoked fish, crab, surimi, or cooked shrimp.

The combination of leftover rice and blue cheese is a revelation. The recipe comes from pediatrician Jon Demos of Glennallen, who inherited it from his Italian grandmother.

3 cups cooked rice
2 tablespoons olive oil
2 tablespoons white wine vinegar
1½ cups blue cheese dressing
1 tablespoon chopped parsley
Freshly ground black pepper to taste
6 large, ripe tomatoes
2 cups cooked, diced fish
6 tablespoons mild salsa
Salt to taste
Raw spinach or other salad greens
1 cucumber, thinly sliced

Shortly before serving, toss the cooked rice with the olive oil and 1 tablespoon of the vinegar. This will separate the grains. Then toss with the blue cheese dressing and parsley. Grind fresh pepper on top and toss again. Allow the mixture to stand while preparing the tomatoes.

Halve the tomatoes horizontally. Remove the interior rib, juice, and seeds with a teaspoon or melon baller, forming cups. Chop the removed tomato flesh. Fill the tomato cups with half of the rice mixture.

Mix the fish, salsa, remaining 1 tablespoon vinegar, and chopped tomato flesh with the remaining rice. Add salt to taste, and then mound into the tomato cups. Serve on a bed of torn raw spinach within ½ hour of filling the cups. Lay a circle of sliced cucumber around each pair of tomato halves.

MAKES 6 SERVINGS.

Wild mustard greens

Tomatoes

Quiche Marine

Rather than clinging to the classic quiche Lorraine, change allegiances; whip up an innovative Quiche Marine, savory with seafood. It's lovely served outside: I serve it on my deck overlooking Delong Lake, where moose browse the shores in the summer—and wander the lake ice in the winter.

1 tablespoon corn oil
1 medium onion, finely diced
4 eggs
1½ cups whole milk, light cream, or half-and-half
1 tablespoon flour
½ teaspoon salt
¼ teaspoon freshly ground black pepper
¼ teaspoon freshly grated nutmeg
1 cup leftover boned, flaked fish, crab, or surimi; or canned, drained
  salmon; or diced, smoked halibut, sablefish, trout, or salmon
1 deep-dish 9-inch unbaked pie shell
1½ cups grated Swiss or Emmentaler cheese

Heat the corn oil in a skillet and sauté the onion until it just begins to brown.

Preheat the oven to 375°F.

Put the eggs, milk, flour, salt, pepper, and nutmeg into a large blender container. Cover and process until well blended. Alternatively, whisk these ingredients together in a large bowl.

Sprinkle the seafood in the bottom of the unbaked pie shell. Distribute the sautéed onions and grated cheese evenly over the top. Pour in the egg mixture.

Bake for 35 to 45 minutes, or until a knife inserted in the center comes out clean.

MAKES 6 MAIN-DISH SERVINGS.

Halibut

Corn-Fish Chowder

The bright colors of yellow, red, and green in this chowder should delight young diners. Teens may even want to try their hand at preparing this recipe themselves.

Leftover grilled corn can be substituted for the fresh corn. Rather than using leftover seafood, raw seafood could be used as well; add it about 5 minutes before the cooked seafood is added.

As the seafood in this satisfying chowder, use one of the following:

- 8 ounces smoked black cod, smoked halibut, smoked trout, or smoked salmon, cut into ½-inch cubes
- 12 ounces chopped, cooked clams
- 8 ounces orange roughy fillets, cut in 1-inch pieces
- 12 to 14 ounces raw medium shrimp, peeled and deveined

8 slices bacon
3 medium onions, diced
3 carrots, diced
4 stalks celery, diced
2 bay leaves
2 teaspoons crumbled dried thyme
4 cups water or low-salt chicken stock
¼ teaspoon freshly ground black pepper
1 green bell pepper, cored, seeded, and sliced
3 potatoes, scrubbed and cut in ¾-inch dice
4 cups fresh corn kernels, cut from 6 to 8 ears
2 cups milk
1 jar (2 ounces) pimientos, drained and diced
8 to 14 ounces cooked seafood (see above)
Salt and pepper to taste

In a large skillet, fry the bacon until crisp. Remove to paper towels. Pour off all but 2 tablespoons of the bacon fat.

In the same skillet, sauté the onions, carrots, and celery. When limp and transparent, stir in the bay leaves and thyme.

In a 5-quart Dutch oven, bring the water or chicken stock to a boil. Stir in the sautéed vegetables. Simmer until the vegetables are tender. Remove the bay leaves.

Purée the mixture in a blender or food processor until smooth.

Corn

Return the purée to the Dutch oven. Add the black pepper, green bell pepper, potatoes, and corn kernels. Bring to a simmer over medium-high heat. Reduce the heat to low and cook for 8 minutes, or until the potato cubes are nearly tender.

Add the milk, pimientos, and the cooked seafood, and bring just to serving temperature. Adjust the seasoning with salt and pepper as needed.

MAKES 6 TO 8 SERVINGS.

Onions

Salmon purse seiner in Chatham Strait, 1975

NOTE: ALASKABITS™ (see page 284) may be sprinkled on at the last minute, as a garnish and flavor enhancer.

DESSERTS

After a meal including seafood, I often turn to my first love, fruit. Dessert can be very simple—a handful of honey-sweet dates, a crisp McIntosh apple, a meltingly ripe Bosc pear with a wedge of blue cheese, a bowl of pineapple sorbet garnished with lemon thyme.

However, if you want an Alaskan finish to your meal, consider warm wild blueberry pie, or one of the following sweet solutions.

Maxim's "Agutaq"

On any festive Alaskan occasion, whether a winter dance celebrating a young man's first successful polar bear hunt or a summer reunion, Eskimos serve *agutaq,* popularly known as "Eskimo ice cream."

Traditionally, *agutaq* (pronounced something like ah-GOO-duck) was made with melted caribou tallow whipped by hand until fluffy, seal oil, freshly fallen snow, and roots gathered on the tundra.

Today, *agutaq* may be made with hydrogenated shortening plus sugar and favorite berries. It is usually served with dried trout or salmon strips.

During the holidays a decade ago, a young boy named Maxim whose ancestors hail from both McGrath and the Pribilofs asked me to make this recipe, his grandma's modern version of *agutaq.*

1 quart vanilla ice cream
2 cups frozen blueberries

Soften the ice cream until it can be stirred but is not melting or soupy. Stir in the blueberries, distributing thoroughly. Refreeze until the ice cream is the proper serving consistency.

MAKES 6 SERVINGS.

Blueberries

Red Currant Sponge

The northern red currant (*Ribes* species) is prized by Alaska berry pickers, including the Athabascans of Nanwalek, who use the juice of the fruit as a medicine for irritated eyes.

This flavorful fruit is delicious in a sponge, a light and fluffy dessert similar in texture to chiffon pie filling. My grandmother gave me this recipe—which I had never tried until the '70s, when I was able to gather wild currants growing behind my house in Chugiak. A fruity or citrusy dessert makes a refreshing finish to a fish dinner.

1 envelope unflavored gelatin
2 cups orange juice
1 cup sugar
Juice and grated zest of 1 lemon
4 egg whites, at room temperature (see Cautionary Note)
1 cup fresh, raw, red currants

CAUTIONARY NOTE: Because of the presence of *salmonella* bacteria, raw eggs are consumed at your own risk.

Soak gelatin in ½ cup of the orange juice for 5 minutes. Then stir over low heat until gelatin is dissolved. Mix with sugar, lemon juice and zest, and remaining orange juice. Allow to cool. Then refrigerate until mixture is the consistency of unbeaten egg white—about 1 hour.

Beat the orange mixture.

In a separate bowl, beat the egg whites until stiff. Fold into the orange mixture. Fold in the currants, being careful not to mash them. Turn into a mold or serving dish and chill until set, about 4 hours.

Serve with sweetened whipped cream.

MAKES 4 TO 6 SERVINGS.

Currants

Coconut-Almond-Chocolate Tart

Craig McMahon, a magistrate employed by the state court system in Bethel, has lived in the Arctic for 19 years. Craig's hobby is cooking: "When I was going to law school, the only way I could eat the way I wanted to on a budget was to do it myself."

Craig's specialty is desserts. He annually whips up some of his delectable sweets for Just Desserts, a fund-raising concert and bake sale sponsored by the Bethel Arts Council. Coconut-Almond-Chocolate Tart is representative of his talents.

Crust:
> 1½ cups whole almonds
> ¼ cup brown sugar
> ¼ cup unsalted butter

Filling:
> ½ cup canned coconut milk
> 3 ounces white chocolate
> ¼ cup sour cream
> ¼ cup unsalted butter
> 1¼ cups shredded, sweetened coconut

Topping:
> ¼ cup whipping cream
> 3 tablespoons unsalted butter
> 2 tablespoons light corn syrup
> 4 ounces semisweet chocolate

Decoration:
> 2 ounces white chocolate
> 26 whole almonds (about)

To make the Crust, chop the almonds in a food processor or blender. Add the brown sugar and butter, and continue processing until the nuts are finely chopped and the mixture is well blended. Press the mixture onto the bottom of a 9-inch tart pan.

To make the Filling, bring the coconut milk to a simmer in a heavy saucepan. Reduce the heat to low, add the white chocolate, and stir until melted. Remove from the heat. Whisk in the sour cream until incorporated. Add the butter and stir until it melts. The mixture should be smooth. Stir in the coconut. Chill until the filling is cold but not set, about 1 hour. Distribute the filling in the crust and chill until it is set.

To make the Topping, bring the cream, butter, and corn syrup to a simmer in a saucepan. Reduce the heat to low. Add the semisweet chocolate, and stir until melted. (Watch carefully to avoid burning.) Set aside 3 tablespoons of the topping. Pour the remainder over the tart, covering the filling. Smooth it out.

For Decoration, melt the white chocolate and pipe or drizzle it in parallel lines over the top of the tart. Then create a decorative spiderweb pattern by drawing a knife through the lines. Dip the whole almonds in the reserved topping until half covered. Arrange the almonds around the edge of the tart. Chill until set. This tart is best served on the same day it is made.

MAKES 10 TO 12 SERVINGS.

Wild rose

Sitka Picnics, ca. 1860

In the days when Sitka was the capital of Russian Alaska, fine ladies and gentlemen took advantage of sunny summer afternoons to walk out with picnic hampers to Indian River or to row to one of the little islands just offshore in Sitka Sound. The hampers contained imported cheeses, salmon pirog layered with fiddleheads, and fine wines. For dessert, tea cakes, custard, and jellies were the rule.

Raspberry-Rhubarb Tart

This tangy dessert combines two Alaska favorites: raspberries and rhubarb. It is a delightful complement to seafood. The tart was created by Valerie Turnbull, pastry chef at O'Malley's on the Green in Anchorage, a restaurant located on a golf course among rolling hills.

A native of Seattle, Valerie is at home in both city and country. She began baking at À la Francaise Bakery in Seattle. After earning a biology degree at the University of Washington and working 6 years in bakery and pastry production, it was off to 60th Street Desserts, which supplies some of Seattle's finest restaurants. At O'Malley's, she strives for natural sweets—natural not only to the palate but also to the eye. Servings may be topped with a spoonful of French vanilla ice cream.

Cooking spray
2 cups raspberries, fresh or frozen (without sugar) and thawed
3 cups rhubarb, fresh or frozen, cut in 1-inch pieces
1 cup plus 3 tablespoons sugar, or to taste
6 tablespoons sifted flour
1 tablespoon fresh lemon juice
Parchment paper sheets
1 tablespoon cold butter, cut into small pieces
1 egg
1 tablespoon water
Sugar, for sprinkling over the top

Crust:
2½ cups flour
¾ teaspoon salt
1 teaspoon sugar
1 cup cold butter, cut into small pieces
¼ to ½ cup cold water

To make the Crust, put the flour, salt, and sugar in the bowl of a food processor. Add the butter pieces and process until the mixture resembles coarse meal. While the machine is running, add the cold water little by little until the dough holds together but is not sticky. Form the dough into a flat circle, wrap it in plastic, and chill for 1 hour.

Spray a 9-inch tart pan with cooking spray. On a lightly floured surface, roll out half the chilled pastry to a thickness of ⅛ inch. Place the dough in the tart pan and press evenly around the bottom and along the sides. Cut the pastry an inch or so higher than the pan's edge and tuck the excess into the side of the pan for reinforcement. Chill the crust until ready to use.

Put the raspberries and rhubarb in a mixing bowl. Sprinkle the sugar, flour, and lemon juice over the fruit and toss gently. Set aside while preparing the lattice.

Roll out the remaining pastry to a thickness of ⅛ inch. Using a pastry wheel, cut into ½-inch strips. Working on a sheet of parchment paper, weave the strips together, leaving a little room in between for the filling to show through. You should have a 10-inch by 8-inch top. Place another sheet of parchment over the lattice and chill for 15 minutes.

Preheat the oven to 350°F.

Place the tart pan on a baking sheet (to keep the juices from dripping into the oven). Spoon the filling into the crust and sprinkle the butter pieces over the top. With the lattice in your hand (and still between 2 pieces of parchment), fold it in half. Remove the outer sheet of the parchment and place the lattice over half the tart. Carefully unfold the other half of the lattice, covering the filling. Remove the top sheet of parchment. Pinch off the excess lattice and press the lattice ends into the sides of the crust to hold them.

Create an "egg wash" by beating the egg with the water, and brush the crust with the egg wash. Sprinkle sugar over the top and bake for 35 minutes, or until the crust is golden and the filling is thick and bubbling. Cool before serving.

MAKES ONE 9-INCH TART, OR 8 SERVINGS.

Wild raspberries

How the Double Musky
Inn Got Its Name

*In the good old days,the
Double Musky earned its
unusual name from was
a hash joint and pizza
parlor—locally famed for
pouring double shots of
muscatel. When the
current owners took
control more than 17 years
ago, wine list and menu
went dramatically upscale,
but the familiar name
remained.*

Double Musky Pie

A nutty meringue crust filled with rich, fudgy chocolate and topped with whipped cream, the Double Musky Pie is one of the most requested recipes in Alaska. This "secret" recipe has been published several times in the *Anchorage Daily News* and once in the *Bon Appetit* RSVP column. The Double Musky Inn is a popular Girdwood restaurant that does not take reservations, but the food is so good that diners are willing to wait for a table.

First Layer (meringue crust):
3 egg whites, at room temperature
Pinch of salt
1 cup sugar
¼ teaspoon cream of tartar
36 saltine crackers, broken into ½-inch pieces
1 cup coarsely chopped pecans
1 tablespoon vanilla extract

Second Layer (chocolate filling):
2 ounces unsweetened chocolate
½ cup butter
2 eggs
¼ cup flour
1 cup sugar

Third Layer (whipped cream topping):
1 cup heavy cream

To make the First Layer, preheat the oven to 350°F. Beat the egg whites until airy and frothy. While still beating, add the salt. Continue to beat, gradually adding the sugar and cream of tartar. Continue beating until the meringue forms stiff, glossy peaks.

Mix the meringue, cracker pieces, pecans, and vanilla completely together, making sure the crackers are evenly distributed and coated with meringue.

Spread the mixture carefully in a buttered 9-inch pie plate. Smooth out to a thickness of 1 inch. Bake for 12 minutes. The meringue should be slightly brown around the edges and should have a very light crust to the touch. Let cool for 15 minutes.

To make the Second Layer, keep the oven preheated to 350°F. In a double boiler, melt the chocolate and butter slowly over hot water. Add the eggs, 2 tablespoons of the flour, and ½ cup of the sugar, and mix for less than 30 seconds. Then add the remaining 2 tablespoons flour and ½ cup sugar, and stir until just mixed. Don't overmix, or it will be brittle.

Pour the chocolate mixture in a circle from the rim of the meringue crust into the center. Bake for 35 minutes. When done, the pie will be slightly crusty on top. A toothpick inserted into the edge will not come out clean. The center will be moist and will continue cooking after it's removed from the oven.

For the Third Layer, once the pie is completely cool, whip the heavy cream until stiff. Spread it over the top of the pie and refrigerate until ready to serve.

MAKES 6 SERVINGS.

Tlingit fish camp, ca. 1920

Low-Fat Lemon Cheesecake

This refreshing dessert comes from the Rose Room Deli at Providence Alaska Medical Center in Anchorage, a cafeteria that makes a concerted effort to serve food that is both heart-healthy and appetizing. Note that the recipe involves making yogurt cheese the day before the cheesecake is made. This dessert serves a crowd.

Lemon

¼ cup graham cracker crumbs
2 tubs (8 ounces each) softened light cream cheese
1 cup sugar
⅔ cup cholesterol-free egg substitute
2 teaspoons vanilla extract
1 teaspoon grated lemon zest
1 tablespoon lemon juice
16 fresh strawberries; or 4 oranges, sliced; or 4 kiwifruit, sliced

Vanilla Yogurt Cheese:
32 ounces nonfat vanilla yogurt

To make the Vanilla Yogurt Cheese, spoon the yogurt into a strainer lined with a coffee filter or cheesecloth. Place the strainer over a bowl; cover with plastic wrap. Refrigerate and allow to drain overnight. Discard the liquid that has drained out. The yogurt cheese may be covered and stored in the refrigerator for up to 5 days. Makes 2 cups.

Preheat the oven to 350°F.

Spray a 9-inch springform pan with nonstick cooking spray. Sprinkle the bottom with the crumbs. Refrigerate.

In a large bowl, beat the cream cheese until smooth. Gradually add the sugar, beating until smooth. Add the egg substitute, Vanilla Yogurt Cheese, vanilla extract, lemon zest, and lemon juice; beat until smooth. Pour into the crumb-coated pan. Bake for 50 to 60 minutes on the top rack of the oven, or until the edges are set. (To minimize cracking, place a shallow pan half full of hot water on the lower oven rack during baking.)

Remove from the oven; cool to room temperature on a wire rack. Remove the sides of the pan. Refrigerate for 6 hours or overnight. Just before serving, top each slice with the fresh fruit of your choice.

MAKES 16 SERVINGS.

Pineapple Chiffon Cake

This light and luscious cake comes from Tyrone Cephas and Larry Weihs, chefs with the catering service Statewide Services Inc., ARCO, which serves hearty meals to North Slope oil field workers.

½ cup vegetable oil, plus extra for preparing pan
1½ cups sifted cake flour, plus extra for preparing pan
1 cup sugar
2 teaspoons baking powder
¼ teaspoon salt
½ cup frozen pineapple juice concentrate, at room temperature
1 teaspoon vanilla extract
6 large egg whites, at room temperature
2 tablespoons sifted confectioners' sugar
1 20-ounce can unsweetened crushed pineapple

Position a rack in the center of the oven and preheat to 350°F. Brush oil over the inside of a 9-inch Bundt or springform tube pan. Dust with flour and tap out the excess.

Sift together flour, sugar, baking powder, and salt into a large mixing bowl. Make a well in the center of the dry ingredients and add oil, pineapple juice concentrate, and vanilla. Do not mix.

In another large mixing bowl, beat egg whites until light and foamy. Add confectioners' sugar and continue beating until stiff but not dry. Scrape off the beaters and place them in the flour-and-oil mixture and beat at low speed just until well blended. In four additions, gently fold the flour-and-oil mixture into the egg whites, adding a quarter of the crushed pineapple with each addition.

Turn the batter out into the prepared pan and smooth the top with a rubber spatula. Bake for 35 to 40 minutes. Invert the cake onto a rack, lift off the pan, and cool the cake to warm.

Spread Pineapple Glaze on top of the still-warm cake and let it drip down the sides.

MAKES 16 SERVINGS.

Pineapple

PINEAPPLE GLAZE: Combine 1½ cups sifted confectioners' sugar, 4 tablespoons frozen pineapple juice concentrate, 1 teaspoon fresh lemon juice in a medium-sized bowl; beat until smooth.

SUGGESTED MENUS

Quagluk with Irish lord, King Island, ca. 1938

MENUS

The Model Cafe, 1923

The menu of The Model Cafe in Fairbanks for Wednesday, July 11, 1923, offered entrées of Yukon River salmon, Birch Lake whitefish, Chena River grayling, and Norwegian mackerel for $1. Bread, butter, coffee, and potatoes plus pie or cake accompanied each entrée.

NOTE: Mossberries, or crowberries *(Empetrum nigrum),* are low, creeping, subalpine evergreen shrubs with needle-like leaves. They thrive above treeline. The glossy black berries have bland, white flesh—not as juicy as Alaska's bog blueberries but often more plentiful. Apply cinnamon generously when baking Mossberry Pie.

During her Wednesday-afternoon "Talk to the Cook" phone sessions, Linda Sievers, food editor of the *Anchorage Daily News,* regularly fields the question, "What do I serve with it?"

"Readers want menus," Sievers says. "They can pick a main dish—but then what?"

Help is at hand. Step right up and begin a gastronomic tour of Alaskan menus featuring fish. (Page references are supplied for recipes in this volume.)

Dinner at Seven Glaciers Restaurant

Reached by a thrilling train ride up the side of a mountain, the Seven Glaciers is one of Alaska's finest restaurants. This menu was suggested by chef Michael Flynn, creator of two of the recipes.

Pesto Roasted Oysters (page 184)
Sautéed Wolf Fish with Alaskan Cabbage and Lemon-Herb Sauce (page 156)
Individual Sourdough Loaves
Raspberry-Rhubarb Tart (page 254)

Russian Christmas Dinner

A 12-course Russian Christmas dinner is served the evening of January 6 in Orthodox households in Alaska and Russia, or January 24 in other Orthodox communities. Poet and linguist Dick Dauenhauer of Juneau lent his expertise to the compiling of this menu.

Barley-Mushroom Soup
Russian Rye Bread, drizzled with honey and sprinkled with
*   slivers of raw garlic*
Kutiya (a casserole of barley and honey)
Blini (Russian buckwheat pancakes), rolled around fried onions,
*   red caviar, and/or sour cream*
Pea Soup
Two-Color Chilled Borscht (page 222)
Oonalashka Pirog (page 144)
Swede's Pickled Herring (page 87)
Smoked Salmon
Raisin Bread or Kulich
Mossberry Pie (see Note)
Individual Tarts, filled with salmonberry jelly, blueberry jelly, or plum jam

Alaskan Bistro Dinner

A bistro-style menu at home isn't taxing when four easy pieces are combined with a nearly instant dessert. Raspberry jam can be substituted for the rosehip butter.

Bistro 401 Salmon (page 129)
Dill Sauce (page 239)
Bannock with Baking Powder (page 217)
Fried Goosetongue Salad (page 225)
Lemon Sherbet drizzled with Rosehip Butter

Dinner at Sophie Station Hotel

When the temperature is 50 below in Fairbanks, cuddle up to this warming dinner.

Salad of butter lettuce and red cabbage with grapefruit segments and poppy
  seed dressing
Sourdough Rolls
Sophie Station Fettuccine (page 201)
Steamed Snow Peas and Red Pepper Rings
Cranberry Bread with Vanilla Glaze

In the Heat of a Fairbanks Summer Night

Temperatures can reach 90 degrees on a summer night in Alaska's Interior. Then it's time to think of an entrée that can be served at room temperature, and a cool dessert. The dessert was introduced to me by my friend Joanne Townsend; it's amazing what a delicious complement lime juice is to melon.

Tomato-Clam Cocktail
Philippine Escabeche (page 66)
Julienne of Squash and Carrots
Steamed Red Potatoes
Cantaloupe Slices sprinkled with Fresh Lime Juice

The Yukon Arcade Cafe, 1935

The Yukon Arcade Cafe in Dawson printed a special menu for Discovery Day, August 17, 1935, topped with a decorative drawing of a husky pulling a cart loaded with prospector's tools over a roadbed of grapefruit-sized nuggets.

Fish on the menu was "fresh-caught King Salmon, Fishwheel Fry, 75 cents." Entrées included "Baby Moose Steak, Wiley Post's Delight, 75 cents," "Eldorado Caribou Cutlets, Will Rogers' Special, 75 cents," and an "Iceworm Salad," plus the usual T-bones and lamb chops. (Humorist Will Rogers and pilot Wiley Post were on an extended flight together and had landed at the new Matanuska Colony in Palmer a few days before; word may not have reached Dawson before this menu went to press that the famous pair had perished in a crash near Point Barrow on August 15.) "Extras" included "Fresh Cow's Milk, 25 cents."

Sheldon Jackson
School, 1920s

*In the 1920s and 1930s
at Sheldon Jackson School
in Sitka, student and
faculty menus were
simple, according to the
school newspaper* The
Verstovian: Clam
*chowder, pork spareribs,
turnips, and potatoes was
the fare one day. The
supper menu another day
was stewed salmon, carrot
salad, and fruit-flavored
gelatin.*

Meal for a Maharaja

When dinners turn routine, board your magic carpet and travel to foreign parts.

Dal (Lentil Soup)
Prawns Bhuna Masala (page 204)
Raita (page 237)
*Vanilla Ice Cream sprinkled with Grated Semisweet Chocolate and
    Coconut*

A Chowder Luncheon

When the wind is howling around the eaves and blown snow is scouring the picture window, close the drapes and chase away the chill with warming comfort food: chowder and gingerbread.

Corn-Fish Chowder (page 248) or Alaskan Seafood Chowder (page 190)
Lettuce Wedges with Blue Cheese Dressing
Hot Gingerbread

Dinner at Glacier Bay Country Inn

Considered the gateway to Glacier Bay National Park and Preserve, the town of Gustavus lies 48 miles northwest of Juneau, accessible only by boat or plane, like much of Alaska. In this quiet place where beachcombing and kayaking are popular, Al and Annie Unrein host the Glacier Bay Country Inn. To finance their 160-acre homestead, the couple cuts hay and timber, and runs a sawmill in addition to operating their many-gabled inn. The Unreins serve afternoon tea complete with hazelnut shortbread. Dinner features local seafood and fresh garden produce. Here's a sample menu from the inn:

Halibut Bisque
Homemade Bread
Steamed Dungeness Crab (page 171) with Clarified Butter (page 232)
Rhubarb Custard Pie

Oil dish

Dinner on Tutka Bay

A scenic boat ride from Homer, Tutka Bay Lodge offers mossy paths through dense rain forest, seabirds such as cormorants, murres, and puffins, as well as glacier-carved mountain peaks. Lodge menus feature local seafood and homemade desserts, served in a dining room over-looking a changeable tidal inlet—a perfect place to kick back after a strenuous day of kayaking on beautiful Kachemak Bay. This is a typical spread:

Avocado and Mandarin Oranges in Honey Lime Dressing
Whole Wheat Rolls
Salmonberry Jelly
Macadamia Nut-Crusted Halibut (page 83)
Steamed Red Potatoes with Parsley
Baked Herbed Spinach
Wild Blueberry Cream Cheese Torte

Labeling canned salmon, ca. 1907

Trail Food

In Alaska, even food "on the trail" can be mind-boggling. In 1990, chef Al Levinsohn of the Regal Alaskan Hotel in Anchorage began serving a special dinner to the first musher to cross the Yukon River during the annual 1,000-mile Iditarod Trail Sled Dog Race from Anchorage to Nome. Each year, in full chef's whites, Levinsohn himself flies out by bush plane to prepare the special meal. This is the 1991 menu:

Fruits of the Sea (assorted seafood appetizer plate)
Chicken Consommé with Garden Vegetables
Shrimp Martini Style (shrimp sautéed with gin and vermouth)
Black Raspberry Sorbet
Caribbean Lamb Medallions with Fresh Pineapple Relish
Assorted Fresh Fruits and Cheeses
Assorted Ice Cream Tarts

For the musher, the high point of the meal may not be the food but the "after-dinner mint"—the prize of $3,500 in silver.

SEAFOOD BASICS

Eskimo woman, Clara Tiulana, emerging from an "ice cellar," King Island, ca. 1938

SEAFOOD BASICS

Notes on Alaskan Seafood Cooking Methods

Many of the Native peoples of Alaska had the good fortune of living in a habitat that provided for their most basic needs, most notably the bountiful coastline rich with plenty of seafood to nourish both their bodies and their spirits.

In Southeast, there were forests to provide both cooking fuel and material for cooking vessels and utensils. And the abundance of food-stuffs—including berries, roots, and game, in addition to seafood—meant these peoples lived a relatively good life, often spending less time hunting and gathering than other Native American populations, and more time cooking and feasting and creating art.

Throughout Alaska, the early peoples boiled, steamed, baked, toasted, roasted, smoked, and dried most of their food. Few Alaska tribes had knowledge of pottery, so most used bentwood boxes, woven

POTLATCH DISHES

To Alaska Natives, a meal is a gift to those who consume it—a gift from nature, and a gift from those who provide the ingredients and prepare the dishes. It is also a ceremony that expresses family, that defines the world of the host and guests.

The potlatch, a traditional ceremony of extravagant gift-giving and feasting, was a central part of the cultural system of the Pacific Northwest Coast peoples and other Native Alaskans. These feasts involved strict protocols, elaborate dining etiquette, the use of heirloom serving dishes, and special carved ladles to pour hooligan grease over the food. Feast dishes were carved in shapes such as octopus, wolf, eagle, bear, and seal.

At Tlingit potlatches, for example, one might encounter 150 different dishes—almost every possible way to roast, steam, or boil every part of salmon, halibut, octopus, and seal, along with recipes for side dishes of crab apples and gooseberries.

Potlatch dishes would include dried salmon, smoked salmon, smoked salmon in hooligan oil, toasted salmon skin, stick-roasted salmon, dried salmon eggs, salmon eggs simmered in seawater, herring roe on kelp (raw or stewed), roasted salmon backbones, salmon head soup, fermented salmon eggs, black seaweed and clams, and more.

Paimiut Eskimo, Katrina Aloyious, cutting fish with an ulu, 1956

root baskets, birch-bark containers, earth pits, and rock ovens as cooking vessels. Just like modern cooks, indigenous cooks turned out delicious foods by adding just the right touch of seawater, wild onions, and
know-how.

The seafood diet of the Eskimo populations of the northern Arctic
territory, on the other hand, was primarily eaten raw and frozen. For
many years, dictionaries claimed the word "Eskimo" came from the
Algonquian, meaning "eater of raw flesh." In truth, "Eskimo" comes
from the Montagnais Indian language, meaning "snowshoe netter."

Ulu

Tsimshian plaited cedar
bark storage basket

The Eskimo practice of eating foods raw stems from the fact that
the only material for making fires in many arctic villages is driftwood,
the supply of which depends on time and tide; trees do not grow on the
tundra. Eskimos relished their icy, raw fish, often dipping it in seal oil
for extra flavor and nutrition.

Good food carefully prepared has long been part of the Native
Alaskan lifestyle, and this is still true today. Some of the culinary traditions
handed down by the indigenous people of Alaska are discussed below.

BAKING AND THE STEAM PIT

Traditionally, Northwest Coast baking was done in a steam pit or
"earth oven," a method nearly identical to the Wampanoag clambake
and the Hawaiian *imu*. Construction is simple. A fire pit 4 feet deep
and 4 feet wide is dug in the earth and lined with stones. A fire is kin-
dled on the stones and kept burning for 4 to 5 hours. When the stones
are well heated, the coals are brushed aside with leafy boughs.

The hot stones are covered with 4 inches of rockweed and kelp,
while the sides of the pit are lined with skunk cabbage or other large
leaves.

Eskimo women cooking walrus meat on the beach, Nome, 1905

Then clams, chunks of seal, crabs, mussels, limpets, sea urchins, and edible roots are laid on this base. Atop the edibles, fern fronds, thimbleberry leaves, and 6 inches of seaweed are placed.

A stout stick is thrust down through the center, then pulled up, creating a shaft for pouring water down onto the hot rocks. The pit is sealed with cedar or rush mats and earth, so that steam builds up and cooks the food to a tender succulence.

BOILING IN BASKETS AND BOXES

Early Pacific Northwest coastal peoples including the Tlingit and Haida used boiling as a method for tenderizing dried fish. They first soaked the fish overnight, and then boiled it in a watertight basket or bentwood box, both very clever creations. They also boiled fresh fish and shellfish by this method.

The baskets were woven from cedar bark, spruce roots, and cedar root, which was favored because of its rigid strength and its resistance to saltwater rot. When tightly woven, these baskets became watertight containers for cooking. In openwork form, the tough cedar-root basket was perfectly suited for collecting shellfish, hooligan, sea urchins, and sea cucumbers. Openwork baskets could double as colanders—immersed in the sea and shaken so that sand washed away. (To improvise a gathering basket for tidal seafoods, use the tough red or purple mesh bags in which 5 pounds of garlic or 15 pounds of potatoes are marketed.)

Bentwood boxes were marvels of craftsmanship made by the Northwest Coast tribes. The boxes were formed from wide hand-adzed cedar boards, kerfed (cut part of the way through) at the corners, wet and steamed so that they became flexible, and bent (kerf-side in) to form square-cornered, watertight vessels. They were used for storing all possessions and foods, including hooligan grease for trade, and also as cooking vessels.

For cooking, the boxes were filled with clean water. Hot cooking stones, selected from rock that would not crack or explode when heated or cooled quickly, were placed in the boxes along with raw food. Each stone was lifted from the fire with long wooden tongs and rinsed before going into the cooking liquid. By replacing the stones as they cooled, steady boiling could be maintained. This same method was used with tightly woven baskets.

By 1800, European traders' iron and brass pots began to replace the traditional cooking boxes. The Tsimshian of north-central British

Tlingit spruce-root basket

Aleut twined fish basket

Counting the Catch

The number 40 was an important one when laying up supplies. The Athabascans harvested ground squirrel skins for parkas in bundles of 40. The Gitskan, a people closely related to the Tlingit, tied bunches of dried fish into bundles of 40 for final smoking, and stacked the finished product in a gap—*a pile of 40. The significance of 40 is simply twice the total of fingers and toes, the earliest abacus.*

Columbia called the old cooking boxes *anjam,* or "a place-where-to-cook-in-water." The name for the new iron pot was *anjam*-Russian, "a place-where-to-cook-in-water-Russian."

Early Alaskans were sophisticated about their cooking. For instance, Gitskan culinary usage includes the phrase *hagul jam* or "slow boil," probably equivalent to the modern "simmer."

So the poaching of today really isn't far from the method ingenious Native Alaskans employed long ago. Poaching remains a preferred cooking method in Alaska because it helps preserve seafood's desirable moistness.

STICK-ROASTING

When Alaskans moved from winter camps to temporary summer fish camps, they left their "kitchens" behind. Busy for the season, rather than using pots which required tending, they opted for simple methods like stick-roasting—an ancient outdoor cooking method still favored today by connoisseurs. Tongs and green sticks hold and splay freshly caught fish in the radiant heat of a flameless bed of coals.

Small fish are simply skewered from end to end, with one end of the sharp stick protruding from the mouth.

Large salmon are halved, as if for drying; the heads are removed and skewered for cooking separately. Sturdy, stiff sticks about 3 feet long are split about halfway along their length to create "tongs." A salmon side is sandwiched between each set of "tongs," the tops of the tongs are lashed together, and the side is spread flat with smaller, horizontal, split cedar sticks.

The tong sticks are stuck into the ground, leaning toward the coals. When cooked on one side, the fish is turned around. One dependable child could simultaneously tend a number of stick-roasting fish.

The fish is roasted slowly to preserve the juices, while the smoke enhances the flavor. When the skin begins to break or appear burnt, the flesh is cooked. This is an outdoor dish anyone would relish.

A related method, toasting, was popular during the winter as a way to make dry fish more appetizing. Bits of dried fish were held at the end of a stick over the house fire pit, marshmallow-wise, until hot and crisp.

Fish toasting is immortalized in *The Inside of a Habitation in Nootka Sound,* an engraving from James Cook's *Third Voyage Around the World* (1784). This engraving of a house interior also shows fish hanging from drying racks below the ceiling and dried fish stacked in the corner like beaver pelts.

Tlingit fish camp, ca. 1920

PRESERVING

Because fish runs were limited to the warm months and many Alaskan tribes relied on fish as their main source of food year-round, preserving fish for the winter was crucial for survival. Before cans and freezers were invented, Alaskans used drying, fermenting underground in cold earth, and a combination of smoking and drying as their preservation methods.

Today, however, freezers can be found even in remote settlements like the Siberian Yup'ik village of Gambell—although they may not be connected to electricity, relying on nature's own freezing temperatures outside. Instead, these freezers serve as an animal-proof storage container.

Labeling canned salmon, ca. 1907

Other Alaskans, who operate their freezers with electricity or generators, can freeze dozens of jars or cartons of fish, wild greens, berries, and other foods to last through a long northern winter.

For complete directions on canning or freezing fish, refer to *Canning, Freezing & Drying, Pickling, Smoking* (Sunset, 1981); the latest edition of *The Ball Blue Book* (Ball Corp., Muncie, IN 47302); or the *Better Homes and Gardens' Home Canning Cook Book* (Meredith Corp., 1973). Write for Bulletin #93, "Freezing Meat & Fish in the Home," U.S. Department of Agriculture, or consult publications of the Cooperative Extension Service, in Alaska a division of the University of Alaska. Publications available include "Fish: Canning the Catch," "Smoking Fish at Home," "Storing and Mailing Vacuum Packaged Fish," "Home Freezing of Fish," and "Home Canning Smoked Fish and Home Smoking Fish for Canning."

Inupiat woman hanging arctic char to dry, Eskimo village of Kaktovik, 1993

A Pilot's Secret

A pilot and river guide in Gakona (who wished to remain anonymous) revealed the secret of his subtly flavored, moist smoked salmon: willow. "I don't know what kind of wood other people use," he said, "but willow does it for me." Reds are his salmon of choice. He freezes his catch very fresh, then smokes it early the following summer—when he has more time on his hands than during the runs themselves.

SMOKING

Alaskans have been smoking fish for untold centuries. When Vitus Bering's physician/naturalist, Georg Wilhelm Steller, explored the west side of Kayak Island (east of modern Cordova) on July 20, 1741, he found many signs of human habitation, including an underground cache of smoked fish, seaweed straps, and arrows. Steller pronounced the fish better than the ship's stores of smoked fish processed in Kamchatka.

Today, many Alaskans are avid fish smokers, often with their own smoker or smokehouse in the backyard where they can create smoked foods to their own personal tastes and preferences. Urban Alaskans who lack the suburbanite's smokehouse use small commercial backyard smokers, which in the hands of experts can turn out wonderful smoked fish.

Fruitwoods and hardwoods are the fuels of choice for smoking fish. In Alaska, alder, hickory, and apple are preferred. Evergreen is unsuitable for smoking because it yields bitter resins.

There are two basic methods: hot-smoked and cold-smoked. In both cases, the fish is first salted or brined. Soaking in brine allows salt to permeate the tissue, drawing out water and thus decreasing the chance of spoilage by harmful bacteria. Since the salt also flavors the fish, the length of time the fish remains in the brine is a subject of considerable debate.

Hot-smoked fish is also called "smoke-cooked" or "kippered." First, the fish are cured in a brine to which flavorings (and sometimes colorings or preservatives) have been added. Second, the fish are air-dried until the surface seals—at least 1 hour, depending on temperature and humidity. Third, the fish are placed in a smoker capable of a temperature range of 150°F to 225°F, and smoked until the internal temperature of the fish rises above 150°F—usually to 180°F. Monitor internal temperature with an instant-read food thermometer, inserting it in the thickest part of the fish.

Hot-smoking takes 6 to 15 hours, depending on the desired finished product. Although "cooked," hot-smoked fish is still perishable and should be refrigerated, canned, or frozen. Its refrigerator shelf life is 10 days.

Halibut, trout, sablefish, grayling, smelt, and salmon are delicious hot-smoked. In Native Alaskan fish camps, the gutted fish first may be "newspaper cut"—sliced repeatedly down their length at intervals of about an inch, producing the illusion of a series of staggered ☞

Smoked Salmon

This smoked salmon recipe comes from Rachel Holzwarth's brochure *Menu Planning Guide for the Backcountry,* which features recipes suitable for hikers and mountain climbers. Oilier salmon, such as king and sockeye, are best for smoking.

10 pounds salmon fillets or sides

Brine:
   ¼ cup lemon juice
   ½ cup brown sugar
   ¼ cup noniodized salt (see Note)
   2 cups soy sauce
   1 cup water
   ½ teaspoon onion powder
   ½ teaspoon minced garlic
   ½ teaspoon pepper
   ½ teaspoon Tabasco sauce
   1 cup dry white wine
   ½ teaspoon red pepper flakes

To make Brine, combine the lemon juice, brown sugar, salt, soy sauce, water, onion powder, garlic, pepper, Tabasco sauce, wine, and red pepper flakes in a large bowl and stir to mix well. Distribute the brine evenly among gallon-sized, zipper-top bags. Divide the salmon among the bags. Soak the salmon in the brine, refrigerated, for 8 hours; turn the bags occasionally to distribute the brine.

Take the salmon from the bags, place on wire racks, and let air-dry for 1 hour. Smoke the salmon over moistened hickory chips (see the smoking information on the preceding page) for 12 hours or until done.

NOTE: For smoked salmon brine, use only kosher salt, vacuum-dried salt, dairy salt, pickling or canning salt, or flake salt. Rock salt, sea salt, and iodized salt all contain impurities and additives that can cause bitterness and off-flavors.

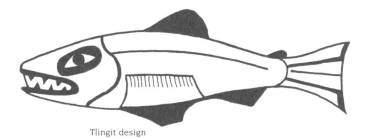

Tlingit design

A Hearty Breakfast, 1878

December 5th [1878], at 1:00 a.m., we arose, and after a hasty breakfast of bread, tea, and dried fish, left our camp and proceeded directly to the coast, along which we traveled . . . when the darkness was rendered more intense by the rising wind filling the air with flying snow. This forced us to hug the shore closely, and make our way by following the line of driftwood which marks the beach in the vicinty of the Yukon mouth.

—Diary by Edward W. Nelson of a sledge journey along the Yukon and Kuskowim rivers. Most of this area had never before been visited by an outsider. A self-trained naturalist, Nelson collected 10,000 Eskimo artifacts as well as specimens of rocks, birds, mammals, and fish; these and the knowledge he gleaned formed the basis of his seminal work The Eskimo About Bering Strait.

"pages" and leaving just enough flesh or skin to hold the sides together. This technique opens more surface area to wind and smoke, thus ensuring even drying. Small whole fish, such as hooligan, are prepared for smoking by gutting and rinsing in water. In the Eskimo fish camps of Kwethluk, large king salmon are often air-dried for a week before being hung in the smokehouse.

Cold-smoked salmon is processed at a temperature (below 80°F) which does not cook the meat. The fish is slowly dried, producing a moist, easily sliced product known as lox, Nova, Nova Scotia, Danish-smoked, Scotch-smoked, Irish-smoked, and Indian-cure.

In cold-smoking, smoke and summer's dry air currents cure the fish, shrinking it, flavoring it, and coating it with chemicals (aldehydes and ketones) that inhibit the growth of unwanted bacteria. The amount of time needed depends on the ambient temperature, the temperature in the smokehouse, and the desired dryness of the salmon. The process can take anywhere from 6 hours to 6 days, depending on these factors. Generally, cold-smoking is reserved for early and late runs of salmon, when the weather affords an ideal ambient temperature of 30°F to 40°F. Cod, bass, salmon, sablefish, pike, mackerel, squid, and octopus all are good cold-smoked.

Indian hard-cure, or fish jerky, is made by salting, drying, and slow-smoking thick strips of fish for an extended period, up to 6 days.

For complete smoking directions, see sources listed under Preserving (see page 273), or consult the publications of the Cooperative Extension Service. Also, *The Joy of Cooking* (1975 ed.) contains a diagram and directions for constructing a backyard smoker from two metal drums.

Smoked seafoods, particularly cold-smoked, are still perishable and must be refrigerated—with the exception of canned or foil-pouched products that are cooked and sealed during the packaging process. Refrigerated, smoked seafood is best consumed within a week; harmful bacteria can begin growing after 2 weeks. For long-term storage, smoked fish must be canned or frozen.

BARBECUING

Prepare barbecue coals according to the directions on a bag of briquets (or, light your gas grill). The coals should be lighted about 45 minutes before you begin to cook, so that there are no visible flames and the "perfume" of any fire starter has dissipated. The coals should have red edges and be covered with gray ash.

Place fish fillets skin side down. (Use a layer of foil under the fillets if they tend to break apart easily, as do sablefish and steelhead.) When the upper side turns opaque or "milky" (about 5 minutes), turn the fillets over gently. Total cooking time will be 10 to 15 minutes, depending on thickness.

Freshness

"The freshest fish are the ones with the seaweed still on them," declares my friend Naomi Warren Klouda of Anchorage, who applies this family axiom when fishing Cook Inlet.

Although aging of game and beef improves their tenderness and taste, aging of fish is quite another matter. The freshest fish is usually considered the most delectable.

On the other hand, some experts in the field say that "fresh" and "frozen" are not the important criteria.

"The real designation is not 'fresh' or 'frozen,' " says Keith Whitehead of the Alaska Seafood Marketing Institute in Juneau. "It's 'fresh' and 'nonfresh.' Bacterial growth is the real issue. Frozen fish is thus really fresher than fresh."

Whitehead's pronouncement takes on new meaning when one considers that some fishing boats stay out catching fish and icing it for 10 days before returning to port. Some boats are equipped to flash-freeze fish almost as soon as it's out of the water, maintaining its peak of freshness for days.

Gustavus Caesar

For an Alaskan take on Caesar Salad, top it with cubes of smoked salmon in the manner of Humpy's Great Alaskan Ale House in Anchorage—or sprinkle on a handy new smoked salmon product, ALASKABITS™. Rechristen the salad "Gustavus Caesar."

REMOVING FISHY ODORS

The simplest way to remove fishy odors from hands is to wash with soap and water, rub them with the cut side of a lemon, then rinse. An Alutiiq method for removing fishy odor from hands involves rubbing them with wild chamomile or pineapple weed.

"To take the odor of fish from a frying pan or baking pan, place a good handful of potato peelings in it, pour boiling water on, and let them boil 10 to 15 minutes."

—The Fairbanks Cookbook
(Women of the First Presbyterian Church, 1910)

Lemon

Eskimo scrimshaw pipe

Buying Seafood

Whenever you purchase seafood, plan to dish it up that very day. To let it wait overnight, no matter how correctly wrapped and carefully refrigerated, is to have a lesser entrée tomorrow.

FISH

When buying fish, look for these general signs of freshness:
1. Lack of odor, or a very slight fresh ocean breeze fragrance. An ammonia odor indicates spoilage.
2. Firm, translucent flesh.
3. Firmly attached scales.

For whole fish, look for:
1. Bright red gills.
2. Eyes that are convex and glossy rather than concave and cloudy.
3. Skin that is shiny.
4. If the head has been removed, browning at the neck signals age rather than wisdom.

For fillets and steaks, look for the above criteria as well as:
1. Flesh that is shiny and translucent.
2. Absence of bruises. The flesh of white fish should be white; pink tones generally indicate bruising or mishandling, which will give the cooked flesh a muddy taste.
3. Ice should not touch flesh directly—either underneath or scattered on top.
4. The darker flesh in shark and swordfish should be bright red or pink; browning is a sign of age.

SHELLFISH

Different shellfish need different criteria for indicating freshness, but in general, start with your nose. Shellfish, like fish, should smell clean, vaguely reminiscent of a sea breeze but not "fishy." Here are some additional criteria.

Fresh abalone, octopus, shucked oysters, scallops, and squid should present a shiny, glistening, almost opalescent surface. The meat should be plump, not wrinkled or dry.

Clams, cockles, and mussels in the shell must be alive when you cook them. If shells are gaping, tap them on a counter: if they shut they are alive; if not they should be tossed. Or, try to slide the two halves of the shell across each other: if they don't budge, they are okay. Avoid clams and mussels with broken shells. Note that the shells of singing scallops remain open even when the scallop is alive and kicking.

For live crab, choose active specimens, and make sure they have all their limbs. Cooked crabmeat should be white and may have red tones on the surface. Raw crabmeat should be translucent. (As crab and shrimp age, they "cook" in their own juices and turn opaque).

Avoid oysters in the shell that are broken or gaping open and unable to close. Oysters in the jar should be free of bits of shell, plump and creamy in appearance, and surrounded by clear liquid (cloudy liquid indicates oysters beyond their prime).

Shrimp in the shell should be slippery, moist, and firm but pliable. Head-on raw shrimp are the best, as they retain their moisture better, but they spoil more quickly. Cooked meat should be white with pink to red tones on the surface, and the shrimp should not be sitting in liquid.

SEASONS

IF YOU PREFER YOUR ALASKA SEAFOOD FRESH, HERE IS
WHAT TO LOOK FOR, SEASON BY SEASON, IN YOUR LOCAL MARKET.

(subsistence catches appear in parentheses)

SPRING	SUMMER	FALL	WINTER
Copper River king salmon	rainbow trout	chum salmon	Dungeness crab
octopus	whitefish	lingcod	scallops
rockfish	sockeye salmon	rockfish	oysters
whitefish	coho salmon	scallops	king salmon
lingcod	king salmon	spot shrimp	lingcod
shrimp	pink salmon	Dungeness crab	rockfish
mussels	rockfish	squid	trout
scallops	flounder	(sea urchin)	mussels
clams	halibut	(steelhead)	halibut
trout	lingcod		clams
land-locked silver salmon	razor clams		(blackfish)
halibut	squid		(pike)
(burbot)	(arctic char)		(eel)
(Dolly Varden)	(grayling)		
(hooligan)	(Dolly Varden)		
	(cockles)		
	(burbot)		

King-Salmon-Month

The Tanaina Athabascans, the people around Cook Inlet, called June "King-Salmon-Month." During this period they caught and preserved their winter supply of salmon. Kings were preferred, but reds and silvers were never scorned. The men caught the fish in basket traps or weirs or from dipnet platforms. Boys and girls washed them. Women gutted and split them, and elders hung them to dry. Later the fish were smoked or pounded into fish meal for storage in caches.

Eskimo woman emerging from an "ice cellar," King Island, ca. 1938

Cutting fish with an ulu, 1956

AMOUNTS PER AVERAGE SERVING

Individual appetites and dietary restrictions have some bearing on how much fish to buy when planning a meal, but these are general guidelines for average main-course servings:

Whole fish: ¾ to 1 pound per person
Dressed/gutted fish: ⅓ pound per person
Fillets/steaks: ⅓ to ½ pound per person
Shellfish meats (scallops, shrimp, squid, shucked oysters):
    ½ to ¾ pound per person
Live crab, lobster, crawfish: 1¼ to 1½ pounds per person
Live mussels or clams: 1½ to 2 pounds per person
Live oysters: 2½ to 3 pounds per person (4 to 6 large oysters)
Whole shrimp with heads and shells on: 1 pound per person

Scaling, Gutting, and Filleting Fish

SCALING

Use a clean, nonslip surface such as a board covered with paper towels. Hold the fish by the tail with one hand. With the other hand, use the blunt side of the knife to scrape scales off, making repeated motions from tail to head. Some cooks like to do this at streamside or outdoors, because the scales tend to jump around like fleas.

GUTTING

Make a shallow slit along the belly from just below the gills to the anus (or about two thirds of the body length). Open the belly, scrape out its contents, and discard them. Be sure to scrape out the black "blood" along the backbone as well. With kitchen shears, clip off the gill covers (the small fins behind the head) on both sides. Remove the tail by cutting through the fish at its thinnest part. Remove the head just behind the gills unless you plan to prepare the fish with head intact.

FILLETING

First scale and gut the fish. Then, with a sharp knife, slice along the back from the head end to the tail end. Make gentle cuts with the knife blade flat against the bones, separating them from the flesh. After one whole fillet of the fish is removed, use the knife to ease the backbone from the second fillet, lifting the backbone as you go.

Frozen Fish

Fish has the most tender texture and most succulent taste when it is purchased fresh and eaten within 24 hours. Freezing, unless done quickly aboard a large processing vessel, tends to give fish the texture of cardboard. If you purchase fresh fish, plan to use it immediately rather than freezing it yourself. If you purchase previously frozen fish, keep it frozen until ready to use and never refreeze it.

I have eaten frozen salmon that was indistinguishable from fresh when cooked. The trick is choosing the best-quality frozen fish. If there are ice crystals on frozen fish, shun it. The crystals indicate that the fish has been thawed and refrozen. When this happens, fish loses not only taste but also nutrients.

A LARGE FROZEN FISH . . .

During the winter of 1931–1932, 21-year-old Leslie Melvin spent 132 days mushing across the top of Alaska, from Martin Point on the Beaufort Sea to Barrow on the Chukchi Sea. He made day-to-day notes—and even gained weight on his diet of rolled oats, frozen reindeer meat, walrus hacked off a carcass with his axe, hot water, seal liver, and coq *(frozen fish dipped in seal oil, Eskimo-style). His journal entry for December 25 [1931], the 63rd day [Barrow], reads:*

We went to dinner at Dr. Greist's house, and in the evening all went to the school. Sat on the floor cross-legged and listened to the Christmas program. The mission had a tree and gifts for all the natives in the village. When Santa Claus gave out the presents, he called Mr. Melvin to come forth. As I stepped up on the stage, he gave me a large frozen fish. All the natives laughed because I had to live on frozen fish so much of the time crossing the Arctic Slope. Morris and I cut the fish up and with the help of several natives ate it up. A great Christmas.

—Leslie Melvin, I Beat the Arctic *(Alaska Northwest Books, 1982)*

If you have fillets or steaks of fish frozen individually, you don't necessarily need to thaw them before cooking. Simply prepare the frozen fish as you would thawed fish, doubling the cooking time. Some feel that cooking fish from a frozen state ensures it will be particularly moist.

To thaw fish, place the wrapped package in the refrigerator on a folded newspaper section or a paper towel (to absorb any fluids produced). A 1-pound package takes about 24 hours to thaw. For faster thawing, set the wrapped package under cold running water; this will take 1 to 2 hours. Do not thaw fish at room temperature on a counter or in warm water. But fish may be speedily and safely thawed at the "defrost" setting of a microwave oven: take care that it does not begin to cook while thawing.

Basic Cooking Times

As fish cooks, its flesh turns from translucent to opaque. A standard cooking time for fish is 10 to 15 minutes per inch of thickness, for all cooking methods except microwaving.

There is no per-inch rule for shellfish. Shrimp and scallops, like fish, will turn from translucent to opaque when done. Live mussels, clams, and oysters pop open when cooked. Shucked oysters firm slightly and their edges curl to indicate that they are cooked.

Seafood Safety

Is there danger in consuming seafood? Very little, according to the statistics. The average American is more likely to be injured skiing or shoveling snow from the driveway than to fall ill from consuming Oysters Rockefeller.

The risk of getting sick from eating cooked seafood is just 1 in 2,500,000, according to a study by the National Academy of Sciences. But the risk increases if the seafood is raw mollusks, the academy says—to about 1 in 1,000. Food poisoning is most likely caused by improper handling, storage, and preparation, rather than chemical contamination, the NAS concludes.

Most bacteria and viruses are rendered harmless by heat. The Food and Drug Administration recommends that fish be cooked to 145°F or until it flakes easily at the center, near the bone; the FDA recommends cooking oysters and clams for 4 to 6 minutes.

Beyond bacteria and viruses, there are additional pests that seafood is heir to: parasites and red tides.

PARASITES

Salmon, halibut, Irish lord, sculpin—almost any fish that swims in the sea can play unwitting host to tapeworms. Freshwater fish can also carry these thread-like, beige worms—an aesthetic affront to the diner, but not a health hazard. But other parasites such as roundworm larvae (common in herring) and nematodes can cause infection in humans if ingested raw.

Parasites should be dealt with in one of three ways. For fish to be served raw (in seviche, sashimi, sushi, cold-smoking, or gravad lax), first freeze the fish to kill the parasites. The Cooperative Extension Service of the University of Alaska at Fairbanks recommends freezing raw fish at a temperature of 0°F for 2 weeks or longer. Another method, when hot-smoking fish, is to ensure that the fish reaches an internal temperature of 150°F while smoking. A third and final method is to simply remove the worms manually with tweezers if you spot them while slicing fish. (When cooked, the worms are barely visible and no longer a threat.)

Alaska's choicest fish, the salmon, commonly carries parasites called *anisakis* (small roundworms). If eaten raw, the worms can cause abdominal pain and nausea. Cooking salmon to an internal temperature of 140°F does the job, as does rapid freezing to minus 40°F (which only commercial freezers can manage) or freezing for 3 to 5 days at minus 4°F.

RED TIDE

The main threat from mussels and clams is red tide, a bloom of phytoplankton in warm water that usually occurs between May 15 and October 15. Red tides contain a toxin that causes paralytic shellfish poisoning (PSP)—a deadly malady that strikes several Alaskans nearly every season. When phytoplankton blooms, it turns the water green, red, orange, or brown, or it can leave the water clear, so visual indications are not valid.

The blooms produce a poison that plankton feeders like clams, oysters, and mussels concentrate in their flesh. The poison does not harm the shellfish themselves, but can reach such concentrations that it harms humans who consume them, paralyzing their respiratory systems and often killing them. So before digging clams or gathering mussels, it is important to check with local fish and game officials. Shellfish sold commercially must come from waters that are regularly certified to be safe from both red tide and typhoid organisms; any retailer should be able to produce a tag confirming that.

Tidal Toxins

Most shellfish dissipate the toxicity of the marine protozoa in red tides within several weeks after exposure. Butter clams, however, can retain the toxin for as long as two years.

There is some evidence that reaction to the red tide toxin is made worse if the shellfish are consumed with alcohol.

FISH BY MAIL

Should you be unable to find Alaskan seafood—whether fresh, frozen, smoked, or prepared—available to you locally, many fish and fish products are as close as your mailbox or fax machine. Most of the following suppliers offer festive gift packs as well as speedy delivery by Federal Express.

ALASKABITS™. c/o Duff Mitchell, Alaska Food Group, Box 3000, Juneau, AK 99802. Phone: (907) 790-2722; fax: (907)790-2722. Alaska Bits is a new smoked red salmon product that can be sprinkled on salads or main dishes; it declines in quality when cooked, so it's added at the last minute. Two-ounce jars.

Alaska Choice Seafoods, 4611 Gambell Street, Anchorage, AK 99503. Phone: (907) 563-4666; fax: (907) 561-8459. Produces low-fat, low-cholesterol, high-protein salmon products from sockeye and chum. Products include salmon franks, pickled salmon franks, deli salmon loaf, and salmon pepperoni sticks.

Alaska Gourmet Seafoods, 1020 West International Airport Road, Anchorage, AK 99518. Phone: (907) 563-3752; fax: (907) 563-2592. Packing, shipping, and canning for the sportfisherman. Canning can be viewed from the retail sales area through a picture window. Gift baskets and boxes, including a complete snow crab and salmon dinner with fish poacher.

Alaska Salmon Snacks, Box 211622, Auke Bay, AK 99821. Phone: (907) 789-3817; fax: (907) 789-5580. These popular all-natural salmon snacks for dogs are vacuum packed in foil wrappers. They are made from alder-smoked pink and chum salmon.

Alaska Sausage and Seafood, 2914 Arctic Boulevard, Anchorage, AK 99518. Phone: (907) 562-3636; fax: (907) 562-7343. Since 1963, Alaska Sausage has specialized in smoking, kippering, and "strips," as well as game

processing. Offers gift packages of smoked salmon and halibut. One Christmas pack, "The Sourdough," contains reindeer sausage, barbecue sauce, smoked salmon, and tea.

Alaska Seafood Company, 5434 Shaune Drive, Juneau, AK 99801. Phone: (907) 780-5111; fax: (907) 780-5140. Handles retorted (metal foil bagged) seafood for the individual customer.

Alaskan Harvest, 320 Seward Street, Sitka, AK 99835. Phone: (800) 824-6389. Whole king crab, smoked silver salmon strips, lox, halibut cheeks, spot shrimp, Dungeness crab sections, scallops, kippered sockeye and king, smoked salmon ham, salmon sausage, smoked sablefish, and more. Gift baskets and boxes available.

Bell's Seafood, Box 1189, Haines, AK 99827. Phone: (800) 446-2950. King salmon, halibut, king crab, and Dungeness crab. Pack and ship anywhere in the U.S.; 48-hour delivery.

Blue Crab Bay Co., Box 180, Onancock, VA 23417. Phone: (800) 221-2722. Seafood marinade and grilling sauce, perfect for tuna, swordfish, shrimp, scallops, vegetables. Bloody Mary mix. Free color catalog.

Carry-On Seafoods, c/o Kirkland Seafoods, 640 Eighth Avenue, Kirkland, WA 98033. Phone: (800) 5-CARRYON; fax (206) 889-9248. Pacific Northwest seafoods packed for travel. Smoked and fresh salmon, canned seafood.

Chinook Planks, Box 78462, Seattle, WA 98178. Phone: (800) 765-4408. Western red cedar and alder baking planks. Aromatic woods enhance natural flavors of fish roasted in the oven.

Discovery Kitchen, 24461 Calvert Street, Box 6325, Woodland Hills, CA 91365. Phone: (800) 367-6865. Handcrafted food products such as fireweed honey, Indian fry bread mix, alder-smoked wild salmon fillets, and solar-cooked strawberry preserves—as well as jars of kelp pickles in both "Spicy Sweet" and "Savory Dill." Gift wrapping and special occasion baskets

available. Catalog available.

Discovery Trading Post, 1975 Discovery Drive, Fairbanks, AK 99709. Phone: (907) 479-6673; fax (907) 479-4613. Gift shop and docking site for the riverboat Discovery, a restored stern-wheeler. Smoked salmon, canned salmon, and cookbooks available.

Ed's Kasilof Seafoods, Inc., Box 18, Kasilof, AK 99610. Phone: (907) 262-7295 or (800) 982-2377. Since 1970, Ed's has furnished seafood gift packs, salmon jerky, canned salmon, smoked salmon, halibut, and lox. Fish processing available for the sportsman.

Gerard & Dominique Seafoods, Bothell, WA. Phone: (800) 858-0449. Smoked salmon, European-style and Northwest-style; seafood sausages, scallops, and gourmet gifts.

Health Sea Inc., a division of Kake Tribal Council, 2211 North Jordan Avenue, Juneau, AK 99801. (907) 586-3333. This company makes a variety of value-added products, including salmon ham and salmon sausages in five flavors.

Indian Valley Meats, HC 52, Box 8809, Indian, AK 99540. Phone: (907) 653-7511; fax (907) 653-7694. Indian Valley Meats is locally renowned for the quality of its preserved meats, made with spices custom-blended by owner/butcher Doug Drumm. Smoked halibut, char, sheefish, sablefish, smoked salmon, musk ox meat, and reindeer sausage are some of the items available. Brochure available.

Katch Seafoods, Box 2677, Homer, AK 99603. Phone and fax: in Alaska (907) 235-7953; elsewhere (800) 368-7400. Katch offers 16 (8-ounce) fresh-frozen halibut steaks, including 2-day delivery, in an insulated box with recipes. Also available are salmon, scallops, king crab, and smoked and canned seafood.

Larry's Smoked Salmon, 14527 Bothell Way, Mill Creek, WA 98012. Phone: (800) 247-8207; fax: (206) 745-5107. A deli, Larry's sends alder-smoked salmon, jerky, turkey, roast beef, and ham anywhere in the U.S.

New Sagaya, 3700 Old Seward Highway, Anchorage, AK 99503. Phone: (907) 561-5173. Outside Alaska: (800) 764-1001. Large variety of seafood from around the world, including live crab, live lobster, herring eggs on kelp, and assorted exotic shellfish such as New Zealand green-lipped mussels. Buys Alaska seafood directly from fishermen.

Norm Thompson, Box 3999, Portland, OR 97208. Phone: (800) 547-1160; fax: (503) 643-1973. Catalog offers "Gifts from the Northwest," such as a seafood-spread sampler composed of cans of crab, salmon, steelhead, and shrimp spreads. Alderwood-smoked Pacific salmon, other smoked seafood.

Original Alaska Birch Syrup Co., Box 29, Ester, AK 99725. Phone: (907) 479-5527. Analogous to maple syrup—except that maple trees don't grow in Alaska—birch syrup tastes just right on sourdough hotcakes. Birch syrup producers have difficulty keeping up with the demand, so Jeff Weltzin has diversified into blueberry, rose hip, fireweed, and cranberry syrups, jellies, and jams.

Pacific Aqua Foods Ltd., 350-601 West Cordova, Vancouver, BC V6B 1G1, Canada. Phone: (800) 667-FISH. Pacific Aqua is the largest producer of off-bottom cultured oysters in North America.

Port Chatham Packing Company, 632 NW 46th Street, Seattle, WA 98107. Phone: (206) 783-8200; fax: (206) 281-4484. Established in 1935, Port Chatham's seafood is cold-smoked over alderwood. Products include smoked lox, smoked salmon strips, kipper smoked salmon, hand-packed sockeye, coho, and pink in cans, salt-free coho, smoked salmon pâté, smoked black cod fillets, and sliced smoked sturgeon, all sold under the "Portlock" trademark.

Salmon, Etc., 322 Mission Street, Ketchikan, AK 99901. Phone: (907) 225-6008; fax: (907) 247-7256. Smoked, canned salmon and fillets. Discount prices available at the Deer Mountain Hatchery. The hatchery was begun by the Ketchikan Chamber of Commerce more than 30 years ago in an attempt to improve local runs of king and coho salmon when they were seriously depleted. The rearing ponds and returning spawners make the hatchery a year-round attraction.

The Salmon River Smokehouse, Box 40, Gustavus, AK 99826. Phone: (907) 697-2330. Award-winning fish smoked homestead-style, lightly smoked and spiced; 2-pound gift boxes with 2-day delivery. Free brochure.

Santa's Smokehouse, *c/o Interior Fish,* 2400 Davis Road, Fairbanks, AK 99701. Phone: (907) 456-3885; fax: (907) 456-3889. Salmon breakfast sausage, salmon hot dogs, salmon hot links, salmon bacon, salmon bratwurst, and smoked salmon.

Sea Sausage, Inc., 18634 Des Moines Memorial Drive, SeaTac, WA 98148. Phone: (800) 3-SALMON; fax: (206) 431-9189. Alder-smoked salmon, vacuum-packed for freshness. Free shipping for two or more gift boxes. Nova-style lox.

Taku Smokeries, 550 South Franklin Street, Juneau, AK 99801. Phone: (907) 463-4617; fax: (907) 463-5209. Smoked sockeye salmon, sockeye lox, and Alaskan salmon jerky. Sampler boxes available. No preservatives. Through an agreement with the Juneau Post Office, Taku's customers can return insulated styrofoam shipping boxes without charge, for recycling. The smokery also has a restaurant. Sandro Lane, owner.

10th & M Seafoods, 1020 M Street, Anchorage, AK 99501. Phone: (907) 272-3474; fax: (907) 272-1685. 10th & M Seafoods offers Alaska seafood fresh or frozen to your door via Federal Express. One-day service is available to most U.S. cities. Seafood gift packs can be made up with king crab, salmon, halibut, shrimp, lox, prawns, smoked salmon, and/or scallops.

Trapper's Creek Smoking Co., 5650 B Street, Anchorage, AK 99518.

Phone: in Alaska (907) 561-8088; elsewhere (800) 770-8088; fax: (907) 561-8389. Smoked salmon, smoked halibut, lox, and sausages. Their "Alaska Banquet" gift pack includes smoked salmon, smoked halibut, reindeer sausage, summer sausage, a hot pad, and serving plate. Catalog available.

Ugashik Wild Salmon Company, 3423 West 100th Avenue, Anchorage, AK 99515. Phone: (907) 277-5932; fax: (907) 277-5935. Salmon in glass, wild berry teas and jellies, and *ulu* knives. Brochure available.

The Ulu Factory, Inc., 298 Ship Creek Avenue, Anchorage, AK 99501. In Alaska, (800) 473-3119; (800) 473-3119; fax, (907) 276-3118. This company makes traditional Eskimo women's chopping knives in a variety of materials.

Wild Alaska Salmon Company, Box 1094, Homer, AK 99603. Phone and fax: (907) 235-7444. Gourmet alderwood-smoked sockeye salmon, vacuum-sealed foil pouches, with no preservatives and no refrigeration necessary. Gift packs come in 3-, 5-, 8-, or 24-ounce sizes. They also offer smoked no-salt sockeye salmon, lox, and kippered sockeye.

Williams-Sonoma, Mail Order Department, Box 7456, San Francisco, CA 94120. Phone (415) 421-7900; fax: (415) 421-5153. Carries Douglas Island salmon sausages produced by Health Sea, Inc., of Juneau. The sausages are 99 percent fat-free and come in five flavors: original, dill, garlic, lemon-pepper, and Cajun.

GLOSSARY

Consult this glossary when you need specifics about the fish species in the recipes. Details about distribution, alternative names, availability, and flesh quality will help you adapt some of your favorite recipes to Alaskan species—or vice versa. Aliases of the common seafood names are listed in quotation marks. Cross-references are to other glossary entries.

Abalone: Red abalone *(Haliotis rufescens)* and pink abalone *(H. kamtschatkana)* are the most important commercial species on the West Coast. Can be tough and need pounding. Unlike most seafood, abalone improves by holding in refrigerator a day or two. Available fresh during summer, canned year-round. Lean, delectable, boneless. Freezes well.

Alaska plaice: *see* Flounder and Sole.

Arctic char *(Salvelinus alpinus)*: Related to trout and salmon. Ranges from Alaska's Arctic coast to southern British Columbia. Wild catch sometimes marketed as "blueback trout," "Quebec red trout"; char sometimes spelled "charr." Available year-round to sportfishermen. Farmed in Norway, Iceland, and Canada. Flesh color of farmed fish varies. Sweet, trout-like, delicate flesh.

Arrowtooth flounder: *see* Flounder and Sole

Atka mackerel: *see* Greenling

Bering wolf fish: *see* Wolf fish

Black cod: *see* Sablefish

Blackfish *(Dallia pectoralis)*: Thrives in tundra ponds and streams in much of Alaska and eastern Siberia. *Atuutaa* (Inupiat Eskimo); *emanguk*. Important subsistence fish; rarely marketed. "Devilfish"

from its color and its unearthly ability to withstand low temperatures. Delicate, slightly oily.

Black rockfish: *see* Rockfish

Brook trout: *see* Trout

Burbot *(Lota lota)*: Widely distributed in North America; similar species in Europe and Siberia; freshwater member of cod family. Chena River, Tanana River. "Eelpout," "lingcod," "freshwater lingcod," "lush," "donzela," "mudshark," "bottatrice." Ice-fishing species. Minor market species. Tender, flaky flesh. Good quality. Edible roe and liver.

California mussel: *see* Mussels

Candlefish: *see* Hooligan

Char: *see* Arctic char

China slipper: *see* Chiton

Chinook: *see* King salmon

Chiton (gumboot): Seven varieties of this single-shell mollusk inhabit Alaska waters. The two best known and largest are the black chiton *(Katharina tunicata)* and giant chiton *(Amicula stelleri,* formerly *Cryptochiton stelleri)*. Brick-red giant chiton, "giant sea cradle," found from Alaska to Southern California and west to Japan. "Japanese abalone"; on Aleutians, *bidarkies* from their resemblance to traditional skin-covered Aleut kayaks; "China slipper," "Chinese slipper" (giant chiton); *uriitaq* (Kodiak Alutiiq). Subsistence food. Fleshy foot similar to abalone. Can be eaten raw.

Chromer: *see* Steelhead

Chub: *see* Mackerel

Chum salmon: *see* Salmon

Clams: Horse or "gaper" clam *(Tresus capax, Schizothaerus nuttalli)*, is up to 10 inches in length; distinguished by a large neck wreathed in tough, black skin; common south of Alaska Peninsula; poor keeping qualities. Butter clam

(Saxidomus giganteus) abundant in Prince William Sound and around the Alaska Peninsula. Littleneck clam *(Protothaca staminea)* found from Alaska down to California; good for chowder. Pacific razor clam *(Siliqua patula)* has an oblong shell up to 6 inches. Geoduck or "king clam" *(Panope generosa)* ranges from California to Alaska and may attain 3 feet in length, including its protruding siphon; geoduck meat is lean, pinkish golden to ivory. A freshwater clam *(Anodonta beringiana)* inhabits streams and lakes throughout Alaska; shells are shiny brown outside, pearly inside, 4 to 12 inches long. The Eastern soft-shell clam of the Atlantic has been introduced to Kachemak Bay near Homer. Clams may need scrubbing and de-sanding. Chewy, tasty flesh.

Cockle: Several varieties are common in Alaska: North Pacific cockle *(Clinocardium californiense),* large Nuttall's or basket cockle *(C. nuttalli),* Greenland cockle *(Serripes groenlandicus)*, and Iceland cockle *(C. ciliatum)*. Meat often consumed raw when fresh; available canned. Use like clams. Firm, chewy.

Cod: True cod *(Gadus macrocephalus)* and pollock *(see* page 288) are important market fish. True cod is also called "Pacific cod," "Alaska cod," "gray cod"; found from Oregon north, harvested in Bering Sea. "Scrod" designates small cod—not a separate species. Tomcod *(Microgadus proximus)* is a subsistence catch. Burbot is a freshwater species of cod *(see* entry this page). True cod is harvested year-round. Snowy white, firm, tender flesh. Excellent quality.

Coho: *see* Salmon

Crab: Alaska is home to several species: giant king (red king *Paralithodes camtschatica* and blue king *P. platypus*), snow crab *(Chionoecetes bairdi* and *C. opilio)*, horsehair *(Erimacrus isenbeckii)*, and Dungeness *(Cancer magister)*. Dungeness is found along Pacific Coast from Aleutian Islands to Mexico; available fresh May through September from Alaska; in winter from Washington and Oregon. Snow crabs are pulled from Bering Sea mid-January through quotas (generally six weeks). King crabs range from Norton Sound to northern British Columbia; available fresh September to January. Crab is also available year-round frozen and canned. Good to excellent quality.

Demersel shelf rockfish: A minor commercial species, caught in Gulf of Alaska.

Devilfish: An alias for both blackfish and octopus. *See* Blackfish; Octopus

Dog salmon: *see* Salmon

Dogfish *(Squalus acanthias)*: Member of shark family; common south of Alaska Peninsula. "Grayfish," "huss," "rigg," "sea-eel," "rock salmon," "flake," "spiny dogfish," "Folkstone beef." Available June to August. Firm, white, boneless, moderately lean.

Dolly Varden *(Salvelinus malma)*: Closely related to arctic char. Brilliantly colored, especially when spawning. Lives both in freshwater and salt water, from Arctic coast of Alaska to southern British Columbia. "Golden fin," "salmon trout." Generally a recreational catch during fall, when entering streams to spawn. Succulent pink flesh.

Dungeness crab: *see* Crab

Eulachon: *see* Hooligan

Flounder and Sole: Vast flatfish family; Alaska species include Alaska plaice *(Pleuronectes quadrituberculatus)* or "lemon sole"; arrowtooth flounder *(Atheresthes stomaias)* or "turbot"; blackback flounder *(Pseudopleuronectes americanus)*, also called "winter flounder," "Georges flounder," "shoals flounder," and "peewee"; Dover sole *(Microstomus pacificus)*; flathead sole *(Hippoglossoides elassodon)*; Greenland turbot *(Reinhardtius hippoglossoides)*, marketed as "Greenland halibut" and "black halibut"; rex sole *(Glyptocephalus zachirus)*; rock sole *(Lepidopsetta bilineata*; and starry flounder *(Platichthys stellatus)*. Generally distributed from Alaska to central California. Arrowhead, yellowtail, winter, and starry flounder are available year-round; commercially important. Light and delicate flesh, mild flavor. Susceptible to dehydration and spoilage.

Geoduck: *see* Clams

Giant sea cradle: *see* Chiton

Grayling *(Thymallus arcticus)*: Common in cold lakes and streams in Alaska, Canada, and Siberia. Popular arctic sport fish and subsistence species; not marketed. "Sailfish of the Arctic" (male). Trout-like flesh. Excellent quality.

Greenling: Primary Alaska greenling species include kelp greenling *(Hexagrammos decagrammus)* or "rock trout," "sea trout"; masked greenling *(H. octogrammus)*; rock greenling *(H. lagocephalus)*; Atka mackerel *(Pleurogrammus monopterygius)* and lingcod *(see* page 288). Greenling favor rocky shallows—the kelp, masked, and rock are found south and north of Alaska Peninsula. Minor market species, chiefly sport fishing; available year-round. Good quality.

Gumboot: *see* Chiton

Halibut *(Hippoglossus stenolepsis)*: A giant flatfish, member of flounder family, Pacific halibut ranges from Kotzebue Bay to Northern California and to northern Japan. Also known as "northern halibut." Important market species. Halibut is available fresh March to November, frozen year-round. Meaty, mild, lean, firm, and tender. Excellent quality.

Herring *(Culpea harengus* or *Culpea pallasii)*: Migratory fish found from Kotzebue to Baja California to Japan and eastern Russia. Roe prized. Pacific herring is a valuable Japanese market species; minor market species in Alaska. Sometimes used as bait. Available fresh December, January, and April. Dark, fatty flesh cooks up ivory. Flesh turns rancid quickly.

Hooligan (eulachon) *(Thaleichthys pacificus)*: Related to smelt, capelin, and grunion. Common north and south of Alaska Peninsula. "Oolachen" or "ooligan," "candlefish," *saak* (Tlingit). Hooligan enter Glacier Bay in late February or early March; enter Cook Inlet in May. Subsistence and sport catch. Delicate, rich, ivory flesh. Extremely perishable. Excellent quality.

Horse clam: *see* Clams

Horse mussel: *see* Mussels

Humpy, humpback: *see* Salmon

Irish lord *(Hemilepidotus hemilepidotus)*: Red Irish lord ("spotted Irish lord," "bullhead") is a member of sculpin family; ranges from Kamchatka (Russia) to Puffin Bay (Alaska) and south to Monterey Bay (California). One of the largest Pacific Coast members of this family, the red grows to 20 inches and bears white and purplish red spots on its olive green body. Freshwater species live in lakes, rivers, and streams. Available year-round to sportfishermen; not generally marketed. Excellent-quality white flesh. *See also* Sculpin.

Kelp greenling: *see* Greenling

King crab: *see* Crab

King salmon: *see* Salmon

Kokanee: A nonmigratory sockeye that spends its whole life cycle in freshwater. Common in lakes of Southeast Alaska and British Columbia. Weighs only about a pound at maturity. Fed on by trophy-size cutthroat trout. Good to excellent flesh.

Lake trout: *see* Trout

Limpet *(Acmaea* genus*)*: A small conical shellfish ranging from fingernail size to 3 inches in diameter. Clings to rocks at sea's edge. "Chinaman's hat," "Chinese hat." Alaska species found from Pribilof and Aleutian islands to Baja California. A subsistence and beachcomber's catch; not marketed. Chewy, but of finer texture than abalone. Eat raw, simmer, sauté in butter, or grind to use in chowder, cakes.

Lingcod *(Ophiodon elongatus)*: A member of greenling family, found south of Alaska Peninsula. Also known as "greenling," "poggie" (Kodiak Island), "blue cod," "green cod," "white cod," "leopard cod," and "cultus cod"—although not a cod. Important market species. When raw, flesh may be pale blue-green, but cooks white. Good quality.

Littleneck: *see* Clams

Mackerel: Chub mackerel *(Scomber japonicus)* or "tinker" is Alaska's native species; Pacific or true mackerel *(Scomberomorus sierra)* are not native to Alaska. Flesh deteriorates rapidly; fair quality fresh. Excellent smoked or canned.

Mako: *see* Shark

Masked greenling: *see* Greenling

Moon snail: *see* Snails

Mussels: Blue mussel *(Mytilus edulis)* is abundant in intertidal zones from Arctic Ocean to Mexico. Horse mussel *(Modiolus modiolus)* can reach 6 inches; found from Pribilof Islands to Southern California. California mussel *(M. californianus)* can reach 10 inches; grows on exposed Aleutian shores; also black mussel *(Musculus niger)* and discord mussel *(M. discors)*; important to subsistence gatherers. Best October through April. Meat is ivory to bright orange, buttery, lean.

Northern pike: *see* Pike

Octopus: Giant Pacific or common octopus *(Octopus dolfleini)* is most common octopus in Alaskan waters. "Devilfish." Marketed frozen year-round, fresh irregularly. White, crisp, lean, milky tentacle meat turns china white when cooked. Good quality.

Oyster: Alaska oyster farming was founded on pearly spat of Pacific oyster *(Crassostrea gigas)* from Japan. Available year-round in limited quantities. Prized market species. Flesh tender, lean, succulent, with a hint of iodine. Perishable, best fresh.

Pacific cod: *see* Cod

Pacific halibut: *see* Halibut

Pacific Ocean perch: *see* Rockfish

Pacific oyster: *see* Oyster

Pacific pollock: *see* Pollock

Perch: *see* Rockfish

Pike *(Esox lucius)*: Widely distributed from Alaska's eastern border north and west to Beaufort and Bering seas. "Northern pike," "arctic pike," "jackfish," "Hechte"; *Siuliglu* or *siilik* (Inupiaq); *luqruuyak* (Yupik). Popular sportfish; not commercially marketed. Delicate, white-meated, lean, flaky, but bony. Excellent quality. Good smoked. Pike liver considered a delicacy.

Pink salmon: *see* Salmon

Pink shrimp: *see* Shrimp

Pollock *(Theragra chalcogramma)*: Member of cod family; abundant both north and south of Alaska Peninsula; dominant bottom fish of this habitat. Also called "Alaska pollock," "walleye pollock," "big-eye cod," "Alaska snow cod." Marketed fresh and frozen year-round. Important commercial species for production of surimi products. White, mild, lean, firm. Fair quality.

Pomfret *(Brama japonica)*: A pelagic species occurring erratically off Alaska Peninsula. A good food fish, but rare in trawl catches.

Quillback: *see* Rockfish

Rainbow trout: *see* Trout

Ray: *see* Skate

Razor clam: *see* Clams

Red Irish lord: *see* Irish lord

Rockfish: Primary Alaska species are black rockfish *(Sebastes melanops)*, found from Gulf of Alaska to Southern California; Pacific Ocean perch *(S. alutus)*, found from Bering Sea to Southern California; sharpchin rockfish or "northern rockfish" *(S. zucentrus)*, harvested in Bering Sea and Aleutians; shortraker rockfish or "rougheye rockfish" *(S. borealis)*, found in Bering Sea and Aleutians; thornyhead or "idiot" *(Sebastolobus alascanus)*, harvested in Gulf of Alaska; and quillback rockfish *(Sebastes maliger)*, found from Southeast Alaska to Southern California. Often called "rockcod," but not members of cod family. Sometimes sold as "red snapper," although not members of snapper family, either. Important market species and good sportfish. Tender flesh, but black and perch both spoil quickly. Good quality.

Sablefish *(Anoplopoma fimbria)*: Found in Bering Sea as well as along

Pacific Coast to Japan. Commonly called "black cod." Important market species, especially smoked. Available year-round smoked; market availability fresh depends on quotas. High fat content. Excellent quality but bony.

Salmon (family *Salmonidae*): Five chief Pacific salmon species are king, chum, sockeye, pink, and silver. Main commercial fishing season for Pacific salmon lasts June to November; availability at other times depends on state quotas. All salmon have good- to excellent-quality flesh, although king is oilier and deeper in flavor. Salmon roe also prized.

Chum salmon *(Oncorhynchus keta)* also known as "dog," "silver bright" (or "brite"), "calico," and "fall"; averages 10 to 15 pounds.

King salmon *(O. tschawytscha)* distinguished by a dark tongue and black gums. Commercially caught kings range between 10 and 80 pounds; found from Sacramento River north to Yukon River and Point Hope in Alaska. Kings also called "Chinook," "spring," "blackmouth," "tyee" (Chinook for "chief"), "tullies," "hog," and "soaker" (specimens over 60 pounds). Main Alaska king salmon season is June and July.

Pink salmon *(O. gorbuscha)* is the smallest Pacific salmon, averaging 2 to 5 pounds; "humpback" or "humpy." Abundant north and south of Alaska Peninsula.

Silver salmon *(O. kisutch)* known as "coho," "hooknose"; spawn from Japan and Siberia to Alaska, and south to Baja California.

Sockeye salmon *(O. nerka)*, "red" or "blueback," is abundant north and south of Alaska Peninsula. Sockeye season begins in Alaska in June and ends on Canada's Fraser River in September.

Salmon trout: *see* Dolly Varden

Scallop: Four main Alaska species are weathervane *(Pecten caurinus)*, up to 12 inches in length; Pacific pink *(Chlamys hastata)*; Hinds' *(C. rubida)*; and arctic pink *(C. pseudoislandica)*. Weathervane most commercially important scallop in northeastern Pacific, common south of Alaska Peninsula. Available frozen year-round but best fresh, July to February. Ivory and lean; tender, sweet, boneless.

Scrod: *see* Cod

Sculpin: A large family with 84 species in North Pacific, 45 of these in Alaskan waters only. Buffalo sculpin *(Enophrys bison)* ranges from Kodiak Island to Monterey Bay; popular subsistence and sportfish. Some sculpins measure a minuscule 4 inches. Cabezon *(Scorpaenichthys marmoratus)* grows to 39 inches and 25 pounds; pale green flesh edible, but roe poisonous. Lean, tender flesh. *See also* Irish lord.

Sea cucumber: An echinoderm—i.e., a creature with a spiny skin. Edible portion is five lean muscles running length of body. Sea football *(Cucumaria fallax)* is largest Alaskan variety; contracted body is football-shaped; brown, orange, or white; up to a foot long. Abundant north and common south of Alaska Peninsula. "Sea sweet potato," *yein* (Tlingit). Season late fall to early spring. Minor market species in Alaska; primarily subsistence catch. Firm, gelatinous, often dried.

Sea urchin: Like sea cucumber, sea urchin is an echinoderm. Giant sea urchin or "red sea urchin" *(Strongylocentrotus franciscanus)* most prized Pacific Coast urchin, up to 6¾ inches in diameter; ranges from Kodiak Island to Mexico. Green sea urchin *(S. droebachiensis)* circumpolar. Pacific purple sea urchin *(S. purpuratus)* a less desirable variety. Available August through April. Rarely marketed in Alaska; primarily subsistence catch. Only fatty "roe" consumed.

Shark: Thresher shark *(Alopius vulpinus)*, mako shark *(Isurus glaucus)*, and dogfish *(see* Dogfish) are most common sharks off Alaska. In warmer waters near Sitka, several shark thrive: salmon shark *(Lamna ditropis)*, angel shark *(Squatina californica)*, white shark *(Carcharodon carcharias)*, and blue shark *(Prionace glauca)*. Shark is available fresh year-round with peak supplies from May through September. Flesh mild, succulent, flaky, and firm. Good quality. If necessary, urea concentration can be reduced by soaking in milk or acidulated water for 1 hour.

Sharpchin: *see* Rockfish

Sheefish *(Stenodus leucichthys)*: A whitefish found in Bering Sea; migrates to Yukon and Kuskokwim drainages in fall. "Shovelnose," "whitefish," "coney," "connie," "Eskimo tarpon," "tarpon of the North." Sportfish, subsistence catch, and local market species in fall. Rich flesh. Excellent smoked.

Shrimp: Pink shrimp *(Pandalus borealis)* account for about 85 percent of total Alaska harvest; also known as "salad shrimp," "tiny Pacific shrimp," "Petersburg shrimp," and "Northern shrimp." Spot shrimp *(P. platyceros)* bear broad white stripes on body with spots on tail and banded legs. Inhabit rocky bottoms and steep undersea slopes from Bering Strait to Southern California, west to

Japan and Korea. Spot prawns or "giant spot shrimp" can attain lengths of 8 inches; available periodically year-round on both sides of North Pacific. Side-stripe shrimp *(Pandalopsus dispar)* named for pale lengthwise bands on abdomen. Found from Alaska to Oregon, harvested in Prince William Sound mid-April until end of July, plus a brief fall season. Coon-stripe shrimp *(P. hypsinotus)* abundant north and south of Alaska Peninsula. Coon-stripe shrimp also known as "humpback" and "raccoon shrimp." Available year-round frozen and canned. Meaty, firm, boneless, and mild.

Silver salmon: *see* Salmon

Skate: Skate in Alaska waters include longnose skate *(Raja rhina)*; big skate *(Raja binoculata)*, which can grow to 94 inches long; Alaska skate *(Bathyraja parmifera)*; and Aleutian skate *(Bathyraja aleutica)*. Alaska and Aleutian most common. Like sharks, skates carry urea in their tissues and blood; urea turns to ammonia when fish dies, thus, for best quality, skate wings must be removed as soon as fish is landed. Shiny, firm; good quality if handled properly.

Snails: Alaska is home to many sea snails. Aleutian moon snail *(Natica aleutica)* variety favored by subsistence gatherers; shell generally resembles common garden snail only bigger. Moon snail "foot" grows to 5 or 6 inches long; can be sliced and pounded like abalone. Large snails can be ground or minced for chowder.

Sockeye salmon: *see* Salmon

Sole: *see* Flounder and Sole

Squid *(Loligo opalescens)*: Cephalopod with a rocket-shaped body and wreath of 10 tentacles around head. Also called "calamari." Available fresh or fresh-frozen year-round. Milky white, cooks up china white; tender, moderately fatty.

Steelhead *(Oncorhynchus mykiss)*: Found in most Alaskan streams from Ketchikan to Yakutat. Freshwater sportfish, anadromous form of rainbow trout. Steelhead runs peak in October. "Chromers," "mint," or "bright." White, delicate, moist flesh. *See also* Trout.

Tanner crab: *see* Crab

Thornyhead: *see* Rockfish

Thresher: *see* Shark

Tomcod: *see* Cod

Trout: Alaska's succulent trout include brook trout *(Salvelinus fontinalis)*, cutthroat trout *(Oncorhynchus clarki,* formerly *Salmo clarki)*, lake trout *(Salvelinus namaycush)*, rainbow trout *(Salmo gairdneri,* formerly *O. mykiss)*, and steelhead *(see* Steelhead). Rainbow is the most popular market trout in U.S.; a farmed species, although not in Alaska. Wild rainbows are coveted by sportfishermen. Brook trout can weigh up to 6 pounds; also called "speckled trout," "squaretail." Cutthroat trout, a speckled seagoing variety, ranges from Prince William Sound to California. Rainbows in Alaska markets are farm-raised, 90 percent from Idaho. All trout have mild-flavored, delicate flesh, pale to deep pink in color. Very popular sportfish. Excellent quality.

Urchin: *see* Sea urchin

Whitefish: Freshwater member of salmon family; flourishes in lakes throughout Alaska. Varieties include cisco and sheefish *(see* Sheefish). "Lake Superior whitefish," "whiting," "shad." White, delicate, sweet flesh; firmer in winter.

Wolf fish *(or* wolffish): Bering wolf fish *(Anarhichas orientalis)* Alaskan species; found north of Alaska Peninsula. Also called "ocean catfish." Minor market fish except in Russia. Excellent quality.

Yellowtail: *see* Flounder and Sole

Boy and king salmon, Juneau, early 1920s

INDEX

Tlingit woman in Chilkat blanket, ca. 1900

TEXT PERMISSIONS

With the permission of *The Anchorage Times*, an article by the author is reprinted here in part: "Fish pie traditional for Russian masquerade ball" (January 25, 1984).

With the permission of Alaska Newspapers, Inc., several recipes and interviews from the author's weekly column, "Alaska Cafe," 1992–1993 are reprinted here, in part.

With the permission of *ALASKA* magazine, eleven of the author's "Frontier Fare" columns are reprinted here, in part: "The Staff of Life" (November 1992); "Sweet Legacy: Christmas recipes passed down from Alaska's Scandinavian Pioneers" (December 1992); "Cut and Dried: Be it moose, buffalo, whale or salmon, jerky tastes good on the trail" (March 1993); "Clams in the Cauldron" (April 1993); "Wild Summer Salads" (May/June 1993); "From Russia with Love" (December 1993); "Casserole Magic" (March 1994); "The Supremes of Shellfish" (April 1994); "Currant Affairs" (July 1994); "Fabulous Fungi" (August 1994); "Skate Picante" (July 1995).

With the permission of *Severnii Prostorii* magazine (Moscow), one article by the author is reprinted here, in part: "Traditional Eskimo and Indian recipes of Alaska" (1990, No. 1)

With the permission of Providence Alaska Medical Center (Anchorage), several recipes are reprinted from the Providence Heart Diet "Guide and Recipes for Healthier Living" booklets (1993, 1994, and 1995). These include "Alaska Creole Ya-Ya" and "Terrine of Leek, Scallops, and Sole."

With the permission of Anchorage's Great Northern Brewers Club, several recipes are reprinted here from *Great Northern Brewing: Alaskan Beer and Food Recipes, 1991.*

With the permission of *Food History News* (Isleboro, Maine), one article by the author is reprinted here: "A Primer for Pirog" (Fall 1995).

The legends of Raven and Moldy End were adapted from text in *The Box of Daylight* by William Hurd Hillyer (Alfred A. Knopf, 1931). These adaptations were reviewed in consultation with the Sealaska Heritage Foundation, a nonprofit 501(c)(3) educational and cultural foundation. Many Raven legends are attributed to the Tlingit. However, "The Legend of Moldy End" has ties to both the Haida and the Tlingit.

The Tanaina Athabascan legend of the Flounder Man was adapted from *Tanaina Tales From Alaska* by Bill Vaudrin (University of Oklahoma Press, 1969). This adaptation was reviewed by Tanaina elders and is used with their written permission.

Note: The original Native legends are considerably longer, but have been abridged here for reasons of space.

Harvesting tanner crab in the Bering Sea, 1981

PHOTO AND ILLUSTRATION PERMISSIONS

Endpapers (pages 1, 2, 311, 312), top, and 29, 69, 93: Haida design from a painted spruce-root mat. *Northwest Coast Indian Art: An Analysis of Form,* Bill Holm (University of Washington Press, 1965). **Endpapers (pages 1, 2, 311, 312), bottom, and 7, 155:** Haida design. **3, left, and 197:** Anchorage Museum of History and Art (AMHA), B70.28.190. **3, lower right, and 7, 268, 291, 303, 304, 306, 310:** Tlingit design. **5, 129, 291:** Whatcom Museum of History and Art, J. W. Sandison Collection, 710. **6, 308:** Haida argillite platter design. **7, 139:** Alaska Historical Library, Case and Draper Collection, PCA 39-135. **8, top, and 10, 227:** Joe Upton. **8, bottom left, and 116:** Winter and Pond photo. Alaska Historical Library, PCA 87-1799. **8, bottom right:** Tlingit halibut club. *Indian Fishing: Early Methods on the Northwest Coast,* Hilary Stewart (University of Washington Press, 1977). **9, top, and 122, 257, 273:** Picture Alaska Art Gallery, 201. **9, bottom, and 269, 280:** Steve McCutcheon. AMHA. **11, top, and 42:** Mendenhall. AMHA, B91.30.63. **11, bottom, and 21:** J. Pennelope Goforth. **12, top:** AMHA. **12, bottom, and 39, 85, 100–103, 135, 142–46:** Tlingit basket design. **13, 32:** *A Field Guide to the Cascades and Olympics,* Stephen R. Whitney (The Mountaineers Books, 1983). **14, top left:** *The Inuit: Life As It Was,* Richard Harrington (Hurtig, 1981). **14, top right, and 16, 17, 21, 115, 157:** Tlingit design. **14, bottom, and 101:** *Discovering Wild Plants: Alaska, Western Canada, the Northwest,* Janice J. Schofield; illustrated by Richard W. Tyler (Alaska Northwest Books, 1989). **15:** *Indian Fishing.* **16, 249:** Joe Upton. **17, top, and 274:** Roger Kaye. **17, bottom:** *Indian Art and Culture of the Northwest Coast,* Della Kew and P. E. Goddard (Hancock House, 1974). **19, 147:** *Indian Art and Culture of the Northwest Coast.* **20:** *Discovering Wild Plants.* **22–23, center, and 74, 80:** Washington State Historical Society, 1664. **22–23, background, and 25, 55, 159, 215, 267:** Tlingit bentwood box design. **25, 236:** Winter and Pond, Alaska State Library, 87-046. **27, top:** Steve Pilz. **28:** J. E. Thwaites. Alaska Historical Library, PCA 18-348. **29, top, and 126, 236:** *Growing and Using Herbs Successfully,* Betty E. M. Jacobs; illustrated by Charles H. Joslin (Storey Communications, 1976). **31, top, and 40, 45, 98, left, 138; 77, background, and 82, 128:** *Indian Art and Culture of the Northwest Coast.* **33, 52, 179, 244:** *Growing and Using Herbs Successfully.* **35, 184:** *Growing and Using Herbs Successfully.* **36, 108, 156, 212, 238:** *Discovering Wild Plants.* **37, 203:** AMHA, Richard M. Jones Collection, B82.51.8. **39, bottom, and 269:** *The Alaska Almanac* (Alaska Northwest Books, 1994). **43:** *Indian Art and Culture of the Northwest Coast.* **44:** *Indian Art and Culture of the Northwest Coast.* **48:** *A Field Guide to the Cascades and Olympics.* **49:** *Discovering Wild Plants.* **55, 72, 146:** Picture Alaska Art Gallery, 68. **57:** *Sea and Cedar: How the Northwest Coast Indians Lived,* Lois McConkey; illustrated by Douglas Tait (Douglas & McIntyre, 1973). **58, 152, 172:** J. Pennelope Goforth. **61, 62, 147, top:** *Indian Art and Culture of the Northwest Coast.* **63, top:** *Discovering Wild Plants.* **63, bottom, and 148, 232:** Haida dogfish design. *Indian Art and*

Culture of the Northwest Coast. **66, 195, 201:** *Discovering Wild Plants.* **69, 304:** Picture Alaska Art Gallery, 199. **70, 170, 231:** *Discovering Wild Plants.* **74:** *Indian Fishing.* **75:** *Indian Fishing.* **76:** *Indian Fishing.* **77:** *Indian Fishing.* **79:** *Indian Fishing.* **80, bottom:** *Sea and Cedar.* **86:** Tlingit basket design. **89:** *Indian Art and Culture of the Northwest Coast.* **91, 261:** Bernard R. Hubbard, SJ, Santa Clara University, KI-38-511. **94:** *Indian Art and Culture of the Northwest Coast.* **95:** Ann Chandonnet. **98:** J. Pennelope Goforth. **102:** *Discovering Wild Plants.* **103, 160:** *Discovering Wild Plants.* **106:** *Indian Art and Culture of the Northwest Coast.* **107, bottom:** Picture Alaska Art Gallery, USGS Collection, 86. **109:** AMHA, B71-X-5-28. **113, bottom:** *Sea and Cedar.* **114:** Alaska Historical Library, Thwaites Collection, 1026. **117:** *Indian Art and Culture of the Northwest Coast.* **118, 125, 136, 143:** *A Field Guide to the Cascades and Olympics.* **124, top, and 193, 265, 273:** Winter and Pond photo. Alaska Historical Library, 87-190. **128, top:** Petroglyph of man. *Guide to Indian Rock Carvings of the Pacific Northwest Coast.* **128, center and bottom:** Petroglyph of fish. *Guide to Indian Rock Carvings of the Pacific Northwest Coast.* **131:** AMHA, Steve McCutcheon Collection. **132:** *Indian Art and Culture of the Northwest Coast.* **154, 306:** J. Pennelope Goforth. **159, 174:** Santa Clara University, Hubbard Collection, KI-38-618. **161:** *Stalking the Blue-Eyed Scallop,* Euell Gibbons; illustrations by Catherine R. Hammond (Alan C. Hood & Co., 1964). **164, 205, 270:** *Indian Baskets of the Pacific Northwest and Alaska,* Allen Lobb; illustrated by Barbara Paxon (Graphic Arts Center, 1990). **168:** *Stalking the Blue-Eyed Scallop.* **171, bottom:** J. Pennelope Goforth. **177, right:** *Growing and Using Herbs Successfully.* **181, left, and 242, 310:** Winter and Pond photo. Alaska Historical Library, 87-070. **181, right, and 183:** *Marine Wildlife of Puget Sound, the San Juans, and the Strait of Georgia,* Steve Yates (Globe Pequot, 1988). **185:** *Marine Wildlife of Puget Sound, the San Juans, and the Strait of Georgia.* **189, 255:** *Discovering Wild Plants.* **193, 267:** Santa Clara University, Hubbard Collection, K1-38-1859. **199, 269:** *Indian Baskets of the Pacific Northwest and Alaska.* **206:** *Growing and Using Herbs Successfully.* **213:** J. Pennelope Goforth. **215:** Alaska Historical Library, Early Prints of Alaska Collection, PCA 01-1892. **216:** Joe Upton. **218:** *Discovering Wild Plants.* **219, 270:** F. H. Nowell. Bancroft Library, University of California Berkeley, YB 95-1251. **221:** *Discovering Wild Plants.* **223 top:** *Discovering Wild Plants.* **223, bottom:** *Alaska's Wilderness Medicines,* Eleanor G. Viereck; illustrations by Dominique Collet (Alaska Northwest Books, 1987). **224, top, and 235, 271:** *Indian Baskets of the Pacific Northwest and Alaska.* **225:** *Discovering Wild Plants.* **228, 253:** *Discovering Wild Plants.* **233:** *Discovering Wild Plants.* **234:** AMHA. **245:** Picture Alaska Art Gallery, USGS Collection, 52. **251:** *Discovering Wild Plants.* **264:** *Indian Art and Culture of the Northwest Coast.* **267:** Santa Clara University, Hubbard Collection, KI-38-1859. **275:** Tlingit design.

ABOUT THE AUTHOR

When ABC's *Good Morning America* was looking for an Alaska cooking authority to stand in the snow on Mount Alyeska to discuss fish and berries, they picked Ann Chandonnet.

A 22-year resident of the Anchorage, Alaska, area and a food columnist for *ALASKA* magazine, Chandonnet is a journalist, poet, and writer who enjoys getting behind the scenes of good food—in the kitchens of chefs and the orchards of fruit growers as well as at a 5,000-year-old Alutiiq fish camp site on Prince William Sound.

Her articles on food history have been published in *Early American Life* magazine, *ALASKA* magazine, *California Girl, Pacific Search,* and *Food History News.*

Chandonnet's previous titles include *The Complete Fruit Cookbook* (1972) and *The Cheese Guide & Cookbook* (1973). She has published two children's books: *Chief Stephen's Parky* (1993) and *The Birthday Party* (1995).